D0440546

No man is an island; he is a 'holon'. Like Janus, the two-faced Roman god, holons have a dual tendency to behave as quasi-independent *wholes*, asserting their individualities, but at the same time as integrated *parts* of larger wholes in the multi-levelled hierarchies of existence. Thus a man is both a unique individual but also part of a social group, which itself is a part of a larger group, and so on. Koestler shows that this polarity between the *self-assertive* and *integrative tendencies* is a universal characteristic of life. Order and stability can prevail only when the two tendencies are in equilibrium. If one of them dominates the other, this delicate balance is disturbed, and pathological conditions of various types make their appearance. These seemingly abstract considerations turn out to be of prime importance when applied to emotive behaviour – the 'paranoid streak' in our species which has played such havoc with its history and now threatens it with extinction. Yet Koestler believes that the two-faced god may guide us to a proper diagnosis and thus provide an 'alternative to despair'.

JANUS is both a summing up and a continuation of Koestler's work over the past twenty-five years, since he turned from politics to the sciences of life – or, more precisely, to the 'evolution, creativity and pathology of the human mind'. The insights gained on that long journey are here assembled in a coherent and comprehensive synthesis, and in the last part of the book, he offers us a tantalizing 'glance through the key-hole' from subatomic physics to metaphysics. He shows that in the light of the new cosmology, the strictly deterministic, mechanistic world-view of the last century, which still dominates many fields of contemporary science, has become a Victorian anachronism. The nineteenth-century clockwork model of the universe is in shambles, and since matter itself has been de-materialized by the physicists, materialism can no longer claim to be a scientific philosophy.

JANUS

JANUS

A Summing Up

Arthur Koestler

Vintage Books
A Division of Random House
New York

ACKNOWLEDGEMENTS

I am indebted to the Editors of the *Encyclopaedia Britannica* (15th edition, 1974) for permission to quote substantial extracts from my article 'Humour and Wit' in that edition.

I wish to thank the Editors of *Mind in Nature: Essays on the Interface of Science and Philosophy,* J. B. Cobb, Jr, and D. R. Griffin (University Press of America, Washington, 1977) for permission to quote passages from my paper, 'Free Will in a Hierarchic Context' which appeared in that book.

I also wish to thank the following for permission to quote extracts from their work: Professor Charles H. Gibbs-Smith, Smithsonian Institution, Washington, and Keeper Emeritus, Victoria and Albert Museum, London, in *Flying Saucer Review* (July/August, 1970); Professor Holger Hyden, University of Gothenburg, in *Control of the Mind* (McGraw-Hill, New York, 1961); Professor Stanley Milgram, *Obedience to Authority: An Experimental View* (Harper and Row, New York, and Tavistock, London, 1974) and in *Dialogue* (Washington, 1975); Dr Lewis Thomas, *The Lives of a Cell* (Viking Press, New York, 1974).

Lastly, I am grateful to Mrs Joan St George Saunders of Writer's and Speaker's Research for giving me invaluable help with this book, as she did with earlier ones.

Library of Congress Cataloging in Publication Data

Koestler, Arthur, 1905—
Janus: a summing up.

Bibliography: p.
Includes index.
1. Philosophy. I. Title.
[B1646.K773J36 1979]   192   78-23626
ISBN 0-394-72886-6

Manufactured in the United States of America

to Daphne

AUTHOR'S NOTE

This book is a summing up (and also a continuation) of works published over the last twenty-five years, since I turned from writing political novels and essays to the sciences of life – i.e., the evolution, creativity and pathology of the human mind.

Such a summing up has its difficulties. When the author puts a summary at the end of a scientific paper or a chapter in a book, he can assume that its contents are still fresh in the reader's mind. Not so in this case, where I have tried to distil the essence of a number of books, which the reader may have read some years ago, if ever at all. Thus I could never be sure how much to take for granted, and had to repeat myself to some extent. The reader may occasionally get a feeling of *déjà vu* – or *déjà lu* – where I cribbed a few lines or even entire paragraphs from earlier books.

What I hope to show is that they add up to a comprehensive system, which rejects materialism and throws some new light on the human condition. In case this sounds over-ambitious, let me quote from the Preface to *The Act of Creation*:

I have no illusions about the prospects of the theory I am proposing; it will suffer the inevitable fate of being proven wrong in many, or most, details, by new advances in knowledge. What I am hoping for is that it will be found to contain a shadowy pattern of truth

London, September 1977

CONTENTS

CONTENTS

PROLOGUE: THE NEW CALENDAR

I

If I were asked to name the most important date in the history and prehistory of the human race, I would answer without hesitation, 6 August 1945. The reason is simple. From the dawn of consciousness until 6 August 1945, man had to live with the prospect of his death as an *individual*; since the day when the first atomic bomb outshone the sun over Hiroshima, mankind as a whole has had to live with the prospect of its extinction as a *species*.

We have been taught to accept the transitoriness of personal existence, while taking the potential immortality of the human race for granted. This belief has ceased to be valid. We have to revise our axioms.

It is not an easy task. There are periods of incubation before a new idea takes hold of the mind; the Copernican doctrine which so radically downgraded man's status in the universe took nearly a century until it penetrated European consciousness. The new downgrading of our species to the status of mortality is even more difficult to digest.

It actually looks as if the novelty of this outlook had worn off even before it had properly sunk in. Already the name Hiroshima has become a historical cliché like the Boston Tea Party. We have returned to a state of pseudo-normality. Only a small minority is conscious of the fact that ever since it unlocked the nuclear Pandora's Box, our species has been living on borrowed time.

Every age had its Cassandras, yet mankind managed to survive their sinister prophecies. However, this comforting reflection is no longer valid, for in no earlier age did a tribe or nation possess the necessary equipment to make this planet unfit for life. They could inflict only limited damage on their adversaries – and did so, whenever given a chance. Now they can hold the entire biosphere to ransom. A Hitler, born twenty years later, would probably have done so, provoking a nuclear *Götterdämmerung*.

The trouble is that an invention, once made, cannot be dis-invented. The nuclear weapon has come to stay; it has become part of the human condition. Man will have to live with it permanently: not only through the next confrontation-crisis and the one after that; not only through the next decade or century, but forever – that is, as long as mankind survives. The indications are that it will not be for very long.

There are two main reasons which point to this conclusion. The first is technical: as the devices of nuclear warfare become more potent and easier to make, their spreading to young and immature as well as old and arrogant nations becomes inevitable, and global control of their manufacture impracticable. Within the foreseeable future they will be made and stored in large quantities all over the globe among nations of all colours and ideologies, and the probability that a spark which initiates the chain-reaction will be ignited sooner or later, deliberately or by accident, will increase accordingly, until, in the long run, it approaches certainty. One might compare the situation to a gathering of delinquent youths locked in a room full of inflammable material who are given a box of matches – with the pious warning not to use it.

The second main reason which points to a low life-expectancy for *homo sapiens* in the post-Hiroshima era is the paranoid streak revealed by his past record. A dispassionate observer from a more advanced planet who could take in human history from Cro-Magnon to Auschwitz at a single glance, would no doubt come to the conclusion that our race is in some respects an admirable, in the main, however, a very sick biological product; and that the consequences of its mental sickness far outweigh its cultural achievements when the chances of prolonged survival are considered. The most persistent sound which reverberates through man's history is the beating of war drums. Tribal wars, religious wars, civil wars, dynastic wars, national wars, revolutionary wars, colonial wars, wars of conquest and of liberation, wars to prevent and to end all wars, follow each other in a chain of compulsive repetitiveness as far as man can remember his past, and there is every reason to believe that the chain will extend into the future. In the first twenty years of the post-Hiroshima era, between the years 0 and 20 P.H. – or 1946–66 according to our outdated calendar – forty wars fought with conventional weapons were tabulated by the Pentagon;[1] and at least on two occasions – Berlin 1950 and Cuba 1962 – we have been on the brink of nuclear war. If we discard the comforts of wishful thinking, we must expect that the focal areas of potential conflict will continue to drift across the globe like high-pressure regions over a meteorological chart. And the only precarious safeguard against the escalating of local into total conflict, mutual deterrence, will, by its very nature, always remain dependent on the restraint or recklessness of fallible key individuals and fanatical regimes. Russian roulette is a game which cannot be played for long.

The most striking indication of the pathology of our species is the contrast between its unique technological achievements and its equally unique incompetence in the conduct of its social affairs. We can control the motions of satellites orbiting distant planets, but cannot control the situation in Northern Ireland. Man can leave the earth and land on the moon, but cannot cross from East to West Berlin. Prometheus reaches out for the stars with an insane grin on his face and a totem-symbol in his hand.

2

I have said nothing about the added terrors of biochemical warfare; nor about the population explosion, pollution, and so forth, which, however threatening in themselves, have unduly distracted the public's awareness from the one central, towering fact: that since the year 1945 our species has acquired the diabolic power to annihilate itself; and that, judging by its past record, the chances are that it will use that power in one of the recurrent crises in the not-too-distant future. The result would be the transformation of space-ship earth into a Flying Dutchman, drifting among the stars with its dead crew.

If this is the probable outlook, what is the point of going on with our piecemeal efforts to save the panda and prevent our rivers from turning into sewers? Or making provisions for our grandchildren? Or, if it comes to that, of going on writing this book? It is not a rhetorical question, as the general mood of disenchantment among the young indicates. But there are at least two good answers to it.

The first is contained in the two words 'as if' which Hans Vaihinger turned into a once-influential philosophical system: 'The Philosophy of As If'.[2] Briefly, it means that man has no choice but to live by 'fictions'; *as if* the illusory world of the senses represented ultimate Reality; *as if* he had a free will which made him responsible for his actions; *as if* there was a God to reward virtuous conduct, and so on. Similarly, the individual must live *as if* he were not under sentence of death, and humanity must plan for its future *as if* its days were not counted. It is only by virtue of these fictions that the mind of man fabricated a habitable universe, and endowed it with meaning.*

The second answer is derived from the simple fact that although our species now lives on borrowed time, from decade to decade as it were, and the signs indicate that it is drifting towards the final catastrophe, we are still dealing in probabilities and not in certainties. There is always a hope of the unexpected and the unforeseen. Since the year zero of the new calendar, man has carried a time-bomb fastened round his neck, and will have to listen to its ticking – now louder, now softer, now louder again – until it either blows up, or he succeeds in de-fusing it. Time is running short, history is accelerating along dizzy exponential curves, and reason tells us that the chances of a successful de-fusing operation before it is too late are slender. All we can do is to act *as if* there was still time for such an operation.

But the operation will require a more radical approach than UNO resolutions, disarmament conferences and appeals to sweet

---

*Vaihinger's (1852–1933) philosophy should not be confused either with Phenomenalism or with American Pragmatism, though it has affinities with both.

reasonableness. Such appeals have always fallen on deaf ears, from the time of the Hebrew prophets, for the simple reason that *homo sapiens* is not a reasonable being – for if he were, he would not have made such a bloody mess of his history; nor are there any indications that he is in the process of becoming one.

3

The first step towards a possible therapy is a correct diagnosis of what went wrong with our species. There have been countless attempts at such a diagnosis, invoking the Biblical Fall, or Freud's 'death wish', or the 'territorial imperative' of contemporary ethologists. None of these carried much conviction, because none of them started from the hypothesis that *homo sapiens* may be an aberrant biological species, an evolutionary misfit, afflicted by an endemic disorder which sets it apart from all other animal species – just as language, science and art set it apart in a positive sense. Yet it is precisely this unpleasant hypothesis which provides the starting point for the present book.

Evolution has made many mistakes; Julian Huxley compared it to a maze with an enormous number of blind alleys leading to stagnation or extinction. For every existing species hundreds have perished in the past; the fossil record is a waste-basket of the Chief Designer's discarded models. The evidence from man's past record and from contemporary brain-research both strongly suggest that at some point during the last explosive stages of the biological evolution of *homo sapiens* something went wrong; that there is a flaw, some potentially fatal engineering error built into our native equipment – more specifically, into the circuits of our nervous system – which would account for the streak of paranoia running through our history. This is the hideous but plausible hypothesis which any serious inquiry into man's condition has to face. The best intuitive diagnosticians – the poets – have kept telling us that man is mad and has always been so; but anthropologists, psychiatrists, and students of evolution do not take poets seriously and keep shutting their eyes to the evidence staring them in the face. This unwillingness to face reality is of course in itself an ominous symptom. It could be objected that a madman cannot be expected to be aware of his own madness. The answer is that he can, because he is not entirely mad the entire time. In their periods of remission, schizophrenics have written astonishingly lucid reports of their illness.

I shall now venture to propose a summary list of some of the outstanding pathological symptoms reflected in the disastrous history of our species, and then proceed from the symptoms to a discussion of their possible causes. I have confined the list of symptoms to four main headings.*

1. In one of the early chapters of Genesis, there is an episode which has inspired many great paintings. It is the scene where Abraham ties his son to a pile of wood and prepares to cut his throat and burn him, out of sheer love of God. From the beginnings of history we are faced with a striking phenomenon to which anthropologists have paid far too little attention: human sacrifice, the ritual killing of children, virgins, kings and heroes to placate and flatter gods conceived in nightmare dreams. It was a ubiquitous ritual, which persisted from the prehistoric dawn to the peak of pre-Columbian civilizations, and in some parts of the world to the beginning of our century. From South Sea islanders to the Scandinavian bog people, from the Etruscans to the Aztecs, these practices arose independently in the most varied cultures, as manifestations of a delusionary streak in the human psyche to which the whole species was and is apparently prone. To dismiss the subject as a sinister curiosity of the past, as is usually done, means to ignore the universality of the phenomenon, the clues that it provides to the paranoid element in man's mental make-up and its relevance to his ultimate predicament.

2. *Homo sapiens* is virtually unique in the animal kingdom in his lack of instinctive safeguards against the killing of con-specifics – members of his own species. The 'Law of the Jungle' knows only one legitimate motive for killing: the feeding drive, and only on condition that predator and prey belong to different species.

---

*This section is based on *The Ghost in the Machine*, Part Three, and its résumé in a paper read to the Fourteenth Nobel Symposium ('The Urge to Self-Destruction', reprinted in *The Heel of Achilles*).

Within the same species competition and conflict between individuals or groups are settled by symbolic threat-behaviour or ritualized duels which end with the flight or surrender-gesture of one of the opponents, and hardly ever involves lethal injury. The inhibitory forces – instinctive taboos – against killing or seriously injuring con-specifics are as powerful in most animals – including the primates – as the drives of hunger, sex or fear. Man is alone (apart from some controversial phenomena among rats and ants) in practising intra-specific murder on an individual and collective scale, in spontaneous or organized fashion, for motives ranging from sexual jealousy to quibbles about metaphysical doctrines. Intra-specific warfare in permanence is a central feature of the human condition. It is embellished by the infliction of torture in its various forms, from crucifixion to electric shocks.*

3. The third symptom is closely linked to the two previous ones: it is manifested in the chronic, quasi-schizophrenic split between reason and emotion, between man's rational faculties and his irrational, affect-bound beliefs.

4. Finally, there is the striking disparity, already mentioned, between the growth-curves of science and technology on the one hand and of ethical conduct on the other; or, to put it differently, between the powers of the human intellect when applied to mastering the environment and its inability to maintain harmonious relationships within the family, the nation and the species at large. Roughly two and a half millennia ago, in the sixth century B.C., the Greeks embarked on the scientific adventure which eventually carried us to the moon; that surely is an impressive growth-curve. But the sixth century B.C. also saw the rise of Taoism, Confucianism and Buddhism – the twentieth

---

*'Torture today is so widespread an instrument of political repression that we can speak of the existence of 'Torture States' as a political reality of our times. The malignancy has become epidemic and knows no ideological, racial or economic boundaries. In over thirty countries, torture is systematically applied to extract confessions, elicit information, penalise dissent and deter opposition to repressive governmental policy. Torture has been institutionalised. . .' (Victor Jokel, Director, British Amnesty, in 'Epidemic: Torture', Amnesty International, London n.d., *c.* 1975).

of Hitlerism, Stalinism and Maoism: there is no discernible growth-curve. As von Bertalanffy has put it:

What is called human progress is a purely intellectual affair . . . not much development, however, is seen on the moral side. It is doubtful whether the methods of modern warfare are preferable to the big stones used for cracking the skull of the fellow-Neanderthaler. It is rather obvious that the moral standards of Laotse and Buddha were not inferior to ours. The human cortex contains some ten billion neurons that have made possible the progress from stone axe to airplanes and atomic bombs, from primitive mythology to quantum theory. There is no corresponding development on the instinctive side that would cause man to mend his ways. For this reason, moral exhortations, as proffered through the centuries by the founders of religion and great leaders of humanity, have proved disconcertingly ineffective.[3]

The list of symptoms could be extended. But I think that those I have mentioned indicate the essence of the human predicament. They are of course inter-dependent; thus human sacrifice can be regarded as a sub-category of the schizophrenic split between reason and emotion, and the contrast between the growth-curves of technological and moral achievement can be regarded as a further consequence of it.

4

So far we have moved in the realm of facts, attested by the historical record and the anthropologist's research into prehistory. As we turn from *symptoms* to *causes* we must have recourse to more or less speculative hypotheses, which again are interrelated, but pertain to different disciplines, namely, neurophysiology, anthropology and psychology.

The neurophysiological hypothesis is derived from the so-called Papez–MacLean theory of emotions, supported by some thirty years of experimental research.* I have discussed it at

*Dr Paul D. Maclean is head of the Laboratory of Brain Evolution and Behaviour, National Institute of Mental Health, Bethesda, Maryland.

length in *The Ghost in the Machine*, and shall confine myself here to a summary outline, without going into physiological details.

The theory is based on the fundamental differences in anatomy and function between the archaic structures of the brain which man shares with the reptiles and lower mammals, and the specifically human neocortex, which evolution superimposed on them – without, however, ensuring adequate coordination. The result of this evolutionary blunder is an uneasy coexistence, frequently erupting in acute conflict, between the deep ancestral structures of the brain, mainly concerned with instinctive and emotional behaviour, and the neocortex which endowed man with language, logic and symbolic thought. MacLean has summed up the resulting state of affairs in a technical paper, but in an unusually picturesque way:

Man finds himself in the predicament that Nature has endowed him essentially with three brains which, despite great differences in structure, must function together and communicate with one another. The oldest of these brains is basically reptilian. The second has been inherited from the lower mammals, and the third is a late mammalian development, which . . . has made man peculiarly man. Speaking allegorically of these three brains within a brain, we might imagine that when the psychiatrist bids the patient to lie on the couch, he is asking him to stretch out alongside a horse and a crocodile.[4]

If we substitute for the individual patient mankind at large, and for the psychiatrist's couch the stage of history, we get a grotesque, but essentially truthful picture of the human condition.

In a more recent series of lectures on neurophysiology, MacLean offered another metaphor:

In the popular language of today, these three brains might be thought of as biological computers, each with its own peculiar form of subjectivity and its own intelligence, its own sense of time and space and its own memory, motor and other functions . . . [5]

The 'reptilian' and 'paleo-mammalian' brains together form the so-called limbic system which, for the sake of simplicity, we may call the 'old brain', as opposed to the neocortex, the specifically human 'thinking cap'. But while the antediluvian structures at the very core of our brain, which control instincts, passions and biological drives, have been hardly touched by the nimble fingers of evolution, the neocortex of the hominids expanded in the last half a million years at an explosive speed which is without precedent in the history of evolution – so much so that some anatomists compared it to a tumorous growth.

This brain explosion in the second half of the Pleistocene seems to have followed the type of exponential curve which has recently become so familiar to us – population explosion, information explosion, etc. – and there may be more than a superficial analogy here, as all these curves reflect the phenomenon of the acceleration of history in various domains. But explosions do not produce harmonious results. The result in this case seems to have been that the rapidly developing thinking cap, which endowed man with his reasoning powers, did not become properly integrated and coordinated with the ancient emotion-bound structures on which it was superimposed with such unprecedented speed. The neural pathways connecting neocortex with the archaic structures of the mid-brain are apparently inadequate.

Thus the brain explosion gave rise to a mentally unbalanced species in which old brain and new brain, emotion and intellect, faith and reason, were at loggerheads. On one side, the pale cast of rational thought, of logic suspended on a thin thread all too easily broken; on the other, the raging fury of passionately held irrational beliefs, reflected in the holocausts of past and present history.

If neurophysiological evidence had not taught us the contrary, we would have expected it to reveal an evolutionary process which gradually transformed the primitive old brain into a more sophisticated instrument – as it transformed gill into lung, or the forelimb of the reptilian ancestor into the bird's wing, the flipper of the whale, the hand of man. But instead of *transforming* old brain into new, evolution *superimposed* a new superior structure on an old one with partly overlapping functions, and without providing the new brain with a clear-cut power of control over the old.

To put it crudely: evolution has left a few screws loose between the neocortex and the hypothalamus. MacLean has coined the term *schizophysiology* for this endemic shortcoming in the human nervous system. He defines it as

. . a dichotomy in the function of the phylogenetically old and new cortex that might account for differences between emotional and intellectual behaviour. While our intellectual functions are carried on in the newest and most highly developed part of the brain, our affective behaviour continues to be dominated by a relatively crude and primitive system, by archaic structures in the brain whose fundamental pattern has undergone but little change in the whole course of evolution from mouse to man.[6]

The hypothesis that this type of schizophysiology is part of our genetic inheritance, built into the species as it were, could go a long way towards explaining some of the pathological symptoms listed before. The chronic conflict between rational thought and irrational beliefs, the resulting paranoid streak in our history, the contrast between the growth-curves of science and ethics, would at last become comprehensible and could be expressed in physiological terms. And any condition which can be expressed in physiological terms should ultimately be accessible to remedies – as will be discussed later on. For the moment let us note that the origin of the evolutionary blunder which gave rise to man's schizophysiological disposition appears to have been the rapid, quasibrutal *superimposition* (instead of *transformation*) of the neocortex on the ancestral structures and the resulting *insufficient coordination* between the new brain and the old, and *inadequate control* of the former over the latter.

In concluding this section, it should be emphasized once more that to the student of evolution there is nothing improbable in the assumption that man's native equipment, though superior to that of any animal species, nevertheless contains some serious fault in the circuitry of that most precious and delicate instrument, the nervous system. When the biologist speaks of evolutionary 'blunders', he does not reproach evolution for having failed to attain some theoretical ideal, but means something quite simple and precise: some obvious deviation from Nature's own standards of engineering efficiency, which deprives an organ of its effectiveness – like the monstrous antlers of the Irish elk, now defunct. Turtles and beetles are well protected by their armour, but it makes them so top-heavy that if in combat or by misadventure they fall on their back, they cannot get up again, and starve to death – a grotesque construction fault which Kafka turned into a symbol of the human predicament.

But the greatest mistakes occurred in the evolution of the various types of brain. Thus the invertebrates' brain evolved around the alimentary tube, so that if the neural mass were to evolve and expand, the alimentary tube would be more and more compressed (as happened to spiders and scorpions, which can only pass liquids through their gullets and have become bloodsuckers). Gaskell, in *The Origin of Vertebrates*, commented:

At the time when vertebrates first appeared, the direction and progress of variation in the Arthropoda was leading, owing to the manner in which the brain was pierced by the oesophagus, to a terrible dilemma – either the capacity for taking in food without sufficient intelligence to capture it, or intelligence sufficient to capture food and no power to consume it.[7]

And another great biologist, Wood Jones:

Here, then, is an end to the progress in brain building among the invertebrates . . . The invertebrates made a fatal mistake when they started to build their brains around the oesophagus. Their attempt to develop big brains was a failure . . . Another start must be made.[8]

The new start was made by the vertebrates. But one of the main divisions of the vertebrates, the Australian marsupials (who, unlike us placentals, carry their unfinished newborn in pouches) again landed themselves in a cul-de-sac. Their brain is lacking a vital component, the *corpus callosum* – a conspicuous nerve tract which, in placentals, connects the right and left cerebral hemispheres.* Now recent brain research has discovered a fundamental

*More precisely, the higher (non-olfactory) functional areas.

division of functions in the two hemispheres which complement each other rather like Yin and Yang. Obviously the two hemi-spheres are required to work together if the animal (or man) is to derive the full benefit of their potentials. The absence of a *corpus callosum* thus signifies *inadequate coordination* between the two halves of the brain – a phrase which has an ominously familiar ring. It may be the principal reason why the evolution of the marsupials – though it produced many species which bear a striking resemblance to their placental cousins – finally got stuck on the evolutionary ladder at the level of the koala bear.

I shall return to the fascinating and much neglected subject of the marsupials later on. In the present context they and the arthropoda, as well as other examples, may serve as cautionary tales, which make it easier to accept the possibility that *homo sapiens*, too, might be a victim of faulty brain design. We, thank God, have a solid *corpus callosum* which integrates the right and left halves, horizontally; but in the vertical direction, from the seat of conceptual thought to the spongy depths of instinct and passion, all is not so well. The evidence from the physiological laboratory, the tragic record of history on the grand scale, and the trivial anomalies in our everyday behaviour, all point towards the same conclusion.

5

Another approach to man's predicament starts from the fact that the human infant has to endure a longer period of helplessness and total dependence on its parents than the young of any other species. The cradle is a stricter confinement than the kangaroo's pouch; one might speculate that this early experience of depen-dence leaves its life-long mark, and is at least partly responsible for man's willingness to submit to authority wielded by individ-uals or groups, and his suggestibility by doctrines and moral imperatives. Brain-washing starts in the cradle.

The first suggestion the hypnotist imposes on his subject is that he should be open to the hypnotizer's suggestions. The subject is being conditioned to become susceptible to conditioning. The helpless infant is subjected to a similar process. It is turned into a willing recipient of ready-made beliefs.* For the vast majority of mankind throughout history, the system of beliefs which they accepted, for which they were prepared to live and to die, was not of their own making or choice; it was shoved down their throats by the hazards of birth. *Pro patria mori dulce et decorum est*, whichever the *patria* into which the stork happens to drop you. Critical reasoning played, if any, only a secondary part in the process of adopting a faith, a code of ethics, a *Weltanschauung*; of becoming a fervent Christian crusader, a fervent Moslem engaged in Holy War, a Roundhead or a Cavalier. The continuous disasters in man's history are mainly due to his excessive capacity and urge to become identified with a tribe, nation, church or cause, and to espouse its credo uncritically and enthusiastically, even if its tenets are contrary to reason, devoid of self-interest and detrimental to the claims of self-preservation.

We are thus driven to the unfashionable conclusion that the trouble with our species is not an excess of *aggression*, but an excess capacity for fanatical *devotion*. Even a cursory glance at history should convince one that individual crimes committed for selfish motives play a quite insignificant part in the human tragedy, compared to the numbers massacred in unselfish loyalty to one's tribe, nation, dynasty, church, or political ideology, *ad majorem gloriam dei*. The emphasis is on unselfish. Excepting a small minority of mercenary or sadistic disposition, wars are not fought for personal gain, but out of loyalty and devotion to king, country or cause. Homicide committed for personal reasons is a statistical rarity in all cultures, including our own. Homicide for *un*selfish reasons, at the risk of one's own life, is the dominant phenomenon in history.

At this point I must insert two brief polemical remarks:

Firstly, when Freud proclaimed *ex cathedra* that wars were caused by pent-up aggressive instincts in search of an outlet, people tended to believe him because it made them feel guilty,

---

*Konrad Lorenz talks of 'imprinting', and puts the critical age of receptivity just after puberty.[9] He does not seem to realize that in man, unlike his geese, susceptibility for imprinting stretches from the cradle to the grave.

although he did not produce a shred of historical or psychological evidence for his claim. Anybody who has served in the ranks of an army can testify that aggressive feelings towards the enemy hardly play a part in the dreary routines of waging war. Soldiers do not hate. They are frightened, bored, sex-starved, homesick; they fight with resignation, because they have no other choice, or with enthusiasm for king and country, the true religion, the righteous cause – moved not by hatred but by *loyalty*. To say it once more, man's tragedy is not an excess of aggression, but an excess of devotion.

The second polemical remark concerns another theory which recently became fashionable among anthropologists, purporting that the origin of war is to be found in the instinctive urge of some animal species to defend at all costs their own stretch of land or water – the so-called 'territorial imperative'. It seems to me no more convincing than Freud's hypothesis. The wars of man, with rare exceptions, were not fought for individual ownership of bits of space. The man who goes to war actually *leaves* the home which he is supposed to defend, and does his shooting far away from it; and what makes him do it is not the biological urge to defend his personal acreage of farmland or meadows, but his devotion to symbols derived from tribal lore, divine commandments and political slogans. Wars are not fought for territory, but for words.

6

This brings us to the next item in our inventory of the possible causes of the human predicament. Man's deadliest weapon is *language*. He is as susceptible to being hypnotized by slogans as he is to infectious diseases. And when there is an epidemic, the group-mind takes over. It obeys its own rules, which are different from the rules of conduct of individuals. When a person identifies himself with a group, his reasoning faculties are diminished and his passions enhanced by a kind of emotive resonance or positive feedback. The individual is not a killer, but the group is, and by identifying with it the individual is transformed into a killer.

16 PROLOGUE: THE NEW CALENDAR

This is the infernal dialectic reflected in man's history of wars, persecution and genocide. And the main catalyst of that transformation is the hypnotic power of the word. The words of Adolf Hitler were the most powerful agents of destruction at his time. Long before the printing press was invented, the words of Allah's chosen Prophet unleashed an emotive chain-reaction which shook the world from Central Asia to the Atlantic coast. Without words there would be no poetry – and no war. Language is the main factor in our superiority over brother animal – and, in view of its explosive emotive potentials, a constant threat to survival.

This apparently paradoxical point is illustrated by recent field-observations of Japanese monkey-societies which have revealed that different tribes of a species may develop surprisingly different habits – one might almost say, different cultures. Some tribes have taken to washing potatoes in the river before eating them, others have not. Sometimes migrating groups of potato-washers meet non-washers, and the two groups watch each other's strange behaviour with apparent bewilderment. But unlike the inhabitants of Lilliput, who fought holy crusades over the question at which end to break the egg, the potato-washing monkeys do not go to war with the non-washers, because the poor creatures have no language which would enable them to declare washing a divine commandment and eating unwashed potatoes a deadly heresy.

Obviously the quickest way to abolish war would be to abolish language, and Jesus seems to have been aware of this when he said: 'Let your communication be Yea, yea, Nay, nay, for anything beyond that cometh from the devil.' And in a sense mankind *did* renounce language long ago, if by language we mean a method of communication for the whole species. The Tower of Babel is a timeless symbol. Other species do possess a single method of communication – by signs, sounds or by secreting odours – which is understood by all members of that species. When a St Bernard meets a poodle they understand each other without needing an interpreter, however different they look. *Homo sapiens*, on the other hand, is split into some 3,000 language groups. Each language – and each dialect thereof – acts as a cohesive force within the group and a divisive force between groups. It is one of the reasons why the disruptive forces are so much stronger than the cohesive forces in our history. Men show a much greater variety in physical appearance and behaviour than any other species (excepting the products of artificial breeding); and the gift of language, instead of bridging over these differences, erects further barriers and enhances the contrast. We have communication satellites which can convey a message to the entire population of the planet, but no *lingua franca* which would make it universally understood. It seems odd that, except for a few valiant Esperantists, neither UNESCO nor any international body has as yet discovered that the simplest way to promote understanding would be to promote a language that is understood by all.

7

In his *Unpopular Essays*, Bertrand Russell has a telling anecdote:

F. W. H. Myers, whom spiritualism had converted to belief in a future life, questioned a woman who had lately lost her daughter as to what she supposed had become of her soul. The mother replied: 'Oh well, I suppose she is enjoying eternal bliss, but I wish you wouldn't talk about such unpleasant subjects . . .'[10]

The last item on my list of factors which could account for the pathology of our species is the discovery of death, or rather its discovery by the intellect and its rejection by instinct and emotion. It is yet another manifestation of man's split mind, perpetuating the divided house of faith and reason. Faith is the older and more powerful partner, and when conflict arises, the reasoning half of the mind is compelled to provide elaborate rationalizations to allay the senior partner's terror of the void. Yet not only the naive concept of 'eternal bliss' (or eternal torment for the wicked) but also the more sophisticated parapsychological theories of survival present problems which are apparently beyond the reasoning faculties of our species. There may be millions of other cultures on planets that are millions of years older than ours, to whom death no longer is a problem; but the fact remains that, to use computer jargon, we are not 'programmed' for the task. Confronted with a task for which it is not programmed, a computer is either reduced to silence, or it goes haywire. The latter seems to have happened, with distressing repetitiveness, in the most varied cultures. Faced with the intractable paradox of consciousness emerging from the pre-natal void and drowning in the post-mortem darkness, their minds went haywire and populated the air with the ghosts of the departed, gods, angels and devils, until the atmosphere became saturated with invisible presences which at best were capricious and unpredictable, but mostly malevolent and vengeful. They had to be worshipped, cajoled and placated by elaborately cruel rituals, including human sacrifice, Holy Wars and the burning of heretics.

For nearly two thousand years, millions of otherwise intelligent people were convinced that the vast majority of mankind who did not share their particular creed or did not perform their rites were consumed by flames throughout eternity by order of a loving god. Similar nightmarish fantasies were collectively shared by other cultures, testifying to the ubiquity of the paranoid streak in the race.

There is, once again, another side to the picture. The refusal to believe in the finality of death made the pyramids rise from the sand; it provided a set of ethical values, and the main inspiration for artistic creation. If the word 'death' were absent from our vocabulary, the great works of literature would have remained unwritten. The creativity and pathology of man are two faces of the same medal, coined in the same evolutionary mint.

8

To sum up, the disastrous history of our species indicates the futility of all attempts at a diagnosis which do not take into account the possibility that *homo sapiens* is a victim of one of evolution's countless mistakes. The example of the arthropods and marsupials, among others, shows that such mistakes do occur and can adversely affect the evolution of the brain.

I have listed some conspicuous symptoms of the mental disorder which appears to be endemic in our species: (a) the ubiquitous rites of human sacrifice in the prehistoric dawn; (b) the persistent pursuit of intra-specific warfare which, while earlier on it could only cause limited damage, now puts the whole planet in jeopardy; (c) the paranoid split between rational thinking and irrational, affect-based beliefs; (d) the contrast between mankind's genius in conquering Nature and its ineptitude in managing its own affairs – symbolized by the new frontier on the moon and the minefields along the borders of Europe.

It is important to underline once more that these pathological phenomena are specifically and uniquely human, and not found in any other species. Thus it seems only logical that our search for explanations should also concentrate primarily on those attributes of *homo sapiens* which are exclusively human and not shared by the rest of the animal kingdom. But however obvious this conclusion may seem, it runs counter to the prevailing reductionist trend. 'Reductionism' is the philosophical belief that all human activities can be 'reduced' to – i.e., explained by – the behavioural responses of lower animals – Pavlov's dogs, Skinner's rats and pigeons, Lorenz's greylag geese, Morris's hairless apes; and that these responses in turn can be reduced to the physical laws which govern inanimate matter. No doubt Pavlov or Lorenz provided us with new insights into human nature – but only into those rather elementary, non-specific aspects of human nature which we share with dogs, rats or geese, while the specifically and exclusively human aspects which define the uniqueness of our species are left out of the picture. And since these unique characteristics are manifested both in the creativity and pathology of man, scientists of the reductionist persuasion cannot qualify as competent diagnosticians any more than they qualify as art critics. That is why the scientific establishment has so pitifully failed to define the predicament of man. If he is really an automaton, there is no point in putting a stethoscope to his chest.

Once more, then: if the symptoms of our pathology are

species-specific, i.e., exclusively human, then the explanations for them must be sought on the same exclusive level. This conclusion is not inspired by *hubris*, but by the evidence provided by the historical record. The diagnostic approaches that I have briefly outlined, were: (*a*) the explosive growth of the human neocortex and its insufficient control of the old brain; (*b*) the protracted helplessness of the newborn and its consequent uncritical submissiveness to authority; (*c*) the twofold curse of language as a rabble-rouser and builder of ethnic barriers; (*d*) lastly, the discovery of, and the mind-splitting fear of death. Each of these factors will be discussed in more detail later on.

To neutralize these pathogenic tendencies does not seem an impossible task. Medicine has found remedies for certain types of schizophrenic and manic-depressive psychoses; it is no longer utopian to believe that it will discover a combination of benevolent enzymes which provide the neocortex with a veto against the follies of the archaic brain, correct evolution's glaring mistake, reconcile emotion with reason, and catalyse the breakthrough from maniac to man. Still other avenues are waiting to be explored and may lead to salvation in the nick of time, provided that there is a sense of urgency, derived from the message of the new calendar – and a correct diagnosis of the condition of man, based on a new approach to the sciences of life.

The chapters that follow are concerned with some aspects of this new approach which in recent years have begun to emerge from the sterile deserts of reductionist philosophy. Thus we shall now leave the pathology of man, and turn from disorder to a fresh look at biological order and mental creativity. Some of the questions raised in the previous pages will be taken up again as we go along – and eventually, I hope, fall into a coherent pattern.

PART ONE

Outline of a System

I

The Holarchy

I

Beyond Reductionism – New Perspectives in the Life Sciences was the title of a symposium which I had the pleasure and privilege to organize in 1968, and which subsequently aroused much controversy.* One of the participants, Professor Viktor Frankl, enlivened the proceedings by some choice examples of reductionism in psychiatry, quoted from current books and periodicals. Thus, for instance:

Many an artist has left a psychiatrist's office enraged by interpretations which suggest that he paints to overcome a strict bowel training by free smearing. . . .

We are led to believe that Goethe's work is but the result of pre-genital fixations. Goethe's struggle does not really aim for an ideal, for

*It is usually referred to as the 'Alpbach Symposium' after the Alpine resort where it was held. The participants were: Ludwig von Bertalanffy (*Faculty Professor, State University of New York at Buffalo*), Jerome S. Bruner (*Director, Center for Cognitive Studies, Harvard University*), Blanche Bruner (*Center for Cognitive Studies, Harvard University*), Viktor E. Frankl (*Professor of Psychiatry and Neurology, University of Vienna*), F. A. Hayek (*Professor of Economics, University of Freiberg, Germany,*), Holger Hyden (*Professor and Head of the Institute of Neurobiology and Histology, University of Gothenburg, Sweden*), Bärbel Inhelder (*Professor of Developmental Psychology, University of Geneva*), Seymour S. Kety (*Professor of Psychiatry, Harvard University*), Arthur Koestler (*Writer, London*), Paul D. MacLean (*Head of the Laboratory of Brain Evolution and Behaviour, NIMH, Bethesda, Maryland*), David McNeill (*Professor of Psychology, University of Chicago*), Jean Piaget (*Professor of Experimental Psychology, University of Geneva*) J. R. Smythies (*Reader in Psychiatry, University of Edinburgh*), W. H. Thorpe (*Director, Sub-Department of Animal Behaviour, Department of Zoology, University of Cambridge*), C. H. Waddington (*Professor and Chairman, Department of Genetics, University of Edinburgh*), Paul A. Weiss (*Emeritus Member and Professor, Rockefeller University, New York*).

beauty, for values, but for the overcoming of an embarrassing problem of premature ejaculation. . . .[1]

Now it is quite possible that some sexual (or even scatological) motivation may enter into an artist's work; yet it is absurd to proclaim that art is 'nothing but' goal-inhibited sexuality, because it begs the question of what makes Goethe's art a work of genius, quite unlike other premature ejaculators'. The reductionist attempt to explain artistic creation by the action of sex-hormones is futile, because that action, though biologically vital, does not give us an inkling of the aesthetic criteria which apply to a work of art. Those criteria pertain to the level of conscious mental processes, which cannot be reduced to the level of biological processes without losing their specifically mental attributes in the course of the operation. Reductionist psychiatry is a Procrustean host to the weary traveller.

It is easy to make fun of those latter-day orthodox Freudians who have reduced the master's teaching to a caricature. In other fields, however, the reductionist fallacy is more discreetly implied, less obvious and therefore more insidious. Pavlov's dogs, Skinner's rats, Lorenz's geese, each served for a while as fashionable paradigms of the human condition. Desmond Morris's bestselling book *The Naked Ape* opened with the statement that man is a hairless ape 'self-named *homo sapiens* . . . I am a zoologist and the naked ape is an animal. He is, therefore, fair game for my pen.' To what extremes this zoomorphic approach may lead is illustrated by a further quotation from Morris:

The insides of houses or flats can be decorated and filled with ornaments, bric-à-brac and personal belongings in profusion. This is usually explained as being done to make the place 'look nice'. In fact, it is the exact equivalent to another territorial species depositing its personal scent on a landmark near its den. When you put a name on a door, or hang a painting on a wall, you are, in dog or wolf terms, for example, simply cocking your leg on them and leaving your personal mark there.[2]

On a more serious level (though the passage quoted was

obviously meant to be taken in all seriousness) we are faced with two impressive strongholds of reductionist orthodoxy. One is the neo-Darwinian (or 'Synthetic') theory which holds that evolution is the outcome of 'nothing but' chance mutations retained by natural selection – a doctrine recently exposed to growing criticism* which nevertheless is still taught as gospel truth. The other is the behaviourist psychology of the Watson–Skinner school which holds that all human behaviour can be 'explained, predicted and controlled' by methods exemplified in the conditioning of rats and pigeons. 'Values and meanings are nothing but defence mechanisms and reaction formations' is another of Frankl's telling quotes from a behaviourist textbook.

By its persistent denial of a place for values, meaning and purpose in the interplay of blind forces, the reductionist attitude has cast its shadow beyond the confines of science, affecting our whole cultural and even political climate. Its philosophy may be epitomized by a last quote from a recent college textbook, in which man is defined as 'nothing but a complex biochemical mechanism, powered by a combustion system which energises computers with prodigious storage facilities for retaining encoded information'.[3]

Now the reductionist fallacy lies not in comparing man to a 'mechanism powered by a combustion system' but in declaring that he is 'nothing but' such a mechanism and that his activities consist of 'nothing but' a chain of conditioned responses which are also found in rats. For it is of course perfectly legitimate, and in fact indispensable, for the scientist to try to analyse complex phenomena into their constituent elements – provided he remains conscious of the fact that in the course of the analyses something essential is always lost, because the whole is more than the sum of its parts, and its attributes as a whole are more complex than the attributes of its parts. Thus the analysis of complex phenomena elucidates only a certain segment or aspect of the picture and does not entitle us to say that it is 'nothing but' this or that. Yet such 'nothing-but-ism' as it has been called, is still the – explicit or

* See below, Part Three.

implied – world-view of reductionist orthodoxy. If it were to
be taken literally, man could be ultimately defined as consisting
of nothing but 90 per cent water and 10 per cent minerals – a
statement which is no doubt true, but not very helpful.

2

Nevertheless, reductionism proved an eminently successful
method within its limited range of applicability in the exact
sciences, while its antithesis, holism, never really got off the
ground. Holism may be defined by the statement that the whole
is more than the sum of its parts. The term was coined by Jan
Smuts in the 1920s in a remarkable book[4] which for a while
enjoyed great popularity. But holism never got a grip on academic science* – partly because it went against the *Zeitgeist*, partly
perhaps because it represented more of a philosophical than an
empirical approach and did not lend itself to laboratory tests.

   In fact both reductionism and holism, if taken as sole guides,
lead into a cul-de-sac. 'A rose is a rose is a rose' may be regarded
as a holistic statement, but it tells us no more about the rose than
the formulae of its chemical constituents. For our inquiry we
need a third approach, beyond reductionism and holism, which
incorporates the valid aspects of both. It must start with the
seemingly abstract yet fundamental problem of the relations
between the whole and its parts – any 'whole', whether the
universe or human society, and any 'part', whether an atom or
a human being. This may seem an odd, not to say perverse, way
to get at a diagnosis of man's condition, but the reader will
eventually realize, I hope, that the apparent detour through the
theoretical considerations in the present chapter may be the
shortest way out of the labyrinth.

3

To start with a deceptively simple question: what exactly do we
mean by the familiar words 'part' and 'whole'? 'Part' conveys

*Except indirectly through *Gestalt* psychology.

the meaning of something fragmentary and incomplete, which by itself has no claim to autonomous existence. On the other hand, a 'whole' is considered as something complete in itself which needs no further explanation. However, contrary to these deeply ingrained habits of thought and their reflection in some philosophical schools, 'parts' and 'wholes' in an absolute sense do not exist anywhere, either in the domain of living organisms, or in social organizations, or in the universe at large.

A living organism is not an aggregation of elementary parts, and its activities cannot be reduced to elementary 'atoms of behaviour' forming a chain of conditioned responses. In its bodily aspects, the organism is a whole consisting of 'sub-wholes', such as the circulatory system, digestive system, etc., which in turn branch into sub-wholes of a lower order, such as organs and tissues – and so down to individual cells, and to the organelles inside the cells. In other words, the structure and behaviour of an organism cannot be explained by, or 'reduced to', elementary physico–chemical processes; it is a multi-levelled, stratified hierarchy of sub-wholes, which can be conveniently diagrammed as a pyramid or an inverted tree, where the sub-wholes form the nodes, and the branching lines symbolize channels of communication and control: see diagram overleaf.

The point first to be emphasized is that each member of this hierarchy, on whatever level, is a sub-whole or '*holon*' in its own right – a stable, integrated structure, equipped with self-regulatory devices and enjoying a considerable degree of *autonomy* or self-government. Cells, muscles, nerves, organs, all have their intrinsic rhythms and patterns of activity, often manifested spontaneously without external stimulation; they are subordinated as *parts* to the higher centres in the hierarchy, but at the same time function as quasi-autonomous *wholes*. They are Janus-faced. The face turned upward, toward the higher levels, is that of a dependent part; the face turned downward, towards its own constituents, is that of a whole of remarkable self-sufficiency.

The heart, for instance, has its own pacemakers – actually several pacemakers, capable of taking over from each other when the need arises. Other major organs are equipped with different

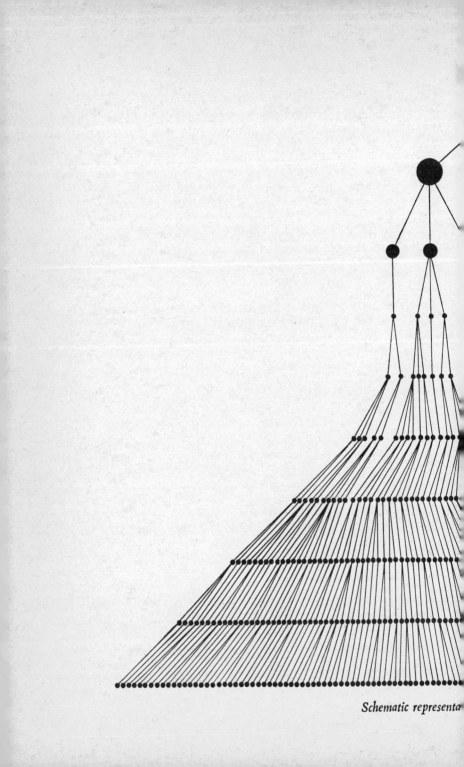

Schematic representa

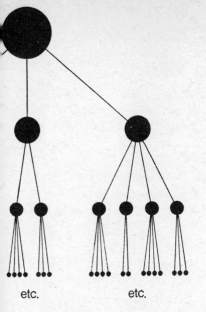

organisms

organ
systems
(respiratory,
digestive,
etc.)

organs

tissues

etc.   etc.

cells

organelles
(ribsomes,
mitochondria,
etc.)

molecules

atoms

sub-atomic
particles

???

the organismic hierarchy

types of coordinating devices and feedback controls. Their autonomy is convincingly demonstrated by transplant surgery. At the beginning of our century, Alexis Carrell showed that a minute strip of tissue taken from the heart of a chicken embryo and put into a nutrient solution will go on pulsating for years. Since then, whole organs were shown to be capable of functioning as quasi-independent wholes when taken out of the body and kept *in vitro*, or transplanted into another body. And as we descend the steps of the hierarchy to the lowest level observable through the electron microscope, we come upon sub-cellular structures – organelles – which are neither 'simple' nor 'elementary', but systems of staggering complexity. Each of these minuscule parts of a cell functions as a self-governing whole in its own right, each apparently obeying a built-in *code of rules*. One type, or tribe, of organelles looks after the cell's growth, others after its energy supply, reproduction, communication, and so on. The mitochondria, for instance, are power plants which extract energy from nutrients by a chain of chemical reactions involving some fifty different steps; and a single cell may have up to five thousand such power plants. The activities of a mitochondrion can be switched on or off by controls on higher levels; but once triggered into action it will follow its own code of rules. It cooperates with other organelles in keeping the cell happy, but at the same time each mitochondrion is a law unto itself, an autonomous unit which will assert its individuality even if the cell around it is dying.

4

Science is only just beginning to rid itself of the mechanistic preconceptions of the nineteenth century – the world as a billiard table of colliding atoms – and to realize that hierarchic organization is a fundamental principle of living nature; that it is 'the essential and distinguishing characteristic of life' (Pattee);[5] and that it is 'a real phenomenon, presented to us by the biological object, and not the fiction of a speculative mind' (P. Weiss).[6] It is at the same time a conceptual tool which on some occasions acts as an Open Sesame. *All complex structures and processes of a relatively stable character display hierarchic organization*, regardless whether we consider galactic systems, living organisms and their activities, or social organizations. The tree diagram with its series of levels can be used to represent the evolutionary branching of species into the 'tree of life'; or the stepwise differentiation of tissues and integration of functions in the development of the embryo. Anatomists use the tree diagram to demonstrate the locomotor hierarchy of limbs, joints, individual muscles, and so down to fibres, fibrils and filaments of contractile proteins. Ethologists use it to illustrate the various sub-routines and action-patterns involved in such complex instinctive activities as a bird building a nest; but it is also an indispensable tool to the new school of psycholinguistics started by Chomsky. It is equally indispensable for an understanding of the processes by which the chaotic stimuli impinging on our sense organs are filtered and classified in their ascent through the nervous system into conscious-ness. Lastly, the branching tree illustrates the hierarchic ordering of knowledge in the subject-index of library catalogues – and the personal memory stores inside our skulls.

The universal applicability of the hierarchic model may arouse the suspicion that it is logically empty. I hope to show that this is not the case, and that the search for the fundamental properties, or laws, which all these varied hierarchies have in common amounts to more than a play on superficial analogies – or to riding a hobby horse. It should rather be called an exercise in General Systems Theory – that relatively recent inter-disciplinary school, founded by von Bertalanffy, whose purpose is to construct theoretical models and discover general principles which are universally applicable to biological, social and symbolic systems of any kind – in other words, a search for common denominators in the flux of phenomena, for unity-in-diversity.

As early as 1936, Joseph Needham wrote:

The hierarchy of relations, from the molecular structure of carbon compounds to the equilibrium of species and ecological wholes, will perhaps be the leading idea of the future.[7]

Even earlier Lloyd Morgan, C. D. Broad, and J. Woodger among others emphasized the importance of recognizing hierarchically ordered 'levels of organization', and the emergence on each higher level of new 'organizing relations' between (sub) wholes of greater complexity, whose properties *cannot be reduced to, nor predicted from, the lower level*. To quote Needham again:

Once we adopt the general picture of the universe as a series of levels of organisation and complexity, each level having unique properties of structure and behaviour, which, though depending on the properties of the constituent elements, appear only when these are combined into the higher whole, we see that there are qualitatively different laws holding good at each level.[8]

But such a multi-levelled view went against the materialist *Zeitgeist*, because it implied that the biological laws which govern life are qualitatively different from the laws of physics which govern inanimate matter, and that accordingly life cannot be 'reduced' to the blind dance of atoms; and similarly, that the mentality of man is qualitatively different from the conditioned responses of Pavlov's dogs or Skinner's rats, which the dominant school in psychology considered as the paradigms of human behaviour. Harmless as the word 'hierarchy' sounded, it turned out to be subversive. It did not even appear in the index of most modern textbooks of psychology or biology.

Yet there have always been voices in the wilderness, insisting that the concept of hierarchic organization was an indispensable prerequisite – a *conditio sine qua non* – of any methodical attempt to bring unity into the diversity of science, and might eventually lead to a coherent philosophy of nature – which at present is conspicuous by its absence.

To this minority chorus there was also added the small voice of the author, expressed in several books in which 'the ubiquitous hierarchy'[9] played a major, and often dominant part. Taken together, the relevant passages would add up to a fairly comprehensive textbook on hierarchic order (which may see the light some day). But this is not the purpose of the present volume. As already said, the hierarchic approach is a conceptual tool – not an end in itself, but a key capable of opening some of nature's combination-locks which stubbornly resist other methods.*

However, before attempting to use the key, it is necessary to gain some insight into the way it works. The present chapter is meant to convey some of the basic principles of hierarchic thought in order to provide a platform or runway for the more speculative flights that follow.

5

To say it once more: if we look at any form of stable social organization, from the insect state to the Pentagon, we shall find that it is hierarchically structured; the same applies to the individual organism, and, less obviously, to its innate and acquired skills. However, to prove the validity and significance of the model, it must be shown that there exist specific principles and laws which apply (*a*) to all levels of a given hierarchy, and (*b*) to hierarchies in different fields – in other words, which define the term 'hierarchic order'. Some of these principles might appear self-evident, others rather abstract; taken together, they form the stepping stones for a new approach to some old problems.

'A good terminology', someone has said, 'is half the game.' To get away from the traditional misuse of the words 'whole' and 'part', one is compelled to operate with such awkward terms as 'sub-whole', or 'part-whole', 'sub-structures', 'sub-skills', 'sub-assemblies', and so forth. To avoid these jarring expressions, I proposed, some years ago,[10] a new term to designate those Janus-faced entities on the intermediate levels of any hierarchy, which can be described either as wholes or as parts, depending on the way you look at them from 'below' or from 'above'. The term I proposed was the '*holon*', from the Greek *holos* = whole, with the suffix *on*, which, as in proton or neutron, suggests a particle or part.

The holon seems to have filled a genuine need, for it is gradually

*cf. also Jevons: 'The organisation hierarchy, forming as it does a bridge between parts and whole, is one of the really vital, central concepts of biology.'[11]

finding its way into the terminology of various branches of science, from biology to communication theory. It was particularly gratifying to discover that it has also insinuated itself into French: in Professor Raymond Ruyer's much discussed book *La Gnose de Princeton*[12] there is a chapter entitled: '*Les accolades domaniales et les holons*' – with a footnote which says: 'If I am not mistaken, the word originated with Koestler.' New words are like parvenus: once their origin is forgotten, they have made it.

Unfortunately, the term 'hierarchy' itself is rather unattractive and often provokes a strong emotional resistance. It is loaded with military and ecclesiastic associations, or evokes the 'pecking hierarchy' of the barnyard, and thus conveys the impression of a rigid, authoritarian structure, whereas in the present theory a hierarchy consists of autonomous, self-governing holons endowed with varying degrees of flexibility and freedom. Encouraged by the friendly reception of the holon, I shall occasionally use the terms 'holarchic' and 'holarchy', but without undue insistence.

6

We have seen that biological holons, from organisms down to organelles, are self-regulating entities which manifest both the independent properties of wholes and the dependent properties of parts. This is the first of the general characteristics of all types of holarchies to be retained; we may call it the *Janus principle*. In social hierarchies it is self-evident: every social holon – individual, family, clan, tribe, nation, etc. – is a coherent whole relative to its constituent parts, yet at the same time part of a larger social entity. A society without holarchic structuring would be as chaotic as the random motions of gas molecules colliding and rebounding in all directions.*

Not quite as obvious at first glance is the hierarchic organization of our skilled activities. The skill of driving a motor-car does not consist in the conscious activation of individual muscles by the driver's brain, but in the triggering of sub-routines like

---

*However, the situation is somewhat obscured by the fact that complex societies are structured by *several* interlocking hierarchies – see below, section 12.

accelerating, braking, steering, changing gears, etc., each of which represents a quasi-autonomous pattern of activities – a behavioural holon which is so self-reliant that once you have mastered the skill of driving a particular car, you can drive any car.

Or, take the skill of communicating ideas by speech. The sequence of operations starts at the apex of the hierarchy with the *intention* of conveying the idea or message. But that idea is as often as not of a pre-verbal nature; it may be a visual image, a feeling, a vague impression. We are familiar with the frustrating experience of knowing what we want to say, but not knowing how to express it; and this refers not only to the search for the right word, but preceding that, to the structuring of the intended message and arranging it in a sequential order; processing it according to the laws of grammar and syntax; and lastly, activating coordinated patterns of muscle contractions in the tongue and vocal chords. Thus speaking involves the stepwise concretization, elaboration and articulation of originally inarticulate mental contents. Although these operations follow each other very fast and to a large extent automatically, so that we are not consciously aware of them, they nevertheless require a succession of different activities on different levels of the mental hierarchy. And each of these levels has its own laws: the laws of enunciation, the rules of grammar and syntax, the canons of semantics, etc.

From the listener's point of view the sequence of operations is reversed. It starts at the lowest level – the perceptual skills of recognizing phonemes (speech sounds) in the air-vibrations reaching the ear-drums, amalgamating them into morphemes (syllables, prefixes, etc.) and so forth, through words and sentences, finally reconstituting the speaker's message at the apex of the hierarchy.

Let us note that nowhere on the upward or downward journey through the linguistic holarchy do we encounter hard and indivisible 'atoms of language'. Each of the entities on various levels – phonemes, morphemes, words, sentences – is a whole relative to its parts, and a subordinate part of a more complex entity on the next higher level. For instance, a morpheme

like /men/ is a linguistic holon which can be put to many uses –
menace, mental, mention, mentor, etc.; and which particular
meaning it will assume depends on the context on the higher level.

Psycholinguists use the branching tree as a convenient model
for this step-by-step process of spelling out an implicit thought
in explicit terms, of converting the potentialities of an amorphous
idea into the actual motion-patterns of the vocal chords. This
remarkable process has been compared to ontogenesis – the
development of the embryo; first, there is the fertilized egg,
which contains all the potentialities defining the finished product,
the 'idea', as it were, of the future individual: these potentials
are then 'spelt out' in successive stages of differentiation. It may
also be compared to the process by which a military action is
carried out: the order 'Eighth Army will advance in the direction
of Tobruk', issued from the apex of the hierarchy by the general
in command is concretized, articulated and spelt out in more
detail at each of the successive lower echelons.

Generally speaking, the performance of any purposeful action,
whether instinctive, like the nest-building of birds, or acquired
as most human skills are, follows the same pattern of spelling out
a general intent by the stepwise activation or triggering of
functional holons – sub-routines – on successively lower levels of
the hierarchy. This rule is universally applicable to all types of
'output hierarchies', regardless whether the 'output' is a human
baby, a sentence spoken in English, the playing of a piano
sonata or the action of tying one's shoelaces. (For input hierarchies, as we shall see later, the reverse sequence holds.)

7

The next point to emphasize is that every level in a hierarchy
of any type is governed by a set of fixed, *invariant rules*, which
account for the coherence, stability, and the specific structure and
function of its constituent holons. Thus in the *language* hierarchy
we found on successive levels the rules which govern the activities
of the vocal chords, the laws of grammar and above them the
whole semantic hierarchy concerned with meaning. The codes

which govern the behaviour of *social* holons, and lend them coherence, are written and unwritten laws, traditions, belief-systems, fashions. The development of the *embryo* is governed by the 'genetic code'. Turning to *instinctive activities*, the web which the spider weaves, the nest which the blue tit builds, and the courting ceremony of the greylag goose all conform to fixed, species-specific patterns, produced according to certain 'rules of the game'. In *symbolic operations*, the holons are rule-governed cognitive structures variously called 'frames of reference', 'associative contexts', 'universes of discourse', 'algorithms', etc., each with its specific 'grammar' or canon. We thus arrive at a tentative definition: the term 'holon' may be applied to any structural or functional sub-system in a biological, social or cognitive hierarchy, which manifests rule-governed behaviour and/or structural *Gestalt*-constancy.* Thus organelles and homologous organs are evolutionary holons; morphogenetic fields are onto-genetic holons; the ethologist's 'fixed action-patterns' and the sub-routines of acquired skills are behavioural holons; phonemes, morphemes, words, phrases are linguistic holons; individuals, families, tribes, nations are social holons.†

---

*The 'or' is necessary to include configurations in symbolic hierarchies – which do not manifest 'behaviour' in the usual sense.

†Various authors have pointed to certain affinities between the concept of the holon and Ralph Gerard's 'org'. Thus D. Wilson in *Hierarchical Structures*: 'Koestler (1967) elects to designate these "Janus-faced" entities by the term *holon* . . . We note that Gerard uses the term *org* to designate the same concept (Gerard, 1957).' This of course amounts to a veiled hint at plagiarism. The two quotations from Gerard that follow indicate the similarities and differences between his *org* and the *holon* (my italics): 'Those *material* systems or entities which are individuals at a given level but are composed of subordinate units, lower level orgs'.[13] The limitation to 'material systems' is made more explicit in the second quotation, where he defines the *org* as 'that sub-class of systems composed of material systems, in which matter enters into the picture; this excludes formal systems, for example.'[14] Thus the term 'org' cannot be applied to be-havioural or linguistic or cognitive hierarchies where the concept of the holon proved especially useful. Orgs, as defined by Gerard, represent a sub-category of holons confined to material systems.

8

The set of fixed rules which govern a holon's structure or function we shall call its *code* or *canon*. However, let us note at once
that while the canon imposes constraints* and controls on the
holon's activities, it does not exhaust its degrees of freedom, but
leaves room for more or less flexible strategies, guided by the
contingencies of the environment. This distinction between
fixed (invariant) codes and *flexible (variable) strategies* may sound at
first a little abstract, but it is fundamental to all purposeful
behaviour; a few examples will illustrate what is meant.

The common spider's web-making activities are controlled by
a fixed inherited canon (which prescribes that the radial threads
should always bisect the laterals at equal angles, thus forming a
regular polygon); but the spider is free to suspend his web from
three, four or more points of attachment – to choose his strategy
according to the lie of the land. Other instinctive activities –
birds building nests, bees constructing their hives, silkworms
spinning their cocoons – all have this dual characteristic of con-
forming to an *invariant code* or rule-book which contains the
blueprint of the finished product, but using amazingly *varied
strategies* to achieve it.

Passing from the instinctive activities of the humble spider to
sophisticated human skills like playing chess, we again find a code
of fixed rules which define the *permissible* moves, but the choice
of the *actual* move is left to the player, whose strategy is guided by
the environment – the distribution of the chessmen on the board.
Speech, as we saw, is governed by various canons on various
levels, from semantics through grammar down to phonology,
but on each of these levels the speaker has a vast variety of
strategic choices: from the selection and ordering of the material
to be conveyed, through the formulation of paragraphs and
sentences, the choice of metaphors and adjectives, right down to
enunciation – the selective emphasis placed on individual vowels.

*'Constraint' is a rather unhappy scientific term (reminiscent of the strait-
jacket) which refers to the rules which govern organized activity.

Similar considerations apply to the pianist improvising variations on a theme. The fixed 'rule of the game' in this case is the given melodic pattern, but he has almost infinite scope for the strategic choices in phrasing, rhythm, tempo or transposition into a different key.* A lawyer's activities are very different from a pianist's but the lawyer, too, operates within fixed rules laid down by statute and precedent, while he disposes of a vast range of strategies in interpreting and applying the law.

9

In *ontogenesis* – the development of the embryo – the distinction between 'rules' and 'strategies' is at first sight less obvious, and requires a slightly longer explanation.

The apex of the hierarchy in this case is the fertilized egg; the axis of the inverted tree represents time: and the holons on successive lower levels represent successive stages in the differentiation of tissues into organs. The growth of the embryo from a shapeless blob to a 'roughed in' form and through various stages of increasing articulation has been compared to the way in which a sculptor carves a figure out of a block of wood – or, as already mentioned, to the 'spelling out' of an amorphous idea into articulate phonemes.

The 'idea' to be spelt out in ontogeny is contained in the genetic code, housed in the double helix of nucleic acid strands in the chromosomes. It takes fifty-six generations of cells to produce a human being out of a single, fertilized egg-cell. The cells in the growing embryo are all of identical origin, and carry the *same* set of chromosomes, i.e., the same hereditary dispositions. In spite of this, they develop into such diverse products as muscle cells, kidney cells, brain cells, toe-nails. How can they do this if they are all governed by the same set of laws, by the same hereditary canon?

This is a question which, as W. H. Thorpe recently wrote, 'we

---

*Incidentally, transposition of a musical theme into a different key on the piano, where the sequence of finger movements is totally different, amounts to a complete refutation of the behaviourists' chain-response theory.

are not yet within sight of being able to answer'.[15] But at least
we can approach it by a rough analogy. Let the chromosomes be
represented by the keyboard of a grand piano – a very grand
piano with a few thousand million keys. Then each key will
represent a gene or hereditary disposition. Every single cell in the
body carries a complete keyboard in its nucleus. But each specialized cell is only permitted to sound *one* chord or play *one* tune,
according to its speciality – the rest of the keyboard having been
sealed off by scotch-tape.*

But this analogy immediately poses a further problem: *quis
custodiet ipsos custodes* – who or what agency decides which keys
the cell should activate at what stage and which should be sealed
off? It is at this point that the basic distinction between fixed
codes and adaptable strategies comes in once again.

The genetic code, defining the 'rules of the game' of ontogeny,
is located in the *nucleus* of each cell. The nucleus is bounded by
a permeable membrane, which separates it from the surrounding
cell-body, consisting of a viscous fluid – the cytoplasm – and the
varied tribes of organelles. The cell-body is enclosed in another
permeable membrane, which is surrounded by body-fluids and
by other cells, forming a *tissue*; this, in turn, is in contact with
other tissues. In other words, the genetic code in the cell-nucleus
operates within a *hierarchy of environments* like a nest of Chinese
boxes packed into each other.

Different types of cells (brain cells, kidney cells, etc.) differ
from each other in the structure and chemistry of their cell-
bodies. These differences are due to the complex interactions
between the genetic keyboard in the chromosomes, the cell-body
itself, and its external environment. The latter contains physico–
chemical factors of such extreme complexity that Waddington
coined for it the expression 'epigenetic landscape'. In this landscape the evolving cell moves like an explorer in unknown
territory. To quote another geneticist, James Bonner, each
embryonic cell must be able to 'test' its neighbour-cells 'for

*This sealing-off process also proceeds step-wise, as the hierarchic tree branches
out into more and more specialized tissues – see *The Ghost in the Machine*, Ch. IX,
and below, Part Three.

strangeness or similarity, and in many other ways'.[16] The information thus gathered is then transferred – 'fed back' – via the cell-body to the chromosomes, and determines which chords on the keyboard should be sounded, and which should be temporarily or permanently sealed off; or, to put it differently, which rules of the game should be applied to obtain the best results. Hence the significant title of Waddington's important book on theoretical biology: *The Strategy of the Genes*.[17]

Thus ultimately the cell's future depends on its position in the growing embryo, which determines the strategy of the cell's genes. This has been dramatically confirmed by experimental embryology: by tampering with the spatial structure of the embryo in its early stages of development, the destiny of a whole population of cells could be changed. If at this early stage the future tail of a newt embryo was grafted into a position where a leg should be, it grew not into a tail, but into a leg – surely an extreme example of a flexible strategy within the rules laid down by the genetic code. At a later stage of differentiation the tissues which form the rudiments of future adult organs – the 'organ-buds' or 'morphogenetic fields' – behave like autonomous self-regulating holons in their own right. If at this stage half of the field's tissue is cut away, the remainder will form, not half an organ, but a complete organ. If the growing eye-cup is split into several parts, each fragment will form a smaller, but normal eye.

There is a significant analogy between the behaviour of embryos at this advanced stage and that very early, blastular stage, when it still resembles a hollow ball of cells. When half the blastula of a frog is amputated, the remainder will develop not into half a frog but a smaller normal frog; and if a human blastula is split by accident, the result will be twins or even quadruplets. Thus the holons which at that earliest stage behave as parts of the potentially *whole organism* manifest the same self-regulating characteristics as the holons which at a lower (later) level of the developmental hierarchy are parts of a potential *organ*; in both cases (and throughout the intermediary stages) the holons obey the rules laid down in their genetic code but retain sufficient freedom to follow one or another developmental pathway, guided by the contingencies of their environment.

These self-regulating properties of holons within the growing embryo ensure that whatever accidental hazards arise during development, the end-product will be according to norm. In view of the millions and millions of cells which divide, differentiate, and move about, it must be assumed that no two embryos, not even identical twins, are formed in exactly the same way. The self-regulating mechanisms which correct deviations from the norm and guarantee, so to speak, the end-result, have been compared to the homeostatic feedback devices in the adult organism – so biologists speak of 'developmental homeostasis'. The future individual is potentially predetermined in the chromosomes of the fertilized egg; but to translate this blueprint into the finished product, billions of specialized cells have to be fabricated and moulded into an integrated structure. It would be absurd to assume that the genes of that one fertilized egg should contain built-in provisions for each and every particular contingency which every single one of its fifty-six generations of daughter-cells might encounter in the process. However, the problem becomes a little less baffling if we replace the concept of the 'genetic blueprint', which implies a plan to be rigidly copied, by the concept of a genetic *canon of rules* which are fixed, but leave room for alternative choices, i.e., adaptive strategies guided by feedbacks and pointers from the environment.

Needham once coined a phrase about 'the striving of the blastula to grow into a chicken'. One might call the strategies by which it succeeds the organism's 'pre-natal skills'. After all, the development of the embryo and the subsequent maturation of the newborn into an adult are continuous processes; and we must expect that pre-natal and post-natal skills have certain basic principles in common with each other and with other types of hierarchic processes.

The foregoing section was not intended to describe embryonic development, only one aspect of it: the combination of *fixed rules and variable strategies*, which we also found in instinctive skills (such as nest-building, etc.) and learnt behaviour (such as *language, etc.). It seems that life in all its manifestations, from morphogenesis to symbolic thought, is governed by rules of the game which lend it order and stability but also allow for flexibility; and that these rules, whether innate or acquired, are represented in coded form on various levels of the hierarchy, from the genetic code to the structures in the nervous system associated with symbolic thought.*

10

Ontogeny and phylogeny, the development of the individual and the evolution of species, are the two grand *hierarchies of becoming*. Phylogeny will be discussed in Part Three, but an anticipatory remark is required in our present context of 'rules and strategies'.

Motor-car manufacturers take it for granted that it would make no sense to design a new model from scratch; they make use of already existing sub-assemblies – engines, batteries, steering systems, etc. – each of which has been developed from long previous experience, and then proceed by small modifications of some of these. Evolution follows a similar strategy. Compare the front wheels of the latest model with those of an old vintage car or horse-cart – they are based on the same principles. Compare the anatomy of the fore-limbs of reptiles, birds, whales and man – they show the same structural design of bones, muscles, nerves and blood-vessels and are accordingly called 'homologous' organs.

The functions of legs, wings, flippers and arms are so different that one would expect them to have quite different designs. Yet they are merely modifications, strategic adaptations of an already existing structure – the forelimb of the common reptilian ancestor. Once Nature has taken out a patent on a vital component or process, she sticks to it with amazing tenacity: the organ or device has become a stable *evolutionary holon*. It is as if she felt compelled to provide unity in variety. Geoffroy de St Hilaire, one of the pioneers of modern biology, wrote in 1818: 'Vertebrates are built upon one uniform plan – e.g., the forelimb may be modified for running, climbing, swimming, or flying, yet the arrangement of the bones remains the same.'[18] That basic arrangement is part of the invariant *evolutionary canon*. Its utilization for swimming or flying is a matter of *evolutionary strategy*.

This principle holds all along the line, through all the levels of the evolutionary hierarchy down to the organelles inside the cell, and the DNA chains in the chromosomes. The same standard models of organelles function in the cells of mice and men; the same ratchet-device using a contractile protein serves the motion of amoeba and of the concert-pianist's fingers; the same four chemical molecules constitute the basic alphabet in which heredity is encoded throughout the animal and plant kingdoms – only the words and phrases formed by hem are different for each creature.

If evolution could only create novelties by starting each time afresh from the 'primeval soup', the four thousand million years of the earth's history would not have been long enough to produce even an amoeba. In a much quoted paper on hierarchic structures, H. G. Simon concluded: 'Complex systems will evolve from simple systems much more rapidly if there are stable intermediate forms than if there are not. The resulting complex forms in the former case will be hierarchic. We have only to turn the argument around to explain the observed predominance of hierarchies among the complex systems Nature presents to us. Among possible complex forms, hierarchies are the ones that have the time to evolve.'[19]

We do not know what forms of life exist on other planets, but we can safely assume that wherever there is life, it is hierarchically organized.

II

Neglect of the hierarchic concept, and the failure to make a categorical distinction between *rules* and *strategies* of behaviour, has caused much confusion in academic psychology.* Since its

*It is interesting to note the intense reluctance of academic psychologists – even those who have outgrown the cruder forms of behaviourist S–R theory – to come to grips with reality. Thus Professor G. Miller writes in an article on

primary concern for the last fifty years was the study of rats in confined spaces ('Skinner boxes'), this failure is hardly surprising. Yet to any spectator of a game of football or chess it is at once obvious that each player obeys rules which determine what he *can* do, and uses his strategic skills to decide what he *will* do. In other words, *the code defines the rules of the game, strategy decides the course of the game.* The examples cited in the previous section indicate that this categorical distinction between rules and strategies is universally applicable to innate and acquired skills, to the hierarchies which make for social coherence, as well as to the hierarchies of becoming.

The nature of the code which regulates behaviour varies of course according to the nature and level of the hierarchy concerned. Some codes are innate – such as the genetic code, or the codes which govern the instinctive activities of animals; others are acquired by learning – like the kinetic code in the circuitry of my nervous system which enables me to ride a bicycle without falling off, or the cognitive code which defines the rules of playing chess.

Let us now turn from codes to *strategies*. To repeat it once more: the code defines the permitted moves, strategy decides the choice of the actual move. The next question is: how are these choices made? We might say that the chess-player's choice is 'free' – in the sense that it is not determined by the rule-book. In fact the number of choices confronting a player in the course of a game of forty moves (while calculating the potential varia-

---

psycholinguistics: 'As psychologists have learnt to appreciate the complexities of language, the prospect of reducing it to the laws of behaviour so carefully studied in lower animals [he means Skinner's rats] has grown increasingly remote. We have been forced more and more into a position that non-psychologists probably take for granted, namely, that language is rule-governed behaviour characterized by enormous flexibility and freedom of choice. Obvious as this conclusion may seem, it has important implications for any scientific theory of language. If rules involve the concepts of right and wrong, they introduce a normative aspect that has always been avoided in the natural sciences.... To admit that language follows rules seems to put it outside the range of phenomena accessible to scientific investigation.'[20] What a very odd notion of the purpose and methods of 'scientific investigation'!

tions which each move might entail two moves ahead) is astronomical. But though his choice is 'free' in the above sense of not
being determined by the rules, it is certainly not *random*. The
player tries to select a 'good' move, which will bring him nearer
to a win, and to avoid a bad move. But the rule-book knows
nothing about 'good' or 'bad' moves. It is, so to speak, ethically
neutral. What guides the player's choice of a hoped-for 'good'
move are strategic precepts of a much higher complexity – on
a higher level of the cognitive hierarchy – than the simple rules
of the game. The rules a child can learn in half an hour; whereas
the *strategy* is distilled from past experience, the study of master
games and specialized books on chess theory. Generally we find on
successively higher levels of the hierarchy increasingly complex,
more flexible and less predictable patterns of activity with more
degrees of freedom (a larger variety of strategic choices); while
conversely every complex activity, such as writing a letter,
branches into sub-skills which on successively lower levels of
the hierarchy become increasingly mechanical, stereotyped and
predictable.* The original choice of subjects to be discussed in the
letter is vast; the next step, phrasing, still offers a great number of
strategic alternatives but is more restricted by the rules of grammar; the rules of spelling are fixed with no elbow-room for
flexible strategies, and the muscle-contractions which depress the
keys of the typewriter are fully automatized.

If we descend even further down into the basement of the
hierarchy, we come to visceral processes which are self-regulating,
controlled by homeostatic feedback devices. These, of course,
leave little scope for strategic choices; nevertheless, my conscious
self can interfere to some extent with the normally unconscious,
automated functioning of my respiratory system by holding my
breath or applying some Yoga technique. Thus the distinction
between rules and strategies remains in principle valid even on
this basic physiological level. But the relevance of this distinction
will only become fully apparent in later chapters when we apply
it to such fundamental problems as the theory of evolution; free

*cf. the ethologist's 'fixed action patterns'.

will versus determinism; and the pathology and creativity of the human mind.

12

As already mentioned, the purpose of this chapter is not to provide a manual of hierarchies, but to convey some idea of the conceptual framework on which this inquiry is based, and to give the reader the 'feel' of hierarchic thinking as opposed to the current reductionist and mechanistic trends. To conclude this summary survey, I must mention, however briefly, a few more principles which all hierarchic systems have in common.

One obvious point is that hierarchies do not operate in a vacuum, but interact with others. This elementary fact has given rise to much confusion. If you look at a well-kept hedge surrounding a garden like a living wall, the rich foliage of the entwined branches may make you forget that the branches originate in separate bushes. The bushes are vertical, *arborizing* structures. The entwined branches form horizontal *networks* at numerous levels. Without the individual plants there would be no entwining, and no network. Without the network, each plant would be isolated, and there would be no hedge and no integration of functions. '*Arborization*' and '*reticulation*' (net-formation) are complementary principles in the architecture of organisms and societies. The circulatory system controlled by the heart and the respiratory system controlled by the lungs function as quasi-autonomous, self-regulating hierarchies, but they interact on various levels. In the subject-catalogues in our libraries the branches are entwined through cross-references. In cognitive hierarchies – universes of discourse – arborization is reflected in the 'vertical' denotation (classification) of concepts, reticulation in their 'horizontal' connotations in associative nets.

The complementarity of arborization and reticulation yields relevant clues to the complex problem of how memory works.*

*The section that follows is a summary of *The Act of Creation*, Book II, Ch. x, *The Ghost in the Machine*, Ch. v and vi, and of a paper read to the Harvard Medical School Symposium on 'The Pathology of Memory'.[21]

13

In Stevenson's novel *Kidnapped*, Alan Breck makes the casual remark: 'I have a grand memory for forgetting, David.' He speaks for all of us, and not only those afflicted with aphasia or senility. Painful as it is, we have to admit that a large proportion of our memories resembles the dregs in a wine glass, the dehydrated sediments of experiences whose flavour has gone – or, to change the metaphor, they are like dusty abstracts of past events on the shelves of a dimly lit archive. Fortunately this applies only to one type or category of memories, which I shall call *abstractive memory*. But there is another category, derived from our capacity to recall past episodes, or scenes, or details of scenes, with almost hallucinatory vividness. I shall call this the *spotlight* type of memory, and I shall contend that 'abstractive memory' and 'spotlight memory' are different classes of phenomena, based on different neural mechanisms.

Take abstractive memory first. The bulk of what we can remember of our life history, and of the knowledge we have accumulated in the course of it, is of the abstractive type.

The word 'abstract' has, in common usage, two main connotations: it is the opposite of 'concrete', in the sense that it refers to a general concept rather than a particular instance; in the second place, an 'abstract' is a condensation of the essence of a longer document. Memory is abstractive in both senses. I watch a television play. The exact words of each actor are forgotten within a few seconds; only their abstracted meaning is retained. The next morning I can only remember the sequence of scenes which constituted the story. A month later, all I can remember is that the play was about a gangster on the run. Much the same happens to the mnemic residues of books one has read and whole chapters of one's own life-story. The original experience has been stripped of detail, skeletonized, reduced to a colourless abstract before being confined to the memory store. The nature of that store is still a complete mystery in brain-research, but it is obvious that if stored knowledge and experience are to be retrievable (for otherwise they would be useless), they must be ordered according to the hierarchic principle – like a thesaurus or a library subject-catalogue, with headings and sub-headings but also with a wealth of cross-references to assist the process of retrieval (the former representing arborization, the latter the reticulation of the hierarchic structure). If we pursue for a moment the metaphor of a library representing our memory stores, we arrive at rather depressing conclusions. Quite apart from the countless volumes that are left to rot away or fall to dust, there is a hierarchy of librarians at work who ruthlessly condense long texts into short abstracts and then make abstracts of the abstracts.

This process of sifting and abstracting actually starts long before a lived experience is confined to the memory store. At every relay station in the perceptual hierarchy through which the sensory input must pass before being admitted to consciousness it is analysed, classified and stripped of irrelevant detail.* This enables us to recognize the letter R in an almost illegible scrawl as 'the same thing' as a huge printed R in a newspaper headline, by a sophisticated scanning process which disregards all details and abstracts only the basic geometrical design – the 'R-ness' of the R – as worth signalling to higher quarters. This signal can now be transmitted in a simple code, like a message in Morse, which contains all the relevant information – 'it's an R' – in a condensed, skeletonized form; but the wealth of calligraphic detail is of course irretrievably lost, as the inflections of the human voice are lost in the Morse message. The wistful remark 'I have a memory like a sieve' may be derived from an intuitive grasp of these filtering devices which operate all along the input channels and storage channels of the nervous system.

Yet even the chosen few among the multitude of potential stimuli incessantly bombarding our receptor organs which have successfully passed all these selective filters and have attained the

*The psychologist distinguishes on the lower levels of the hierarchy lateral inhibition, habituation, and efferent control of the receptors; on the higher levels the mechanisms responsible for the visual and auditory constancy phenomena, and the scanning and filtering devices that account for pattern recognition and enable us to abstract universals.

status of consciously perceived events, must submit, as we have
seen, to further rigorous stripping procedures before being
admitted to the permanent memory store; and as time passes,
they will suffer further decay. Memory is a prize example of the
law of diminishing returns.

This retrospective impoverishment of lived experience is
unavoidable; 'abstractive' memory implies the sacrifice of particulars. If, instead of abstracting generalized concepts, like 'R'
or 'tree' or 'dog', our memories consisted of a collection of all
our particular experiences of R's and trees and dogs encountered
in the past – a storehouse of lantern slides and tape-recordings – it
would be a chaotic jumble, completely useless for mental guidance, for we would never be able to identify an R or understand
a spoken sentence. Without hierarchic order and classification,
memory would be bedlam (or the parroting of sequences learned
by rote, and reinforced by conditioning, which is the behaviourist's model – or caricature – for remembering).

To say it again: the loss of particulars in abstractive memory
is unavoidable. Fortunately this is not the whole story, for there
are several compensating factors which, at least in part, make up
for the loss.

In the first place, the abstractive process can acquire a higher
degree of sophistication by learning from experience. To the
novice, all red wines taste alike, and all Japanese males look the
same. But he can be taught to superimpose more delicate perceptual filters on the coarser ones, as Constable trained himself to
discriminate between diverse types of clouds and to classify them
into sub-categories. Thus we learn to abstract finer and finer
nuances – to make the trees of the hierarchies of perception grow
new shoots, as it were.

Moreover, it is important to realize that abstractive memory
is not based on a single hierarchy but on several interlocking
hierarchies pertaining to different sensory realms such as vision,
hearing, smell. What is less obvious is that there may exist
several distinct hierarchies with different criteria of relevance
operating within the same sense modality. I can recognize a
melody regardless of the instrument on which it was played; but

I can also recognize the sound of an instrument regardless of the melody played on it. We must therefore assume that melodic pattern and instrument sound (timbre) are abstracted and stored independently by separate filtering hierarchies *within the same sensory modality but with different criteria of relevance*. One abstracts melody and disregards timbre, the other abstracts the timbre of an instrument and disregards melody as irrelevant. Thus not all the detail discarded as irrelevant by one filtering system is irretrievably lost, because it may have been retained and stored by another filtering hierarchy with different criteria of relevance.

The recall of an experience would then be made possible by the cooperation of several interlocking hierarchies, which may include different sense modalities, for instance, sight and sound or odour, or different branches within the same modality. You may remember the words of the aria 'Your Tiny Hand is Frozen', but have lost the tune. Or you may remember the tune after having forgotten the words. And you may recognize the unique timbre of Caruso's voice on a gramophone record, regardless of the words and the tune he is singing. But if two, or all three of these features have been abstracted and stored, the recall of the original experience will have more dimensions and be the more complete.

The process could in some respects be compared to multi-colour printing by the superimposition of several colour-blocks. The painting to be reproduced – the original experience – is photographed through different colour-filters on blue, red and yellow plates, each of which retains only those features that are 'relevant' to it: i.e., those which appear in its own colour, and ignores all other features; then they are recombined into a more or less faithful reconstruction of the original input. Each hierarchy would then have a different 'colour' attached to it, the colour symbolizing its *criteria of relevance*. Which memory-forming hierarchies will be active at any given time depends, of course, on the subject's general interests and momentary state of mind.

Although this hypothesis represents a radical departure from both the behaviourist and the *Gestalt* schools' conceptions of memory, some modest evidence for it can be found in a series of experiments carried out in cooperation with Professor J. J. Jenkins in the psychological laboratory of Stanford University;* and more tests on these lines can be designed without much difficulty.

14

The 'colour printing' hypothesis may provide part of the explanation of the complex phenomena of memory and recall, but it is based solely on the *abstractive* type of memory which by itself cannot account for the extreme vividness of the *'spotlight'* type of memory mentioned at the beginning of this chapter. It is a method of retention based on principles which seem to be the exact opposite of memory formation in abstractive hierarchies. It is characterized by the recall of scenes or details with almost hallucinatory clarity. They are rather like photographic close-ups, in contrast to abstractive memory's aerial panorama seen through a haze. The emphasis is on detail, which may be a fragment, torn from its context, that survived the decay of the whole to which it once belonged – like the single lock of hair on the shrivelled mummy of an Egyptian princess. It may be auditory – a line from an otherwise forgotten poem, or a chance remark by a stranger overheard in a bus; or visual – a wart on Nanny's chin, a hand waving farewell from the window of a departing train; or even refer to taste and smell, like Proust's celebrated *madeleine* (the French pastry, not the girl). Though often trivial from a rational point of view, these spotlighted images add texture and flavour to memory, and have an uncanny evocative power. This suggests

---

*See Appendix II. This is a rather technical paper of possible interest to experimental psychologists, which the general reader can safely ignore. The gist of the experiment was to show to each subject for a fraction of a second only (by means of an apparatus called a tachistoscope) a number of seven or eight digits, and then let him try to repeat the sequence. The results of several hundred experiments show that a highly significant number of errors (approximately fifty per cent) consisted in the subject *correctly identifying* all numbers in the sequence, but *inverting the order* of two or three neighbouring digits. This seems to confirm that the identification of individual digits, and the determination of their sequential order, are carried out by different branches of the perceptual hierarchy.

that, although irrelevant by logical criteria, they have some special *emotive* significance (on a conscious or unconscious level) that caused them to be retained.

Nobody, not even computer designers, thinks all the time in terms of abstractive hierarchies. Emotion colours most of our perceptions, and there are indications that our emotive reactions also involve a hierarchy of levels – including archaic structures in the brain which are phylogenetically much older than the structures concerned with abstract conceptualizations. One might speculate that in the formation of 'spotlight memories' these older levels in the hierarchy play a dominant part.

There are some further considerations in favour of such a hypothesis. First, from the neurophysiologist's point of view, they receive strong support from the Papez–MacLean theory of emotions.* Second, from the standpoint of the communication-theorist, abstractive memory generalizes and schematizes, while spotlight memory particularizes and concretizes – which is a much more primitive method of storing information.† Third, from the standpoint of the psychologist, abstractive memory would be related to insightful learning and spotlight memory to a process resembling imprinting. But imprinting in Konrad Lorenz's geese is restricted to a critical period of a few hours, and apparently results in a very coarse and vague imprint. On the human level, imprinting may take the form of eidetic imagery. According to Jaensch[22] and Kluever, [23] a considerable proportion of children have the eidetic faculty – they are able to 'project' a photographically accurate, coloured image of a previously fixated picture onto a blank screen and to repeat this after long intervals, sometimes even years. Penfield and Roberts'[24] experiments, evoking what is claimed to be total recall of past scenes by electrical stimulation of the patient's temporal lobes, may be a related phenomenon.

*See above, Prologue.
†The term 'information' in modern communication-theory is used in a more general sense than in common parlance. Information includes anything from the colour and taste of an apple to the Ninth Symphony of Beethoven. Irrelevant inputs convey no information and are called 'noise' – on the analogy of a noisy telephone line.

But though apparantly quite common in children, eidetic memory tends to vanish with the onset of puberty, and is rare among adults. Children and primitives live in a world of visual imagery. In William Golding's novel *The Inheritors*, the author makes his Neanderthalers say, instead of 'I have thought of something,' 'I have a picture in my head.' The eidetic child's way of 'imprinting' pictures on the mind may represent a phylogenetically and ontogenetically earlier form of memory formation – which is lost when abstractive, conceptual thinking becomes dominant.

To sum up, abstractive memory, operating through multiple interlocking hierarchies, strips down the input to bare essentials according to each hierarchy's criteria of relevance. *Recalling* the experience requires dressing it up again. This is made possible, up to a point, by the cooperation of the hierarchies concerned, each of which contributes those aspects it has deemed worth preserving. The process is comparable to the superimposition of colour-plates in printing. Added to this are 'spotlight' memories of vivid details which may include fragments of eidetic imagery, and carry a strong emotive charge. The results of this exercise in re-creating the past is a kind of collage, with glass eyes and a strand of genuine hair stuck on to the hazy, schematized picture.

15

When the centipede was asked in which precise order it moved its hundred legs, it became paralysed and starved to death because it had never thought of this problem before and had left its legs to look after themselves. When an intent is formed at that top level of the hierarchy which we call the conscious self – an intent such as tying one's shoelaces or lighting a cigarette – it does not directly activate the contractions of individual muscles, but triggers off a coordinated pattern of impulses – functional holons – which activates sub-patterns, and so on. But this can only be done one step at a time; the top echelons in the hierarchy do not normally have direct dealings with the lowly ones, and vice versa. Brigadiers do not concentrate their attention on individual soldiers;

if they did, the operation would go haywire. Signals must be transmitted by 'regulation channels' as the army calls them, i.e., step by step up or down the levels of the hierarchy.

This statement may sound trivial, but ignoring it carries penalties of various kinds. The short-circuiting of intermediary levels by focusing conscious attention on activities which otherwise proceed automatically, usually ends in the centipede's predicament – reflected in symptoms that range from the awkward condition we call 'self-conscious' behaviour to disorders such as impotence, stuttering or spastic colons. Viktor Frankl, the founder of 'logotherapy', coined the term 'hyper-reflection' for disorders of this type.[25]

On the other hand, the ancient practices of Hatha Yoga and some derivative techniques at present much in vogue aim at deliberate control of visceral and neural processes (including the alpha waves of the brain), through meditation aided by biofeedback gadgets. But under normal conditions, the 'one-step rule' holds in all types of hierarchies – from ontogeny and phylogeny to social institutions and the processing of the sensory input on its step-wise ascent from the receptor organs to consciousness.

16

I have repeatedly referred to the 'apex' of the hierarchy. Some hierarchies do indeed have a well-defined apex or peak, and a definite bottom level – e.g., a small business enterprise with a single proprietor and a stable work force. But the grand holarchies of existence – whether social, biological or cosmological – tend to be 'open-ended' in one or both directions. A laboratory chemist, analysing a chemical compound, is engaged in a stepwise operation, where the apex of his tree – the sample to be analysed – is on the molecular level of the hierarchy, branching into chemical radicals, branching into atoms. For his particular purpose this hierarchy of a limited number of levels is sufficient. But from a broader point of view, which takes into account sub-atomic processes, what appears to the chemist as a complete tree turns out to be merely a branch of a more comprehensive hierarchy.

Just as holons are, by definition, sub-wholes, so all branches of a hierarchy are sub-hierarchies, and whether you treat them as 'wholes' or 'parts' depends on the task in hand. The chemist need not bother about the so-called elementary particles which, as somebody remarked, have a disconcerting tendency not to remain elementary for very long, and seem to consist ultimately – or penultimately – of patterns of energy-concentration or stresses in the universal foam of space–time. Our laboratory chemist can safely ignore these surrealistic developments in modern quantum physics; but he must not forget – under the penalty of mental dehydration – that his tidy little hierarchic tree extends only through a very limited number of levels in the great open-ended hierarchies of being.

The same applies at the other end of the scale to the astronomer faced with the wheels-within-wheels display of solar systems, galaxies, galactic clusters and the possibility of parallel universes in hyper-space.

By way of a summary, I would like to call the reader's attention to Appendix I, 'Beyond Atomism and Holism – The Concept of the Holon'. This is the edited text of a paper read at the Alpbach Symposium which attempts to put into concise form the characteristic properties of open hierarchic systems discussed in this chapter (and also some other properties, still to be discussed).

II

BEYOND EROS AND THANATOS

I

One further universal characteristic of holarchic order which
remains to be discussed is of such basic importance that it deserves
a chapter to itself.

The holons which constitute a living organism or a social body
are, as we have seen, Janus-like entities: the face turned towards
the higher levels in the holarchy is that of a subordinate part in
a larger system; the face turned towards the lower levels shows a
quasi-autonomous whole in its own right.

This implies that every holon is possessed of two opposite
tendencies or potentials: an *integrative tendency* to function as part
of the larger whole, and a *self-assertive tendency* to preserve its
individual autonomy.

The most obvious manifestation of this basic polarity is found
in social holarchies. Here the autonomy of the constituent holons
is jealousy guarded and asserted on every level – from the rights
of the individual to those of clan or tribe, from administrative
departments to local governments, from ethnic minorities to
sovereign nations. Every social holon has a built-in tendency to
preserve and defend its corporate identity. This *self-assertive
tendency* is indispensable for maintaining the individuality of
holons on all levels, and of the hierarchy as a whole. Without it,
the social structure would dissolve into an amorphous jelly or
degenerate into a monolithic tyranny. History provides many
examples of both.

At the same time the holon is dependent on, and must function
as an integrated part of the larger system which contains it: its
integrative or self-transcending tendency, resulting from the holon's

partness, must keep its self-assertive tendency in check. Under favourable conditions, the two basic tendencies – *self-assertion and integration* – are more or less equally balanced, and the holon lives in a kind of dynamic equilibrium within the whole – the two faces of Janus complement each other. Under unfavourable conditions the equilibrium is upset, with dire consequences.

We thus arrive at a basic polarity between the *self-assertive tendency* and the *integrative tendency* of holons on every level, and, as we shall see, in every type of hierarchic system. This polarity is a fundamental feature of the present theory and one of its *leitmotifs*. It is not a product of metaphysical speculation, but is in fact *implied* in the model of the multi-levelled holarchy, because the stability of the model depends on the equilibration of the dual aspects of its holons, as wholes and as parts. This polarity or *coincidencia oppositorum* is present in varying degrees in all manifestations of life. Its philosophical implications will be discussed in later chapters; for the time being let us note that *the self-assertive tendency is the dynamic expression of the holon's wholeness, its integrative tendency the dynamic expression of its partness.**

As far as the holons in social hierarchies are concerned, the polarity is obvious – shouting at us from the headlines of the daily newspaper. But in less obvious ways the dichotomy of self-assertion versus integration is ubiquitous in biology, psychology, ecology and wherever we find complex hierarchic systems – which is practically everywhere around us. To paraphrase Gertrude Stein again: a whole is a part is a whole. Each sub-whole is a 'sub' and a 'whole'. In the living animal or plant, as in the body social, each part must assert its individuality, for otherwise the organism would lose its articulation and disintegrate; but at the same time the part must submit to the demands of the whole – which is not always a smooth process.

We have seen earlier on that each part of the living creature, from complex organs down to the organelles inside the cell, has its intrinsic rhythm and pattern of activity, governed by its

*For 'integrative tendency' I shall occasionally use as synonymous: 'participatory' or 'self-transcending' tendency.

own built-in code of rules, which makes it function as a quasi-independent unit. On the other hand, these autonomous activities of the holon are released, inhibited and modified by controls on higher levels of the hierarchy which act on the holon's integrative potential and make it function as a subordinate part. In a healthy organism as in a healthy society, the two tendencies are in equilibrium on every level of the hierarchy. But when exposed to stress, the self-asserting tendency of the affected part of the organism or society may get out of hand – i.e., the part will tend to escape the restraining controls of the whole. This can lead to pathological changes – such as malignant growths with an untrammelled proliferation of tissues which have escaped genetic restraint. On a less extreme level, virtually any organ or function may get temporarily and partially out of control. In rage and panic the sympathico–adrenal apparatus takes over from the higher centres which normally coordinate behaviour; when sex is aroused, the gonads seem to take over from the brain. The *idée fixe*, the obsession of the crank, are cognitive holons running riot. There is a wide range of mental disorders in which some subordinate part in the cognitive hierarchy exerts a tyrannical rule over the whole, or in which some chunks of the personality seem to have 'split off' and lead a quasi-independent existence. The most frequent aberrations of the human mind are due to the obsessional pursuit of some part-truth, treated as if it were the whole truth – a holon masquerading as the whole.

In the routines of everyday existence both tendencies are in constant interplay. The *self-assertive* tendency is manifested on every level of the hierarchies of behaviour: in the stubbornness of instinctive rituals in animals and of acquired habits in men; in tribal traditions and social customs; and even in a person's individual gait, gestures or handwriting, which he might be able to modify, but not sufficiently to fool the expert; the holons of his graphological style defend their autonomy. It is the *integrative* tendency, equally ubiquitous, which prevents us from becoming complete slaves of our habits and freezing into automata; it is manifested in flexible strategies, original adaptations, and creative syntheses which originate higher, more complex and integrated forms of thought and behaviour, adding new levels to the open-ended hierarchy.

2

The basic polarity is much in evidence in the phenomena of *emotive* behaviour on the individual and social scale. No man is an island; he is a holon. Looking inward, he experiences himself as a unique, self-contained, independent whole; looking outward as a dependent part of his natural and social environment. His self-assertive tendency is the dynamic manifestation of his individuality; his integrative tendency expresses his dependence on the larger whole to which he belongs, his partness. When all is well, the two tendencies are more or less evenly balanced. In times of stress and frustration, the equilibrium is upset, manifested in emotional disorders. The emotions derived from the frustrated self-assertive tendencies are of the well-known, adrenergic, *aggressive–defensive* type: hunger, rage and fear, including the possessive components of sex and of parental care. The emotions derived from the integrative tendency have been to a large extent neglected by academic psychology: one may call them the *self-transcending* type of emotions. They arise out of the human holon's need to belong, to transcend the narrow boundaries of the self and to be part of a more embracing whole – which may be a community, a religious creed or political cause, Nature, Art, or the *anima mundi*.

When the need to belong, the urge towards self-transcendence is deprived of adequate outlets, the frustrated individual may lose his critical faculties and surrender his identity in blind worship or fanatical devotion to some cause, regardless of its merits. As we have seen earlier on, it is one of the ironies of the human condition that its ferocious destructiveness derives not from the self-assertive, but from the integrative potential of the species. The glories of science and art, and the holocausts of history caused by misguided devotion, were both nurtured by the self-transcending type of emotions. For the code of rules which defines the corporate identity, and lends coherence to a social holon (its language, laws, traditions, standards of conduct, systems of belief) represents not merely negative constraints imposed on its activities but also positive precepts, maxims and moral imperatives. In normal times, when the social hierarchy is in equilibrium, each of its holons operates in accordance with its code of rules, without attempting to impose it on others; in times of stress and crisis, a social holon may get over-excited and tend to assert itself to the detriment of the whole, just like any over-excited organ or obsessive idea.

3

The dichotomy of wholeness and partness, and its dynamic manifestation in the polarity of the self-assertive and integrative tendencies is, as already said, inherent in every multi-levelled hierarchic system, and implied in the conceptual model. We find it reflected even in inanimate nature: wherever there is a relatively stable dynamic system, from atoms to galaxies, its stability is maintained by the equilibrium of opposite forces, one of which may be centrifugal – i.e., inertial or separative, the other centripetal, i.e., attractive or cohesive, which binds the parts together in the larger whole, without sacrifice of their identity. Newton's first law – 'Every body continues in its state of rest or uniform motion in a straight line unless compelled by a force to change that state' – sounds like a proclamation of the self-assertive tendency of every speck of matter in the universe; while his Law of Gravity reflects the integrative tendency.*

We may venture a step further, and regard the Principle of Complementarity as an even more basic example of our polarity. According to this principle, which dominates modern physics, all elementary particles – electrons, photons, etc. – have the dual character of corpuscles and waves: according to circumstances they

*In a science-fiction play, written many years ago, I had a visiting maiden from an alien planet explain the central doctrine of its religion: '... We worship gravitation. It is the only force which does not travel through space in a rush; it is everywhere in repose. It keeps the stars in their orbits and our feet on our earth. It is Nature's fear of loneliness, the earth's longing for the moon; it is love in its pure, inorganic form.' (*Twilight Bar*, 1945.)

will behave either as compact grains of matter, or as waves without substantial attributes or definable boundaries. From our point of view, the corpuscular aspect of the electron – or any elementary holon – manifests its wholeness and self-assertive potential, while its wave-character manifests its partness and integrative potential.*

<h1 style="text-align:center">4</h1>

Needless to say, the manifestations of the two basic tendencies appear in different guises on different levels of the hierarchy, according to the specific codes – or 'organizing relations' – characteristic of that level. The rules which govern the interactions of sub-atomic particles are not the same rules which govern the interactions between atoms as wholes; and the ethical rules which govern the behaviour of individuals are not the same rules which govern the behaviour of crowds or armies. Accordingly, the manifestations of the polarity of self-assertive and integrative tendencies, which we find in all phenomena of life, will take different forms from level to level. Thus, for example, we shall find the polarity reflected as:

integration ⟷ self-assertion
partness   ⟷ wholeness
dependence   ⟷ autonomy
centripetal ⟷ centrifugal
cooperation ⟷ competition
altruism   ⟷ egotism

Let us further note that the self-assertive tendency is by and large *conservative* in the sense of tending to preserve the individuality of the holon in the here and now of existing conditions; whereas the integrative tendency has the dual function of co-ordinating the constituent holons of a system in its present stage, *and* of generating new levels of complex integrations in evolving

*Another instance of the polarity of inanimate nature is reflected in Mach's Principle, which connects terrestrial inertia with the total mass of the universe; see below, Ch. XIII.

hierarchies – whether biological, social or cognitive. Thus the self-assertive tendency is present-orientated, concerned with self-maintenance, while the integrative tendency may be said to work both for the present and towards the future.

5

As the polarity of the self-assertive and the integrative tendencies plays a crucial role in our theory and will keep cropping up in later chapters, a brief comparison with Freud's metaphysical system, which achieved such immense popularity, may be of some interest.

Freud postulated two basic *Triebe* ('drives', or loosely, 'instincts') which he conceived as mutually antagonistic universal tendencies inherent in all living matter: Eros and Thanatos, or libido and death-wish. A close reading of the relevant passages (in *Beyond the Pleasure Principle, Civilisation and its Discontents*, etc.) reveals, surprisingly, that both his drives are *regressive*: they both aim at the restoration of a past primeval condition. Eros, through the lure of the pleasure principle, tries to re-establish the erstwhile 'unity of protoplasm in the primordial slime', while Thanatos aims even more directly at a return to the inorganic state of matter through the annihilation of self and other selves. As both drives are attempting to turn the clock of evolution backward, one is left wondering how it came about that it moves forward nevertheless. Freud's answer seems to be that Eros is forced to make a long detour in gathering 'the dispersed fragments of living substance'[1] into multicellular aggregates with the final aim of restoring protoplasmic unity; in other words, evolution appears as the product of inhibited regression, the negation of a negation, a backing forward, as it were.

As a curiosity one may note Freud's rather dim view of the working of Eros. According to this view, pleasure is always derived from 'the diminution, lowering, or extinction of psychic excitation' and 'un-pleasure* from an increase of it'. The organism tends towards stability; it is guided by 'the striving of the

---

Unlust, dysphoria, as distinct from physical pain.

mental apparatus to keep the quantity of excitations present in it as low as possible or at least constant. Accordingly, everything that tends to increase the quantity of excitation must be regarded as adverse to this tendency, that is to say, as unpleasurable.'[2]

Now this is of course true, in a broad sense, in so far as the frustration of elementary needs like hunger is concerned. But it passes in silence a whole class of experiences to which we commonly refer as 'pleasurable excitement'. The preliminaries of love-making cause an increase in sexual tension and should, according to the theory, be unpleasant – which they decidedly are not. It is curious that in the works of Freud there is no answer to be found to this embarrassingly banal objection. The sex-drive in the Freudian system is essentially something to be disposed of – through the proper channels or by sublimation; pleasure is derived not from its pursuit, but from getting rid of it.*

Freud's concept of Thanatos – the *Todestrieb* – is as puzzling as his Eros. On the one hand, the death-wish 'works silently, within the organism towards its disintegration' by catabolic processes, breaking down living into lifeless matter. This aspect of it may in fact be equated with the Second Law of Thermo-dynamics† – the gradual dispersion of matter and energy into a state of chaos. But, on the other hand, Freud's death-instinct, which works so quietly *within* the organism, appears, when projected outward, as active destructiveness or sadism. How these two aspects of Thanatos can be harmonized and causally connected is difficult to see. For the first aspect is that of a physico–chemical process which tends to reduce living cells to quiescence and ultimately to dust; while the second aspect shows a coordi-nated, violent aggression of the whole organism against other

---

*One might argue that in Freud's universe there is no place for amorous love-play because Freud, like D. H. Lawrence, was basically a puritan with a horror of frivolity, who treated sex '*mit tierischem Ernst*'. Ernest Jones says in his biography: 'Freud partook in much of the prudishness of his time, when allusions to lower limbs were improper.' He then gives several examples – such as Freud 'sternly forbidding' his fiancée to stay 'with an old friend, recently married, who as she delicately put it, "had married before her wedding"'.[3]

†We shall see later that this famous law applies only to so-called 'closed systems' in physics, and not to living organisms; but this is a relatively recent discovery which Freud could not know.

organisms. The process by which the silent sliding towards senescence and disintegration is converted into the infliction of violence on others is not explained by Freud; the only link he provides is the ambiguous use of words like 'death-wish' and 'urge to destruction'.

Not only is the connection between these two aspects of the Freudian Thanatos missing, but each in itself is highly questionable. Taking the second aspect first, nowhere do we find in nature destruction for destruction's sake. Animals kill to devour, not to destroy; and – as already mentioned – even when they fight in competition for territory or mates, the fight is ritualized like a fencing bout and is hardly ever carried to a lethal end. To prove the existence of a primary 'destructive instinct', it would have to be shown that destructive behaviour regularly occurs *without* external provocation, as hunger and the sex-drive make themselves felt regardless of the absence of external stimuli. To quote Karen Horney (once an eminent, but critical psychoanalyst):[4]

Freud's assumption implies that the ultimate motivation for hostility or destructiveness lies in the impulse to destroy. Thus he turns into its opposite our belief that we destroy in order to live: we live in order to destroy. We should not shrink from recognizing error, even in an age-old conviction, if new insight teaches us to see it differently, but this is not the case here. If we want to injure or to kill, we do so because we are or feel endangered, humiliated, abused; because we are or feel rejected or treated unjustly; because we are or feel interfered with in wishes which are of vital importance to us.

It was, after all, Freud himself who taught us to seek out in apparently wanton, unprovoked acts of destructiveness, by disturbed children or adults, the hidden motive – which usually turns out to be a feeling of being rejected, jealousy, or hurt pride. In other words, cruelty and destructiveness are to be regarded as pathological extremes of the self-assertive tendency when frustrated or provoked beyond a critical limit – without requiring the gratuitous postulate of a death-instinct, for which there is not a trace of evidence anywhere in biology.

Turning once more to the other aspect of Freud's Thanatos, the outstanding characteristic of living substance is, as already mentioned, that it seems to ignore the Second Law of Thermodynamics. Instead of dissipating its energy into the environment, the living animal extracts energy from it, eats environment, drinks environment, burrows and builds in environment, sucks information out of noise and meaning out of chaotic stimuli. 'Neither senescence nor natural death are necessary, inevitable consequences of life,' as Pearl summed it up;[5] the protozoa are potentially immortal; they reproduce by simple fission, 'leaving behind in the process nothing corresponding to a corpse'. In many primitive, multicellular animals senescence and natural death are absent; they reproduce by fission or budding, again without leaving any dead residue behind. 'Natural death is biologically a relatively new thing';[6] it is the cumulative effect of some, as yet little understood, deficiency in the metabolism of cells in complex organisms – an epiphenomenon due to imperfect integration, and not a basic law of nature.

Thus Freud's primary drives, sexuality and the death-wish, cannot claim universal validity; both are based on biological novelties which appear only on a relatively high level of evolution: sex as a new departure from asexual reproduction and sometimes (as in certain flatworms) alternating with it; death as a consequence of imperfections arising with growing complexity. In the theory proposed here there is no place for a 'destructive instinct' in organisms; nor for regarding sexuality as the *only* integrative force in human or animal society. Eros and Thanatos are relatively late arrivals on the stage of evolution; a host of creatures which multiply by fission (or budding) are ignorant of both. In our view, *sexuality is a specific manifestation of the integrative tendency, aggressiveness an extreme form of the self-assertive tendency*; while Janus appears as the symbol of the two irreducible properties of living matter: wholeness and partness, and their precarious equilibrium in the hierarchies of nature.

To say it once more, this generalized schema is not based on metaphysical assumptions but built in, as it were, into the architecture of complex systems – physical, biological or social – as a necessary precondition of the coherence and stability of their multilevelled assemblies of holons. Not by chance did Heisenberg call his autobiographical account of the genesis of modern physics *The Part and the Whole*.* Where indeed in micro-physics do we find the ultimate 'elementary' parts which do not turn out to be composite wholes? Where in the macro-world of astrophysics do we locate the boundaries of our universe of multidimensional space-time? Infinity yawns both at the top and bottom of the stratified hierarchies of existence, and the dichotomy of self-assertive wholeness and self-transcending partness is present on every level, from the trivial to the cosmic. The earthiest aspect of hierarchic order is reflected in what one might call 'Swift's paradigm';

> So, naturalists observe, a flea
> Hath smaller fleas that on him prey;
> And these have smaller fleas to bite 'em,
> And so proceed *ad infinitum*. . .

6

I am aware that this chapter may have seemed to oscillate between the over-obvious and the apparently abstract and speculative; yet one of the tests of a theory is that, once grasped, it appears self-evident.

There is a further difficulty inherent in the subject. The postulate of a universal self-assertive tendency needs no apology; it has an immediate appeal to commonsense, and has many forerunners – such as the 'instinct of self-preservation', 'survival of the fittest', and so forth. But to postulate as its counterpart an equally universal integrative tendency, and the dynamic interplay between the two as the key to a general systems theory, smacks of old-fashioned vitalism and runs counter to the *Zeitgeist*, epitomized in books like Monod's *Chance and Necessity* or Skinner's *Beyond Freedom and Dignity*. It may therefore be appropriate to wind up

Der Teil und das Ganze in the German original. In the English translation this was changed to *Physics and Beyond*.

this chapter with a few quotations from a recent book by an eminent clinician, Dr Lewis Thomas (President of the Sloan-Kettering Cancer Centre), who can hardly be accused of an unscientific attitude. The passage starts with a fascinating description of the parasite *myxotricha paradoxa*, a single-celled creature which inhabits the digestive tract of Australian termites:

At first glance, he appears to be an ordinary, motile protozoan, remarkable chiefly for the speed and directness with which he swims from place to place, engulfing fragments of wood finely chewed by his termite host. In the termite ecosystem, an arrangement of Byzantine complexity, he stands at the epicenter. Without him, the wood, however finely chewed, would never get digested; he supplies the enzymes that break down cellulose to edible carbohydrate, leaving only the nondegradable lignin, which the termite then excretes in geometrically tidy pellets and uses as building blocks for the erection of arches and vaults in the termite nest. Without him there would be no termites, no farms of the fungi that are cultivated by termites and will grow nowhere else. . . [7]

But this tiny creature inside the termite's digestive tracts turns out to consist of whole populations of even tinier creatures living in symbiosis with each other, yet retaining their autonomous individuality. Thus . . .

. . . the flagellae that beat in synchrony to propel myxotricha with such directness turn out, on closer scrutiny with the electron microscope, not to be flagellae at all. They are outsiders, in to help with the business: fully formed, perfect spirochetes that have attached themselves at regularly spaced intervals all over the surface of the protozoan.[8]

Thomas then enumerates the various types of other organelles and bacteria which form a kind of cooperative zoo inside *myxotricha*, and cites evidence that the cells which constitute the *human body* evolved by a similar process 'of being made up, part by part, by the coming together of just such prokaryotic animals'. Thus the lowly myxotricha becomes a paradigm for our integrative tendency.

The whole animal, or ecosystem, stuck for the time being halfway along in evolution, appears to be a model for the development of cells like our own. . . . There is an underlying force that drives together the several creatures comprising myxotricha, and, then drives the assemblage into union with the termite. If we could understand this tendency, we would catch a glimpse of the process that brought single separate cells together for the construction of metazoans, culminating in the invention of roses, dolphins, and, of course, ourselves. It might turn out that the same tendency underlies the joining of organisms into communities, communities into ecosystems, and ecosystems into the biosphere. If this is, in fact, the drift of things, the way of the world, we may come to view immune reactions, genes for the chemical marking of self, and perhaps all reflexive responses of aggression and defense as secondary developments in evolution, necessary for the regulation and modulation of symbiosis, not designed to break into the process, only to keep it from getting out of hand.

If it is in the nature of living things to pool resources, to fuse when possible, we would have a new way of accounting for the progressive enrichment and complexity of form in living things.[9]

III

THE THREE DIMENSIONS OF EMOTION

I

Emotions can be described as mental states accompanied by intense feelings and associated with bodily changes of a widespread character – in breathing, pulse, muscle tone, glandular secretion of hormones such as adrenalin, etc. They have also been described as 'over-heated' drives. They can be classified, in the first place, according to the *nature of the drive* which gives rise to them: hunger, sex, curiosity (the 'exploratory drive'), conviviality, protection of the offspring, and so on.

In the second place, a conspicuous feature of all emotions is the feeling of *pleasureableness or unpleasureableness*, the 'hedonic tone', attached to them. In the third place, there is the polarity between the *self-assertive and self-transcending* tendencies which enter into every emotion.

We thus arrive at a three-dimensional conception of human emotions. I have proposed★ a coarse but homely analogy for it: imagine your mental scenery transformed into the saloon bar of a tavern, equipped with a variety of taps, each serving a different kind of brew; these are turned on and off as the need arises. Then each tap would represent a different *drive*, while the pleasure–unpleasure rating would depend on the *rate of flow* through the tap – whether it is nice and smooth, or gurgles and splutters because there is too little or too much pressure behind it. Lastly, the ratio of self-assertive to self-transcending impulses in emotive behaviour could be represented by the *acid–alkaline scale*. This is not a very engaging metaphor, but it may help to visualize the three variables (or parameters) of emotion which the present theory suggests. Let us take a closer look at each, and particularly at those features which distinguish it from other theories.

★In *The Ghost in the Machine*, Ch. XV.

2

One of the difficulties inherent in the subject is that we rarely experience a pure emotion. The barman tends to mix the liquids from the various taps: sex may be combined with curiosity and with virtually any other drive. The point is too obvious to need further discussion.

The second variable, the pleasure–unpleasure scale or 'hedonic tone', also gives rise to ambiguous, 'mixed feelings'. Earlier on (in Chapter II) I quoted Freud's dictum that pleasure is always derived from 'the diminution, lowering or extinction of psychic excitation and unpleasure from an increase of it'. This view (which was held throughout the first half of our century by the major schools in psychology, including American behaviourism* and Continental psychoanalysis) is no doubt true for the frustration of 'over-heated' primitive drives which arise, for instance, from the pangs of starvation; but it is palpably untrue for that class of complex emotions encountered in everyday life, which we call pleasurable excitement, thrill, arousal, suspense. Reading an erotic passage in a book leads, in Freud's words, to an 'increase in psychic excitation' and should therefore be unpleasant; in fact it arouses a complex emotion in which *frustration is combined with pleasure*.

The answer to this paradox lies in the important part played by *imagination* in human emotions. Just as an imagined stimulus in an erotic reverie is sufficient to arouse physiological impulses, so, vice versa, imagined satisfaction may lead to a pleasurable experience – the 'internalized' consummation of those components in the complex drive which can be lived out in fantasy.

Another gateway through which imagination enters into the emotional drive is *anticipation* of its reward. In the previous example the reward was fictional, yet emotionally real, i.e., pleasurable; now we are talking of the imagined anticipation of the *factual* reward. When one is thirsty, the sight of the publican pouring beer into one's glass is pleasurable, although it 'increases

*Where Thorndike's 'Law of Effect', which asserted the same fallacy, reigned as supreme dogma.

psychic excitation'. The same applies to the preliminaries of love-making, or watching a thriller: the anticipation of the happy ending mediates the 'internal consummation' of some components of the emotive drive while the excitation of other components increases; we are impatient to get over the preliminaries which at the same time we enjoy.

Although the 'internalization' and 'internal consummation' of emotive drives are triggered by acts of imagination, they have their physiological concomitants in visceral and glandular processes, and are as 'real' as the muscular activities of 'external' or overt behaviour. The memory of a French three-star meal can be sufficient to re-activate one's gastric juices.

The more sublimated the drive (i.e., the closer the coordination between the higher, cortical, and the lower, visceral levels of the hierarchy) the more it is amenable to internalization. This sounds rather abstract, but consider two players in a chess competition facing each other across the board. The simplest way of defeating the opponent is to club him over the head. A player may occasionally experience this urge (particularly if this opponent is Bobby Fischer), but he will never seriously entertain the idea: the competitive drive can express itself only according to the 'rules of the game'. Instead of resorting to violence, the player visualizes in his imagination the possibilities of deriving an advantage from his next move, and this mental activity provides him with a series of pleasurable anticipatory, partial satisfactions, even if in the end victory is not achieved. Hence the sporting pleasure in competitive games, regardless – up to a point – of the final outcome. Stevenson saw deeper than Freud when he wrote that to travel hopefully is better than to arrive.

Romantic lovers have always been aware of this. Longing is a bitter-sweet emotion with painful and pleasurable components. Sometimes the imagined presence of the beloved person can be more gratifying than the real one. Emotions have a many-coloured spectrum of components, each with its own hedonic tone. To ask whether to love is pleasurable or not is as meaningless as to ask whether a Rembrandt painting is bright or dark.

We can now turn to the third source of ambivalence in our

emotions. The first, we remember, was the biological origin of the drive, the second the pleasure–unpleasure tone attached to it, the third is the polarity of self-assertion versus self-transcendence which is manifested in all our emotions.

Take love first – an ill-defined but heady cocktail of emotions with countless variations. (Sexual, platonic, parental, oedipal, narcissistic, patriotic, botanistic, canine-directed or feline-orientated, as the textbooks would say.) But whatever its target and method of wooing, there is always present an element of self-transcending devotion in varying proportions. In *sexual* relationships, domination and aggression are blended with empathy and identification; the outcome ranges from rape to platonic worship. *Parental love* reflects, on the one hand, a biological bond with 'one's own flesh and blood' which transcends the boundaries of the self; while domineering fathers and over-protective mothers are classic examples of self-assertiveness. Less obvious is the fact that even *hunger*, an apparently simple and straightforward biological drive, can contain a self-transcending component. Everyday experience tells us that appetite is enhanced by congenial company and surroundings. On a less trivial level, ritual commensality is intimately related to magic and religion among primitive people. By partaking of the flesh of the sacrificed animal, man or god, a process of transubstantiation takes place; the virtues of the victim are ingested and a kind of mystic communion is established which includes all who participated in the rite. Transmitted through the Orphic mystery cult, the tradition of sharing the slain god's flesh and blood, entered in a symbolic guise into the rites of Christianity. To the devout, Holy Communion is the supreme experience of self-transcendence; and no blasphemy is intended by pointing to the continuous tradition which connects ritual feeding with transubstantiation as a means of breaking down the ego's boundaries.

Other echoes of this ancient communion survive in such rites as baptismal and funeral meals, symbolic offerings of bread and salt, or the blood-brother ceremony among some Arab tribes, performed by drinking a few drops of the elected brother's blood. We can only conclude that even while eating, man does not live by bread alone: that *even the apparently simplest act of self-preservation may contain an element of self-transcendence.*

And vice versa, such admirably altruistic pursuits as caring for the sick or poor, protecting animals against cruelty, serving on committees and joining protest marches, can serve as wonderful outlets for bossy self-assertion, even if unconscious. Professional do-gooders, charity tigresses, hospital matrons, missionaries and social workers are indispensable to society, and to inquire into their motives, often hidden to themselves, would be ungrateful and churlish.

3

Thus leaving apart the extremes of blind rage and mystic trance at opposite ends of the spectrum, all our emotional states show combinations of the two basic tendencies: one reflecting the individual holon's wholeness, the other his partness, with a mutually restraining influence on one another. But it may also happen that the integrative tendency, instead of restraining its antagonist, acts *as a trigger or catalyst* for it. We shall discuss in Chapter IV the disastrous consequences of self-transcending identification of the individual with the group-mind, its leaders, slogans and beliefs. For the moment we shall turn to the happier aspects of the self-same catalysing process, when it serves to generate the magic of illusion in art.

How does the process work? Let us consider a simple situation with only two people involved: Mrs A. and her friend, Mrs B. whose little daughter has recently been killed in an accident. Mrs A. sheds tears of sympathy, participating in Mrs B.'s sorrow, partially identifying herself with her friend by an act of empathy, projection or introjection – whatever you like to call it. The same might happen if the 'other person' is merely a heroine on the screen or in the pages of a novel.

But it is essential to distinguish here between two distinct emotional processes involved in the event, although they combine in the lived experience. The first is the spontaneous act of identification itself, characterized by the fact that Mrs A. has for

the moment more or less forgotten her own existence by participating in the experiences of another person, real or imagined.
This is clearly a self-transcending and cathartic experience; while
it lasts, Mrs A. is prevented from thinking of her own worries,
jealousies and grudges against her husband. In other words, the
process of identification temporarily *inhibits* the self-assertive
tendencies.

But now we come to the second process which may have the
opposite effect. The act of identification may lead to the arousal
of *vicarious emotions* experienced, as it were, on the other person's
behalf. In Mrs A.'s case the vicarious emotion was one of sadness
and bereavement. But it can also be anxiety or anger. You
commiserate with Desdemona; as a result, the perfidy of Iago
makes your blood boil. The anxiety which grips the spectator of a
Hitchcock thriller, though vicarious, is physiologically real, accompanied by palpitations, increased pulse rate, sudden jumps of
alarm. And the anger aroused by the ruthless gangster on the
screen – which Mexican audiences have occasionally riddled with
bullets – is real anger, marked by a flow of adrenalin. Here, then,
is the core of the paradox, which is basic to the understanding
of both the delusions of History – and the illusions of Art. Both
derive from man's nature as a belief-accepting animal (as Waddington called it). Both require a – temporary or permanent –
suspension of disbelief.

To recapitulate: we are faced with a process in two steps. At
the first step, the self-transcending impulses of projection, partici-
pation, identification *inhibit* the self-assertive tendencies, purge
us of the dross of our self-centred worries and desires. This leads
to the second step: the process of loving identification may
stimulate – or trigger off – the surge of hatred, fear, vengefulness,
which, though experienced on behalf of another person, or group
of persons, nevertheless increases the pulse rate. The physiological
processes which these vicarious emotions activate are essentially
the same whether the threat or insult is directed at oneself or at
the person or group with whom one identifies. They belong to
the self-assertive category, although the self has momentarily
changed its address – by being, for instance, projected into the

guileless heroine on the stage; or the local soccer team; or 'my country, right or wrong'.

It is a triumph of the imaginative powers of the human mind that we are capable of shedding tears over the death of Anna Karenina, who only exists as printer's ink on paper, or as a shadow on the screen. Children and primitive audiences who, forgetting the present, completely accept the reality of events on the stage, are experiencing a kind of hypnotic trance, with its ultimate origin in the sympathetic magic practised in primitive cultures, where the masked dancer becomes identified with the god or demon he mimes, and the carved idol is invested with divine powers. At a more advanced stage of cultural sophistication we are still capable of perceiving Laurence Olivier as himself and as Prince Hamlet of Denmark at one and the same time, and of manufacturing large quantities of adrenalin to provide him with the required vigour to fight his adversaries. It is the same magic at work, but in a more sublimated form: the process of identification (of spectator via actor with the hero) is transitory and partial, confined to certain climactic moments, a suspension of disbelief which does not entirely abolish the critical faculties or undermine personal identity.

Art is a school of self-transcendence. So is a voodoo session or a Nazi rally. But our responses to the various forms of illusion created by art have undergone a process of sublimation on the road from childhood to maturity and from the worship of icons to their aesthetic appreciation. No comparable process of sublimation can be observed in those forms of behaviour where the urge towards self-transcendence finds its expression in social and political group-formation. In this respect, the stage on which the tragedies of history are played is still populated by heroes and villains, and the vicarious emotions which they arouse are still capable of turning the peaceful audience into homicidal fanatics. This may serve as an illustration of the ambiguous role played by the integrative tendency in man – which may manifest itself in primitive forms of *identification*, as distinct from mature *integration*. Social history is dominated by the former, the history of art by the latter.

IV

AD MAJOREM GLORIAM...

I

The theoretical considerations outlined in previous chapters
enable us to take a closer look at the human predicament.

From the dawn of civilization, there has never been a shortage
of inspired reformers. Hebrew prophets, Greek philosophers,
Chinese sages, Indian mystics, Christian saints, French humanists,
English utilitarians, German moralists, American pragmatists,
Hindu pacifists, have denounced wars and violence and appealed
to man's better nature, without success. As already suggested,
the reason for this failure must be sought in the reformer's mistaken interpretation of the causes which compelled man to make
such a disaster of his history, prevented him from learning the
lessons of the past, and which now puts his survival in question.
The basic fallacy consists in putting all the blame on man's
selfishness, greed and alleged destructiveness; that is to say, on the
self-assertive tendency of the individual. Nothing could be farther
from the truth, as both the historical and psychological evidence
indicate.

No historian would deny that the part played by crimes
committed for personal motives is very small compared to the
vast populations slaughtered in unselfish loyalty to a jealous god,
king, country, or political system. The crimes of Caligula shrink
to insignificance compared to the havoc wrought by Torquemada.
The number of people killed by robbers, highwaymen, gangsters
and other asocial elements is negligible compared to the masses
cheerfully slain in the name of the true religion, the righteous
cause. Heretics were tortured and burned alive not in anger but
in sorrow, for the good of their immortal souls. The Russian and
Chinese purges were represented as operations of social hygiene,

to prepare mankind for the golden age of the classless society. The gas chambers and crematoria worked towards the advent of a different type of millennium. To say it once more: throughout human history, the ravages caused by excesses of individual self-assertion are quantitatively negligible compared to the numbers slain *ad majorem gloriam* out of a self-transcending devotion to a flag, a leader, a religious faith or political conviction. Man has always been prepared not only to kill, but also to die for good, bad, or completely hare-brained causes. What can be a more valid proof for the reality of the urge towards self-transcendence?

Thus the historical record confronts us with the paradox that the tragedy of man originates not in his aggressiveness but in his devotion to transpersonal ideals; not in an excess of individual self-assertiveness but in a malfunction of the integrative tendencies in our species. I think it was Pascal who said: man is neither angel nor devil, but when he tries to act the angel he turns into a devil.

But how did this paradox arise?

2

Let us remember that in the basic polarity underlying all phenomena of life, the self-assertive tendency of a holon is the dynamic expression of its 'wholeness', the integrative tendency the expression of its 'partness', i.e., its subordination to a larger whole on the next higher level of the holarchy. In a well-balanced society both tendencies play a constructive part in maintaining the equilibrium. Thus a certain amount of self-assertiveness – 'rugged individualism', ambition, competitiveness – is indispensable in a dynamic society; without it there could be no social or cultural progress. John Donne's 'holy discontent' is an essential motivating force in the social reformer, the artist and thinker. Only when the balance is disturbed for one reason or another does the self-assertive tendency of the individual manifest its destructive potential and tend to assert itself to the detriment of society. Most civilizations, primitive or advanced, have been by and large quite successful in coping with such contingencies.

However, the vagaries of the *integrative tendency*, which in our view are mainly responsible for man's predicament, are less obvious and more complex. One pathogenic factor I have already alluded to: the human infant is subjected to a longer period of helplessness and total dependence on the adults who rear it than the young of any other species. This protracted experience may be at the root of the adult's ready submission to authority, and his quasi-hypnotic suggestibility by doctrines and ethical commandments – his urge to *belong*, to identify himself with a group or its system of beliefs.

Freud taught that moral conscience – the super-ego – is the residue of identification with the parents, particularly with the father; that parts of their personalities and moral attitudes are 'introjected' – quasi-cemented into the growing child's unconscious mental structure. One does not have to go that far, and accept that the mature adult's moral conscience is 'nothing but' the product of this psychic transplantation, to realize nevertheless that it plays an important part in the immature adult's psychic make-up – and in our present context we are mainly concerned with emotionally immature adults, whose integrative tendency, 'the need to belong', manifests itself in infantile or otherwise aberrant ways.

We can distinguish three overlapping factors in these pathogenic manifestations of the integrative tendency: *submission* to the authority of a father-substitute; unqualified *identification* with a social group; uncritical *acceptance of its belief-system*. All three are reflected in the gory annals of our history.

The first has, since Freud, become such a commonplace that it needs only a brief mention. The leader who incorporates the father-image may be a saint or a demagogue, a sage or a maniac. What qualities make a leader does not concern us here, but obviously he must appeal to some common denominators in the masses under his sway, and the commonest of denominators is infantile submission to authority.

The leader–follower relationship can embrace a whole nation, as in the case of the Hitler cult; or a small sect of devotees; or be confined to a duet as in the hypnotic rapport, on the psychotherapist's couch, or in the Father Confessor's curtained box. The common element is the act of *surrender*.

When we turn to the second and third factors mentioned above – the unqualified identification of an individual with a social group and its system of beliefs – we again have a wide variety of social aggregations which can be designated as 'groups', and described in terms of 'group-mentality' or *Massenpsychologie*. But this branch of psychology tended to concentrate its attention on extreme forms of group behaviour such as the outbreaks of mass-hysteria in the Middle Ages, or Le Bon's classic studies of the behaviour of the heroic and murderous mobs unleashed by the French Revolution (which Freud and others took as their text). This tendency to focus attention on the dramatic manifestations of mass-psychology made them overlook the more general principles underlying group mentality and its dominant influence on human history, past and present. For one thing, a person need not be physically present in a crowd to be affected by the group-mind; emotive identification with a nation, Church or political movement can be quite effective without physical contact. One can be a victim of group-fanaticism even in the privacy of one's bathroom.

Nor does every group need a personal leader or 'father-figure' in whom authority is vested, as discussed under the previous heading. Religious and political movements need leaders to get under way; once established they still benefit from efficient leadership; but the primary need of a group, the factor which lends it cohesion as a social holon, is a credo, a shared system of beliefs, and the resulting code of behaviour. This may be represented by human authority, or by a symbol – the totem or fetish which provides a mystic sense of union among the members of the tribe; by sacred icons as objects of worship; or the regimental flag to which soldiers in battle were supposed to hang on even at the price of their lives. The group-mind may be governed by the conviction that the group represents a Chosen Race whose ancestors made a special covenant with God; or a Master Race whose forebears were blond demi-gods; or whose Emperors were descended from the sun. Its credo may be based on the conviction that observance of certain rules and rites qualifies one for membership in a privileged elite in after-life; or that manual work qualifies one for membership in the elite class of history. Critical arguments have little impact on the group-mind, because identification with a group always involves a certain sacrifice of the critical faculties of the individuals which constitute it, and an enhancement of their emotional potential by a kind of group-resonance or positive feedback.

Let me repeat that in the present theory the term 'group' is not confined to a crowd assembled in one place, but refers to any social holon, governed by a set code of rules (e.g., language, traditions, customs, beliefs, etc.) which defines its corporate identity, lends it cohesion and a 'social profile'. As an autonomous holon, it has its own pattern of functioning and is governed by its own code of conduct, which cannot be 'reduced' to the individual codes which govern the behaviour of its members when acting as autonomous individuals and not as parts of the group. The obvious example is the conscript who as an individual is forbidden to kill, as a disciplined member of his unit is in duty bound to do so.

Thus it is essential to distinguish between the rules which govern individual behaviour and those which guide the behaviour of the group as a whole.*

The group, then, is to be regarded as a quasi-autonomous holon, not simply as a sum of its individual parts; and its activities depend not only on the interactions of its parts, but also on the group's interactions, as a whole, with other social holons on a higher level of the hierarchy. These interactions will again reflect the polarity of the holon's self-assertive and integrative tendencies, oscillating between competition and/or cooperation with other groups. In a healthy social holarchy the two tendencies are in equilibrium; but when tensions arise, this or that social holon

*In a paper on 'The Evolution of Systems of Rules of Conduct' Professor F. A. von Hayek defines as his aim 'to distinguish between the systems of rules of conduct which governs the behaviour of the individual members of a group (or of the elements of any order) and the order or pattern of actions which results from this for the group as a whole. . . That [they] are not the same thing should be obvious as soon as it is stated, although the two are in fact frequently confused.'[1]

may tend to get over-stimulated and impose upon its rivals or usurp the role of the whole. History provides a never-ending list of such tensions, confrontations and conflicts.

Several factors responsible for this chronic disequilibrium have already been mentioned in earlier pages – such as the unique range of diversity in our species with regard to racial character-istics and national temperament, or the divisive effect of the multiplicity of languages – which, in their ensemble, have always made *the disruptive forces in mankind prevail over the cohesive forces on a local or global scale*. An even more important cause of trouble is that the code of conduct of a social holon includes not only the rules which govern the behaviour of its members, but also moral precepts and imperatives with a claim to universal validity. These imperatives carry a high emotional charge, and the group-mind tends to react violently to any threat – real or imaginary – to its cherished beliefs.

All that has been said points to the conclusion that in the group-mind the self-assertive tendencies are more dominant than on the level of the average individual; and that, by identifying himself with the group, the individual adopts a code of behaviour different from his personal code. The individual – *pace* Lorenz – is not a killer, the group is; and by identifying with it, the indi-vidual is transformed into a killer.

We shall see in a moment that this paradox can be observed not only on the battlefield or among lynching mobs, but also in austere psychological laboratories. Its paradoxical nature derives from the fact that the act of identification with the group is a *self-transcending* act, yet it reinforces the *self-assertive* tendencies of the group. Identification with the group is an act of devotion, of loving submission to the interests of the community, a partial or total surrender of personal identity and of the self-assertive tendencies of the individual. In our terminology, he relinquishes his 'wholeness' in favour of his 'partness' in a larger whole on a higher level of the holarchy. He becomes to some extent de-personalized, i.e., unself-ish in more than one sense. He may become indifferent to danger; he feels impelled to perform altruistic, even heroic actions to the point of self-sacrifice, and at the same time to behave with ruthless cruelty towards the enemy – real or imagined – of the group. But his brutality is impersonal and unselfish; it is exercised in the interest, or supposed interest of the whole; he is prepared not only to kill, but also to die in its name. Thus the self-assertive behaviour of the group is based on the self-transcending behaviour of its members; or to put it simply, *the egotism of the group feeds on the altruism of its members*.

The 'infernal dialectics' of this process is reflected on every level of the various social holarchies. Patriotism is the noble virtue of subordinating individual interests to the interests of the nation; yet it gives rise to chauvinism, the militant expression of those higher interests. Loyalty to the clan produces clannishness; *esprit de corps* blossoms into arrogant cliquishness; religious fervour into zealotry; the Sermon on the Mount into the Church militant.

Let us now turn to the experimental confirmation of our theoretical schema which has recently been provided, in a rather surprising manner, by the psychological laboratories in Yale and other universities.

3

The series of highly original experiments, which I propose to describe in some detail, were started by Dr Stanley Milgram at the Psychology Department in Yale University, and repeated by various experimental laboratories in Germany, Italy, Australia and South Africa. The purpose of the experiments was to discover the limits of the average person's obedience to authority, when ordered to inflict severe pain on an innocent victim in the interests of a noble cause. Authority was represented by a figure of professional appearance in a laboratory coat; I shall call him the Prof. The noble cause was Education; more precisely, the experiment was purportedly designed to provide answers to the problem whether punishing the pupil for his mistakes had a positive effect on the learning process. It involved three people: the Prof, who was in charge of the proceedings; the learner or victim; and the experimental subject, who was asked by the Prof to act as teacher and to punish the learner each time he gave the wrong reply. Punishment was by electric shocks of growing severity, administered by the 'teacher' on the Prof's orders. The 'learner' or victim was strapped into a kind of electric chair, with an electrode attached to his wrist. The 'teacher' was seated in front of an impressive shock-generator which had a key-board of thirty switches, ranging from 15 volts to 450 volts (i.e., a 15 volt increment from one switch to the next). There were also verbal inscriptions on the machine ranging from SLIGHT SHOCK TO INTENSE SHOCK to DANGER–SEVERE SHOCK.

In fact the whole gruesome set-up was based on make-believe. The 'victim' was an actor hired by the Prof. The shock-generator was a dummy. Only the 'teacher', at whom the experiment was aimed, believed in the reality of the shocks he was ordered to administer, and of the shrieks of pain and cries for mercy uttered by the 'victim'.

The 'teachers' – i.e., the real subjects of the experiment – were volunteers from all walks of life between the ages of twenty and fifty, who came to the Yale laboratory attracted by newspaper advertisements to participate in 'a scientific study of memory and learning' (they were paid a modest four dollars per hour). Typical subjects were postal clerks, high-school teachers, salesmen, engineers and manual labourers. Altogether, more than a thousand volunteers were tested in Yale alone.

The basic procedure of the experiment was as follows. The 'pupil' was given to read a long list of paired words, e.g., blue box – nice day – wild duck – etc. Then, in the 'examination' he was given one test-word, for instance, 'blue', with four alternative answers, e.g., ink, box, sky, lamp, and had to indicate which was the correct answer. The 'teacher' was instructed by the Prof to administer a shock each time the pupil gave a wrong response, and moreover 'to move one level higher on the shock-generator each time the learner gives the wrong answer'.

To make sure that the 'teacher' was aware of what he was doing, the actor who played the role of the victim uttered complaints which increased in stridency according to the voltage, from 'mild grunts' starting at 75 volts, in a crescendo, until at 150 volts the victim cried out 'Get me out of here! I won't be in the experiment any more! I refuse to go on.' (Remember that the 'teacher' believed that the victim too was a volunteer.) 'At 315 volts, after a violent scream, the victim reaffirmed vehemently that he was no longer a participant. He provided no answers, but screamed in agony whenever a shock was administered. After 330 volts he was not heard from. . . .' Yet the Prof instructed the subject to treat no answer as a wrong answer and to continue to increase the shock level according to schedule. After three shocks of 450 volts he called off the experiment.

How many people, in an average population, do you think would obey the command to carry on with the task of torturing the victim to the limit of 450 volts? The answer seems to be a foregone conclusion: perhaps one in a thousand, a pathological sadist. Before starting his experiments, Milgram actually asked a group of psychiatrists to predict the outcome. 'With remarkable similarity they predicted that virtually all subjects would refuse to obey the experimenter.' The consensus of the thirty-nine psychiatrists who answered the questionnaire was that 'most subjects would not go beyond 150 volts (i.e., when the victim asks for the first time to be released). They expected that only 4% would reach 300 volts, and that only a pathological fringe of about one in a thousand would administer the highest shock on the board.'[2]

In actual fact, *over 60 per cent* of the subjects at Yale continued to obey the Prof to the very end – the 450 volt limit. When the experiment was repeated in Italy, South Africa and Australia, the percentage of obedient subjects was somewhat higher. In Munich it was 85 per cent.

Before going any further, let me clarify a few points relating to the experimental set-up.

First, the Prof had no power over his volunteer subjects comparable to that of an army officer or an office boss or even a school teacher. He had no power to punish the subject who refused to administer further shocks, nor did he have any financial or other incentives to offer. (It was understood that volunteers would only be employed on a single occasion.)

How then did the Prof impose his authority on the 'teacher', and induce him to continue with his gruesome task? There was no bullying, nor any eloquent persuasion. The Prof's procedure was rigidly standardized:

At various points in the experiment the subject would turn to the experimenter [the Prof] for advice on whether he should continue to administer shocks. Or he would indicate that he did not wish to go on.

The experimenter responded with a sequence of 'prods', using as many as necessary to bring the subject into line.

Prod 1: Please continue *or* Please go on.

Prod 2: The experiment requires that you continue.

Prod 3: It is absolutely essential that you continue.

Prod 4: You have no other choice, you *must* go on.

The experimenter's tone of voice was at all times firm, but not impolite.

If the subject asked if the learner was liable to suffer permanent physical injury, the experimenter said: 'Although the shocks may be painful, there is no permanent tissue damage, so please go on.' (Followed by prods 2, 3 and 4, if necessary.)

If the subject said that the *learner* did not want to go on, the experimenter replied: 'Whether the learner likes it or not, you must go on until he has learned all the word pairs correctly. So please go on.' (Followed by Prods 2, 3 and 4, if necessary.)[3]

One could hardly call this technique brain-washing. And yet it worked on nearly two-thirds of all experimental subjects, regardless of country and of the method of soliciting volunteers. It worked even when the 'victim' complained of a heart condition and the maximum shocks seemed to constitute a danger to his life. That humane people are capable of committing inhuman acts when acting as members of an army or a fanatical mob has always been taken for granted. The importance of the experiments was that they revealed *how little* was needed to push them across the psychic boundary which separates the behaviour of decent citizens from dehumanized SS guards. The fragility of that boundary – which two-thirds of the subjects crossed – came as an utter surprise even to psychiatrists, whose recorded predictions turned out to be totally – though understandably – wrong.

A comfortable way to evade the uncomfortable problem with which these results confront us, is to put the blame on the repressed aggressive impulses of the subjects, for which the experiments provide a socially respectable outlet. This interpretation is in the traditional line of Freud's 'urge to destruction', or Lorenz's 'killer-instinct' – a view which, as I have argued before, is contradicted by both the historical and psychological evidence. Milgram found an elegant method to refute this facile explanation, and to demonstrate that

. . . the act of shocking the victim does not stem from destructive urges but from the fact that the subjects have become integrated into a social structure and are unable to get out of it. Suppose the experimenter instructed the subject to drink a glass of water. Does this mean the subject is thirsty? Obviously not, for he is simply doing what he is told to do. It is the essence of obedience that the action carried out does not correspond to the motives of the actor but is initiated in the motive system of those higher up in the social hierarchy.[4]

To prove his point, he carried out a further series of experiments in which the 'teacher' was told that he was free to inflict on the learner *any* shock level of his own choice on any of the trials –

. . . the highest levels on the generator, the lowest, any in between, or any combination of levels . . .[5]

Though given full opportunity to inflict pain on the learner, almost all subjects administered the lowest shocks on the control panel, the mean shock level being 54 volts. [Remember that the victim's first mild complaint came only at 75 volts.] But if destructive impulses were really pressing for release, and the subjects could justify their use of high shock levels in the cause of science, why did they not make the 'learners' suffer? There was little if any tendency in the subjects to do this. One or two, at most [out of 40 subjects],* seemed to derive any

*The experimental series consisted of batches of 40 subjects of mixed ages and professions.

satisfaction from shocking the learner. The levels were in no way comparable to that obtained when the subjects were ordered to shock the victim. There was an order-of-magnitude difference.[6]

In the original experiments, when the teacher acted on the Prof's orders, an average of 25 out of 40 subjects administered the maximum shock of 450 volts. In the free-choice experiment 38 out of 40 did not go beyond 150 volts (victim's first loud protest) and only two subjects went up to 325 and 450 respectively.

To clinch the argument, Milgram quotes other experiments, carried out by his colleagues Buss and Berkowitz in a similar set-up.

In typical experimental manipulations, they frustrated the subject to see whether he would administer higher shocks when angry. But the effect of these manipulations was minuscule compared with the levels obtained under obedience. That is to say, no matter what these experimenters did to anger, irritate or frustrate the subject, he would at most move up one or two shock levels, say from shock level 4 to level 6 [90 volts]. This represented a genuine increment in aggression. But there remained an order-of-magnitude difference in the variation introduced in his behaviour this way, and under conditions where he was taking orders.[7]

The vast majority of the experimental subjects, far from deriving any pleasure from shocking the victim, showed various symptoms of emotional strain and distress. Some broke into a sweat, others pleaded with the Prof to stop, or protested that the experiment was cruel and stupid. Yet two-thirds nevertheless went on to the bitter end.

What made them persist in a task that was obviously distasteful to them and in blatant contradiction to their individual standards of ethics? Milgram's analysis, apart from some differences in terminology, is on the same lines as the theoretical considerations set out in previous chapters. He recognizes the profound implications of the hierarchic concept:* to wit, that

*I was gratified by the generous references in his book to the hierarchic mode proposed in *The Ghost in the Machine*.

... when individuals enter a condition of hierarchic control, the mechanism which ordinarily regulates individual impulses is suppressed and ceded to the higher-level component ...[8]

The individuals who enter into such hierarchies are, of necessity, modified in their functioning ...[9] This transformation corresponds precisely to the central dilemma of our experiment: how is it that a person who is usually decent and courteous acts with severity against another person within the experiment? ...[10]

The disappearance of a sense of responsibility is the most far-reaching consequence of submission to authority ...[11]

Most subjects in the experiment see their behaviour in a larger context that is benevolent and useful to society – the pursuit of scientific truth. The psychological laboratory has a strong claim to legitimacy and evokes trust and confidence in those who perform there. An action such as shocking a victim, which in isolation appears evil, acquires a totally different meaning when placed in this setting ...[12]

Morality does not disappear, but acquires a radically different focus: the subordinate person feels shame and pride depending on how adequately he has performed the actions called for by authority. Language provides numerous terms to pinpoint this type of morality: *loyalty, duty, discipline* ...[13]

Here, then, we have the experimental confirmation of what I have called the 'infernal dialectics' in man's condition. It is not, as the facile catch-phrase goes, his 'innate aggressiveness' (i.e., his self-assertive tendency) which transforms harmless citizens into torturers, but their self-transcending devotion to a cause, symbolized by the Prof in the role of the leader. It is *the integrative tendency acting as a vehicle or catalyst* which induces the change of morality, the abrogation of personal responsibility, the replacement of the individual's code of behaviour by the code of the 'higher component' in the hierarchy. In the course of this fatal process, the individual becomes to a certain extent de-personalized; he no longer functions as an autonomous holon or part-whole, but merely as a part. Janus no longer has two faces – only one is left, looking upward in holy rapture or in a moronic daze.

The final conclusions which Milgram drew from his experiments are in keeping with the present theory:

This is, perhaps, the most fundamental lesson of our study: ordinary people, simply doing their jobs, and without any particular hostility on their part, can become agents in a terrible destructive process. Moreover, even when the destructive effects of their work become patently clear, and they are asked to carry out actions incompatible with fundamental standards of morality, relatively few people have the internal resources needed to resist authority . . .[14]

The behaviour revealed in the experiments reported here is normal human behaviour but revealed under conditions that show with particular clarity the danger to human survival inherent in our make-up. And what is it we have seen? Not aggression, for there is no anger, vindictiveness, or hatred in those who shocked the victim. Something far more dangerous is revealed: the capacity for man to abandon his humanity, indeed, the inevitability that he does so, as he merges his unique personality into larger institutional structures.

This is a fatal flaw nature has designed into us, and which in the long run gives our species only a modest chance of survival.

It is ironic that the virtues of loyalty, discipline, and self-sacrifice that we value so highly in the individual are the very properties that create destructive organizational engines of war and bind men to malevolent systems of authority . . .[15]

4

I said earlier on that the metamorphosis of individual minds into the group-mind does not necessarily require the individual's physical presence in a group or crowd, only an act of identification with the group – its beliefs, traditions, leadership, and/or its emotion-rousing symbols. Thus in the case of Milgram's experiments, the 'teachers' became members of an invisible group – the awe-inspiring academic hierarchy, the priesthood of Science – whose wisdom and authority were represented by the Prof. But once committed, they found themselves in a trap – a 'closed system', easily entered, but difficult to get out of. The integrative tendency, which provides the binding forces within the group, manifests itself in various ways which we have discussed before, but they all carry a high emotive voltage, far beyond rational expectation: Milgram's results drastically refuted the predictions of psychiatrists – and of commonsense.

Some more recent experiments by Henri Tajfel and his team at Bristol University produced equally unexpected phenomena in a different context. Parties of schoolboys aged 14 to 15 were subjected to a quick – and bogus – psychological test; then each boy was told that he was either a 'Julius person' or an 'Augustus person'. No explanation was given of the characteristics of the Julius or Augustus people, nor did the boys know who the other members of their group were. Nevertheless, they promptly identified with their fictitious group, proud to be a Julius person or an Augustus person to such an extent that they were willing to make financial sacrifices to benefit their anonymous group brothers, and to cause discomfort in the other camp.

The procedure followed in this and later experiments was rather complicated; instead of going into more detail I shall quote the summary given by Nigel Calder, who has done much to bring Tajfel's findings to public attention:

The experiments that began with the Bristol schoolboys have given points of reference in a broad ocean of human social behaviour that previously seemed unnavigable for science. Many a theory had been launched in vain. Some, like those of Sigmund Freud and Konrad Lorenz, offered the innate aggressiveness of the individual as the source of conflict between groups – a world war being somehow like a pub brawl that got out of hand . . .[16] Yet the big problem all along has been to explain why well-behaved young men will so readily go out and kill other well-behaved young men, not in a frenzied horde but in disciplined formation. A forceful challenge to the 'individualistic' point of view has come from the social psychologist Henri Tajfel. He points to the drastic shift in the norms of human behaviour, when one group confronts another. What comes into play is the capacity of people to act in unison, in accordance with the laws and structure of society, largely irrespective of individual motives and feelings . . . In a remarkable series of experiments Tajfel and his colleagues at Bristol University have shown that you can alter a person's behaviour predictably, just by telling him he belongs to a group – even a group of which he has never before heard. Almost automatically the participant in these experiments favours anonymous members of his own group and, given the opportunity, he is likely to go out of his way to put

members of another group at a disadvantage . . . People will stick up
for a group to which they happen to be assigned, without any indoctrin-
ation about who else is in the group or what its qualities are supposed to
be . . .[17] Only by grasping the full import of the positive and quick pro-
pensity of human beings to identify with any group they find themselves in can one make a firm base from which to search out the origins
of hostility . . .[18]

I found these experiments extremely revealing, not only on
theoretical grounds but also for personal reasons, related to a
childhood episode which has never ceased to puzzle and amuse
me. On my first day at school, aged five, in Budapest, Hungary,
I was asked by my future class-mates the crucial question: 'Are
you an MTK or an FTC?' These were the initials of Hungary's
two leading soccer teams, perpetual rivals for the League cham-
pionship, as every schoolboy knew – except little me, who had
never been taken to a football match. However, to confess such
abysmal ignorance was unthinkable, so I replied with haughty
assurance: 'MTK, of course!' And thus the die was cast; for the
rest of my childhood in Hungary, and even when my family
moved to Vienna, I remained an ardent and loyal supporter of
MTK; and my heart still goes out to them, all the way across the
Iron Curtain. Moreover, their glamorous blue-and-white striped
shirts never lost their magic, whereas the vulgar green-and-white
stripes of their unworthy rivals still fill me with revulsion. I am
even inclined to believe that this early conversion played a part
in making blue my favourite colour. (After all, the sky is blue,
a primary colour, whereas green is merely the product of its
adulteration with yellow.) I may laugh at myself, but the emotive
attachment, the magic bond, is still there, and to shift my loyalty
from the blue–white MTK to the green–white FTC would be
downright blasphemy. Truly, we pick up our allegiances like
infectious germs. Even worse, we walk through life unaware of
this pathological disposition, which lures mankind from one
historic disaster into the next.

5

From the dawn of recorded history, human societies have always been fairly successful in restraining the *self-assertive* tendencies of the individual – until the howling little savage in its cot became transformed into a more or less law-abiding and civilized member of society. The same historical record testifies to mankind's tragic inability to induce a parallel sublimation of the *integrative tendency*. Yet, to say it again, both the glory and the pathology of the human condition derive from our powers of self-transcendence, which are equally capable of turning us into artists, saints or killers, but more likely into killers. Only a small minority is capable of canalizing the self-transcending urges into creative channels. For the vast majority, throughout history, the only fulfilment of its need to belong, its craving for communion, was identification with clan, tribe, nation, Church, or party, submission to its leader, worship of its symbols, and uncritical, child-like acceptance of its emotionally saturated system of beliefs. Thus we are faced with a contrast between the mature restraint of the self-assertive tendency and the immature vagaries of the integrative tendency, strikingly revealed whenever the group-mind takes over from the individual mind, whether at a political rally or in the psychological laboratory.

To put it in the simplest way: the individual who indulges in an excess of aggressive self-assertion incurs the penalties of society – he outlaws himself, he contracts *out* of the hierarchy. The true believer, on the other hand, becomes more closely knit *into it;* he enters the womb of his Church or party, or whatever social holon to which he surrenders his identity. For the process of identification in its cruder forms always entails, as we have seen, a certain impairment of individuality, an abdication of the critical faculties and of personal responsibility.

This leads us to a basic distinction between primitive or infantile forms of *identification*, and mature forms of *integration* into a social holarchy. In a well-balanced holarchy, the individual retains his character as a social holon, a part–whole who, *qua* whole, enjoys autonomy within the limits of the restraints imposed by the interests of the group. He remains an autonomous whole in his own right, and is even expected to assert his holistic attributes by originality, initiative and, above all, personal responsibility. The same considerations apply to the social holons on the higher levels of the hierarchy – clans and tribes, ethnic and religious communities, professional groups and political parties. They, too, ought ideally to display the virtues implied in the Janus principle: to function as autonomous wholes and at the same time to conform to the national interest; and so on, upwards, level by level, to the world community at the apex of the pyramid. An ideal society of this kind would possess '*hierarchic awareness*', every holon on every level being conscious both of its rights as a whole and its duties as a part.

Needless to say, the mirror of history, past and present, confronts us with a different picture.

6

Those dramatic manifestations of mass-hysteria which so much impressed Freud and Le Bon I have only mentioned in passing, because I meant to focus attention on the process of 'normal' group-formation and its devastating effects on the history of our species. This 'normal' process, as we have seen, involves identification with the group, and acceptance of its beliefs. An important side-effect of the process is to deepen the split between emotion and reason. For the group-mind is dominated by a system of beliefs, traditions, moral imperatives, with a high emotive potential regardless of its rational content; and quite frequently its explosive power is enhanced by its very irrationality. Faith in the group's credo is an emotional commitment; it anaesthetizes the individual's critical faculties and rejects rational doubt as something evil. Moreover, individuals are endowed with minds of varying complexity, while the group must be single-minded if it is to maintain its cohesion as a holon. Consequently, the group-mind must function on an intellectual level accessible to all its members: single-mindedness must be simple-minded. The overall result of this is the *enhancement* of the emotional dynamics of the group and simultaneous *reduction* of its intellectual faculties: a sad caricature of the ideal of hierarchic awareness.

7

I mentioned earlier on the paranoid streak which runs through History. Enlightened people may be quite willing to admit that such a streak existed among the head-hunters of Papua or in the Aztec kingdom, where the number of young men, virgins and children sacrificed to the gods amounted to between 20,000 and 50,000 *per annum*. 'In this state of things,' commented Prescott,

... it was beneficially ordered by Providence that the land should be delivered over to another race, who would rescue it from the brutish superstitions that daily extended wider and wider ... The debasing institutions of the Aztecs furnish the best apology for their conquest. It is true, the conquerors brought along with them the Inquisition. But they also brought Christianity, whose benign radiance would still survive, when the fierce flames of fanaticism should be extinguished...[19]

Prescott must have known, though, that shortly after the Mexican conquest, the 'benign radiance' of Christianity manifested itself in the Thirty Years War, which killed off a goodly proportion of Europe's population. And so on to Auschwitz and Gulag. Yet even clear-sighted people who recognize the mental disorder underlying these horrors are apt to dismiss them as phenomena of the past. It is not easy to love humanity and yet to admit that the paranoid streak, in different guises, is as much in evidence in contemporary history as it was in the distant past, but more potentially deadly in its consequences; and that it is not accidental but inherent in the human condition.

'Chairman Mao's swim across the Yangtze river', wrote the official New China Agency, '... was a great encouragement to the Chinese people and revolutionaries throughout the world, and a heavy blow to imperialism, modern revisionism and the monsters and freaks who are opposed to socialism and Mao Tse-tung's thought.'[20]

The symptoms vary with time, but the underlying pattern of the disorder is the same: the split between faith and reason, rational thought and irrational beliefs. Religious beliefs are derived from ever-recurrent archetypal *motifs*, which seem to be shared by all mankind and evoke instant emotive responses.* But once they become institutionalized as the collective property of a specific group, they degenerate into rigid doctrines which, without losing their emotive appeal, are potentially offensive to the critical faculties. To paste over the split, various forms of double-think have been designed at various times – powerful techniques of self-deception, some crude, some extremely sophisticated. The same fate has befallen the secular religions which go by the name of political ideologies. They too have their archetypal roots – the craving for utopia, for an ideal society; but when they crystallize into movements and parties, they can become distorted to such an extent that the actual policy they pursue is the direct opposite of their professed ideal. This apparently inevitable tendency of both religious and secular ideologies to degenerate into their own caricatures is a direct consequence of the characteristics of the group-mind which we have discussed: its need for intellectual simplicity combined with emotional arousal.

Irrational beliefs are saturated with emotion; they are *felt* to be true. Believing has been described as 'knowing with one's viscera'. And visceral knowledge, whether innate or acquired, is mediated by the 'old brain'. We often describe our affect-charged judgements – mistakenly – as 'instinctive reactions'. They are not. But they have the same elemental, reason-defying, old-brain power as true instincts. At this point the psychological considerations of the present chapter lead straight back to the neurophysiological theories discussed in the Prologue. The schizophysiology of the brain provides an essential clue to the streak of insanity running through the history of man.

Our cherished beliefs are of course neither exclusive products of the human neocortex, nor of the 'old brain' which we share

*See, for instance, William James's *The Varieties of Religious Experience*, still a classic in this field. A more recent treatment is offered by Sir Alister Hardy in *The Divine Flame* and *The Biology of God*.

with the lower mammals, but of their combined activities. Their degree of irrationality varies according to which level dominates and to what extent. Between the theoretical extremes of 'pure logic' and 'blind passion' there are many levels of mental activity, as we find them in primitives at various stages of development, in children at various ages, and in adults in various states of consciousness (lucid, daydreaming, dreaming, hallucinating, etc.). Each of these types of mental activity is governed by its own 'rules of the game' which reflects the complex interactions of the old and new structures in the brain. For interact they must all the time – even if their coordination is inadequate, and deficient in the effective controls which lend stability to a well-ordered holarchy. Thus even abstract verbal symbols become imbued with emotive values and visceral reactions – as the psycho-galvanic lie-detector so dramatically shows. And that applies even more, of course, to doctrines and ideologies amplified by the group-mind. Unfortunately we cannot apply a lie-detector to measure the irrationality of its beliefs, nor its explosive and devastating potential.

V

AN ALTERNATIVE TO DESPAIR

I

As long as we believed that our species was potentially immortal, with an astronomical lifespan before it, we could afford to wait patiently for that evolutionary change in human nature which, gradually or suddenly, would make love and sweet reason prevail. But man's biological evolution came to a virtual standstill in Cro-Magnon days, 50,000 to 100,000 years ago. We cannot wait another 100,000 years for the unlikely chance mutation which will put things right; we can only hope to survive by inventing techniques which supplant biological evolution. That is to say, we must search for a cure for the schizophysiology endemic in our nature, which led into the situation in which we find ourselves. If we fail to find that cure, the old paranoid streak in man, combined with his new powers of destruction, must sooner or later lead to his extinction. But I also believe that the cure is not far beyond the reach of contemporary biology; and that with the proper concentration of efforts it might enable man to win the race for survival.

I am aware that this sounds over-optimistic, in contrast to the pessimistic views expressed in previous chapters, of the prospects ahead of us. Yet I do not think that these fears are exaggerated, and I do not think that the hope for a rescue is entirely utopian. It is not inspired by science fiction, but based on the recent spectacular advances in neuro-chemistry and related fields. They do not yet provide a cure for the mental disorder of our species, but they indicate the area of research that may eventually produce the remedy hopefully invoked in the Prologue: that combination of benevolent hormones or enzymes which would resolve the conflict between the old and recent structures in the brain, by providing the neocortex with the power of hierarchic control over the archaic lower centres, and thus catalyse the transition from maniac to man.

Yet I have learned from painful experience that any proposal which involves 'tampering with human nature' is bound to provoke strong emotional resistances. These are partly based on ignorance and prejudice, but partly on a justified revulsion against further intrusions into the privacy and sanctity of the individual by social engineering, character engineering, various forms of brain-washing, and other threatening aspects of overt or covert totalitarianism. It hardly needs saying that I share this loathing for a nightmare in whose shadow most of my life was spent. But on the other hand it has to be realized that ever since the first cave-dweller wrapped his shivering frame into the hide of a dead animal, man has been, for better or worse, creating for himself an artificial environment and an artificial mode of existence without which he no longer can survive. There is no turning back on housing, clothing, artificial heating, cooked food; nor on spectacles, hearing aids, forceps, artificial limbs, anaesthetics, antiseptics, prophylactics, vaccines and so forth. We start tampering with human nature almost from the moment a baby is born, by the universal practice of dropping a solution of silver nitrate into its eyes as a protection against *ophthalmia neonatorum*, a form of conjunctivitis often leading to blindness, caused by bacilli which lurk in the mother's genital tract. This is followed later by preventive vaccinations, compulsory in most civilized countries, against smallpox and other infectious diseases. To appreciate the value of these tamperings with the course of nature, let us remember that the epidemics of smallpox among American Indians were one of the main reasons why they lost their lands to the white man. It also decimated the population of Europe in the beginning of the seventeenth century – its ravages only equalled, perhaps symbolically, by the massacres, in the name of true religion, of the Thirty Years War.

A less well-known form of tampering, pertinent to our subject, is the prevention of goitre and the variety of cretinism associated with it. When I was a child, the number of people in Alpine mountain valleys with monstrous swellings in the front of their necks, and of cretinous children in their families was quite frightening. On recent trips, revisiting the same regions half a century later, I cannot remember having come across a single cretinous child. Thanks to the progress of biochemistry, it has been discovered that this type of cretinism was caused by a malfunction of the thyroid gland. This in turn was due to the shortage of iodine in the nutrients of the mountainous areas affected. Without sufficient iodine, the gland is unable to synthesize the required quantities of thyroid hormones, with tragic consequences for the mind. Thus iodine in small quantities was added by the health authorities to the common table salt, and goitrous cretinism in Europe became virtually a thing of the past.

Obviously, our species does not possess the biological equipment needed to live in environments with iodine-poor soil, or to cope with the micro-organisms of malaria and smallpox. Nor does it possess instinctual safeguards against excessive breeding: ethologists tell us that every animal species they have studied – from flower beetles through rabbits to baboons – is equipped with such instinctual controls, which inhibit excessive breeding and keep the population density in a given territory fairly constant, even when food is plentiful. When the density reaches a critical limit, crowding produces stress which affects the hormonal balance and interferes with lifespan and reproductive behaviour. Thus there is a kind of feedback mechanism which adjusts the rate of breeding and keeps the population at a more or less stable level. The population of a given species in a given territory behaves in fact as a self-regulating social holon.

But in this respect, too, man is a biological freak, who, somewhere along the way, lost this instinctual control-mechanism. It seems almost as if in human populations the ecological rule were reversed: the more crowded they are in slums, ghettoes and poverty-stricken areas, the faster they breed. What prevented the population from exploding much earlier in history was not the kind of automatic feedback control which we observe in animals, but the death-harvest of wars, epidemics, pestilence and infant mortality. These were factors beyond the control of the masses; but nevertheless conscious attempts to regulate the birth-rate through contraception and infanticide are on record from the very dawn of history. (The oldest recipes to prevent conception are contained in the so-called Petri Papyrus, dating from about 1850 B.C.) Birth control through infanticide was also common from ancient Sparta to quite recently among Eskimos. Compared to these cruel methods, the modern ways of directly 'tampering with Nature' by intra-uterine coils and oral contraceptives are certainly preferable. Yet they interfere in a radical and permanent manner with the vital physiological processes of the oestrous cycle. Applied on a world-wide scale they would amount to the equivalent of an artificially induced adaptive mutation.

There is no end to the list of beneficial 'tamperings with human nature', compared to which the abuses and occasional follies of medicine and psychiatry shrink to relative insignificance. What the sum total of these tamperings amounts to is in fact *correcting* human nature, which without these correctives would in its biological aspect hardly be viable, and which in its social aspect, after countless disasters, is heading for the ultimate catastrophe. Having conquered the worst of the infectious diseases which assail the body of man, the time has come to look for methods to immunize him against the infectious delusions which from time immemorial have assailed the group-mind and made a blood-bath of his history. Neuropharmacology has given us lethal nerve-gases, drugs for brain-washing, others to induce hallucinations and delusions at will. It can and will be put to benevolent use. Let me quote a single example of the type of research pointing in that direction:

In 1961 the University of California San Francisco Medical Centre organized an international symposium on *Control of the Mind*. At the first session, Professor Holger Hyden of Gothenburg University made headlines in the Press with his paper – 'Biochemical Aspects of Brain Activity'. Hyden is one of the leading authorities in that field. The passage which created the sensation is quoted below (the reference to me is explained by the fact that I was a participant at the symposium):

In considering the problem of control of the mind, the data give rise to the following question: would it be possible to change the fundamentals of emotion by inducing molecular changes in the biologically active substances in the brain? The RNA,* in particular, is the main target for such a speculation, since a molecular change of the RNA may lead to a change in the proteins being formed. One may phrase the question in different words to modify the emphasis: do the experimental data presented here provide means to modify the mental state by specifically induced chemical changes? Results pointing in that direction have been obtained; this work was carried out using a substance called tricyano-aminopropene.

. . . The application of a substance changing the rate of production and composition of RNA and provoking enzyme changes in the functional units of the central nervous system has both negative and positive aspects. There is now evidence that the administration of tricyano-aminopropene is followed by an *increased suggestibility* in man. This being the case, a defined change of such a functionally important substance as the RNA in the brain could be used for conditioning. The author is not referring specifically to tricyano-aminopropene, but to any substance inducing changes of biologically important molecules in the neurons and the glia and affecting the mental state in a negative direction. It is not difficult to imagine the possible uses to which a government in a police-controlled state could put this substance. For a time they would subject the population to hard conditions. Suddenly the hardship would be removed, and at the same time, the substance would be added to the tap water and the mass-communications media turned on. This method would be much cheaper, and would create more intriguing possibilities than to let Ivanov treat Rubashov individually for a long time, as Koestler described in his book. On the other hand, a counter-measure against the effect of a substance such as tricyanoamino-propene is not difficult to imagine either.[1]

The last sentence is formulated with caution, but the implications are clear. However shocking this may sound, if our sick species is to be saved, salvation will come, not from UNO resolutions and diplomatic summits, but from the biological laboratories. It stands to reason that a biological malfunction needs a biological corrective.

---

*Ribonucleic acid, a key substance in the genetic apparatus.

2

It would be naive to expect that drugs can present the mind with
gratis gifts, and put into it something which is not already there.
Neither mystic insights, nor philosophical wisdom, nor creative
power can be provided by pill or injection. The biochemist
cannot *add* to the faculties of the brain – but he can *eliminate*
obstructions and blockages which impede their proper use. He
cannot put additional circuits into the brain, but he can improve
coordination between existing ones and enhance the power of
the neocortex – the apex of the hierarchy – over the lower,
emotion-bound levels and the blind passions engendered by them.
Our present tranquillizers, barbiturates, stimulants, anti-depres-
sants and combinations thereof are merely a first step towards
more sophisticated aids to promote a balanced state of mind,
immune against the sirens' song, the barking of demagogues and
false Messiahs. Not the Pop-Nirvana procured by LSD or the
soma pills of *Brave New World*, but a state of dynamic equilibrium
in which the divided house of faith and reason is reunited and
hierarchic order restored.

3

I first published these hopeful speculations – as the only alternative
to despair that I could (and can) see – in the concluding chapter
of *The Ghost in the Machine*. Among the many negative criticisms
which it brought in its wake, the one most frequently voiced
accused me of proposing the manufacture of a little pill which
would suppress all feeling and emotion and reduce us to the
equanimity of cabbages. This charge, sometimes uttered with
great vehemence, was based on a complete misreading of the
text. What I proposed was not the castration of emotion, but
reconciling emotion and reason which through most of man's
schizophrenic history have been at loggerheads. Not an amputation, but a process of harmonization which assigns each level
of the mind, from visceral impulses to abstract thought, its

appropriate place in the hierarchy. This implies reinforcing the
new brain's power of veto against that type of emotive behaviour – *and that type only* – which cannot be reconciled with
reason, such as the 'blind' passions of the group-mind. If these
could be eradicated, our species would be safe.

There are blind emotions and visionary emotions. Who in his
senses would advocate doing away with the emotions aroused
while listening to Mozart or looking at a rainbow?

4

Any individual living today who asserted that he had made a
pact with the devil and had intercourse with succubi would be
promptly dispatched to a mental home. Yet not so long ago,
belief in such things was taken for granted and approved by
'common sense' – i.e., the consensus of opinion, i.e., the group-
mind. Psychopharmacology is playing an increasing part in the
treatment of mental disorders in the clinical sense, such as individual delusions which affect the critical faculties and are *not*
sanctioned by the group-mind. But we are concerned with a cure
for the paranoid streak in what we call 'normal people', which is
revealed when they become victims of group-mentality. As we
already have drugs to increase man's suggestibility, it will soon be
within our reach to do the opposite: to reinforce man's critical
faculties, counteract misplaced devotion and that militant
enthusiasm, both murderous and suicidal, which is reflected in
history books and the pages of the daily paper.

But who is to decide which brand of devotion is misplaced,
and which beneficial to mankind? The answer seems obvious: a
society composed of autonomous individuals, once they are
immunized against the hypnotic effects of propaganda and
thought-control, and protected against their own suggestibility
as 'belief-accepting animals'. But this protection cannot be provided
by counter-propaganda or drop-out attitudes; they are self-
defeating. It can only be done by 'tampering' with human nature
itself to correct its endemic schizophysiological disposition.
History tells us that nothing less will do.

5

Assuming that the laboratories succeed in producing an immunizing substance conferring mental stability – how are we to propagate its global use? Are we to ram it down people's throats, whether they like it or not?

Again the answer seems obvious. Analgesics, pep pills, tranquillizers, contraceptives have, for better or worse, swept across the world with a minimum of publicity or official encouragement. They spread because people welcomed their effects. The use of a mental stabilizer would spread not by coercion but by enlightened self-interest; from then on, developments are as unpredictable as the consequences of any revolutionary discovery. A Swiss canton may decide, after a public referendum, to add the new substance to the iodine in the table salt, or the chlorine in the water supply, for a trial period, and other countries may imitate their example. There might be an international fashion among the young. In one way or the other, the simulated mutation would get under way. It is possible that totalitarian countries would try to resist it. But today even Iron Curtains have become porous; fashions are spreading irresistibly. And should there be a transitional period during which one side alone went ahead, it would gain a decisive advantage because it would be more rational in its long-term policies, less frightened and less hysterical. In conclusion, let me quote from *The Ghost in the Machine*:

Every writer has a favourite type of imaginary reader, a friendly phantom but highly critical, with whom he is engaged in a continuous, exhausting dialogue. I feel sure that my friendly phantom-reader has sufficient imagination to extrapolate from the recent breath-taking advances of biology into the future, and to concede that the solution outlined here is in the realm of the possible. What worries me is that he might be repelled and disgusted by the idea that we should rely for our salvation on molecular chemistry instead of a spiritual rebirth. I share his distress, but I see no alternative. I hear him explain: 'By trying to sell us your Pills, you are adopting that crudely materialistic attitude and naive scientific *hubris* which you pretend to oppose.' I still oppose it. But I do not believe that it is 'materialistic' to take a realistic view of the condition of man; nor is it *hubris* to feed thyroid extracts to children who would otherwise grow into cretins . . . Like the reader, I would prefer to set my hopes on moral persuasion by word and example. But we are a mentally sick race, and as such deaf to persuasion. It has been tried from the age of the prophets to Albert Schweitzer; and Swift's anguished cry: 'Not die here in a rage, like a poisoned rat in a hole,' has acquired an urgency as never before.

Nature has let us down, God seems to have left the receiver off the hook, and time is running out. To hope for salvation to be synthesised in the laboratory may seem materialistic, crankish or naive; it reflects the ancient alchemist's dream to concoct the *elixir vitae*. What we expect from it, however, is not eternal life, but the transformation of *homo maniacus* into *homo sapiens*.[2]

This is the only alternative to despair which I can read into the shape of things to come.

We can now move to more cheerful horizons.

PART TWO

The Creative Mind

VI

HUMOUR AND WIT

I

The theory of human creativity which I developed in earlier books[1] endeavours to show that all creative activities – the conscious and unconscious processes underlying the three domains of artistic originality, scientific discovery and comic inspiration – have a basic pattern in common, and to describe that pattern. The three panels of the triptych on page 110 indicate these three domains, which shade into each other without sharp boundaries. The meaning of the diagram will become apparent as the argument unfolds.

The creative process is, oddly enough, most clearly revealed in humour and wit. But this will appear less odd if we remember that 'wit' is an ambiguous term, relating to both witticism and to ingenuity or inventiveness.* The jester and the explorer both live on their wits, and we shall see that the jester's riddles provide a convenient back-door entry, as it were, into the inner sanctum of creative originality. Hence this inquiry will start with an analysis of the comic.† It may be thought that I have allowed a disproportionate amount of space to humour, but it is meant to serve, as I said, as a back-door approach to the creative process in science and art. Besides, it can also be read as a self-contained essay – and it may provide the reader with some light relief.

---

*'Wit' stems from *witan*, understanding, whose roots go back to the Sanskrit *veda*, knowledge. The German *Witz* means both joke and acumen; it comes from *wissen*, to know; *Wissenschaft*, science, is a close kin to *Fürwitz* and *Aberwitz* – presumption, cheek, and jest. French teaches the same lesson. *Spirituel* may either mean witty or spiritually profound; 'to amuse' comes from 'to muse' (*a-muser*), and a witty remark is a *jeu d'esprit* – a playful, mischievous form of discovery.

†This chapter is based on the summary of the theory which I contributed to the fifteenth edition of the *Encyclopaedia Britannica*.[2]

2

Humour, in all its many-splendour'd varieties, can be simply defined as a type of stimulation which tends to elicit the laughter reflex. Spontaneous laughter is a motor reflex, produced by the coordinated contraction of fifteen facial muscles in a stereotyped pattern and accompanied by altered breathing. Electrical stimulation of the *zygomatic major*, the main lifting muscle of the upper lip with currents of varying intensity, produces facial expressions ranging from the faint smile through the broad grin, to the contortions typical of explosive laughter.[3] (The laughter and smile of civilized man is of course often of a conventional kind where voluntary effort deputizes for, or interferes with, spontaneous reflex activity; we are concerned, however, only with the latter.)

Once we realize that laughter is a humble reflex, we are immediately faced with several paradoxes. Motor reflexes, such as the contraction of the pupil of the eye in dazzling light, are simple responses to simple stimuli, whose value in the service of

The three domains of creativity

survival is obvious. But the involuntary contraction of fifteen facial muscles associated with certain irrepressible noises strikes one as an activity without any practical value, quite unrelated to the struggle for survival. *Laughter is a reflex, but unique in that it has no apparent biological utility.* One might call it a luxury reflex. Its only purpose seems to be to provide temporary relief from the stress of purposeful activities.

The second, related paradox is a striking discrepancy between the nature of the stimulus and that of the response in humorous transactions. When a blow beneath the knee-cap causes an automatic upward kick, both 'stimulus' and 'response' function on the same primitive physiological level, without requiring the intervention of higher mental functions. But that such a complex mental activity as reading a story by James Thurber should cause a specific reflex-contraction of the facial musculature is a phenomenon which has puzzled philosophers since Plato. There is no clear-cut, predictable response which would tell a lecturer whether he has succeeded in convincing his listeners; but when he is telling a joke, laughter serves as an experimental test. *Humour is the only form of communication in which a stimulus on a high level of complexity produces a stereotyped, predictable response on the physiological reflex level.* This enables us to use the response as an indicator for the presence of that elusive quality that we call humour – as we use the click of the Geiger counter to indicate the presence of radioactivity. Such a procedure is not possible in any other form of art; and since the step from the sublime to the ridiculous is reversible, the study of humour provides the psychologist with important clues for the study of creativity in general.

3

The range of laughter-provoking experiences is enormous, from physical tickling to mental titillations of the most varied and sophisticated kinds. I shall attempt to demonstrate that there is unity in this variety, a common denominator of a specific and specifiable pattern which reflects the 'logic' or 'grammar' of humour. A few examples will help to unravel that pattern.

(*a*) A masochist is a person who likes a cold shower in the morning, so he takes a hot one.

(*b*) An English lady, on being asked by a friend what she thought of her departed husband's whereabouts: 'Well, I suppose the poor soul is enjoying eternal bliss, but I wish you wouldn't talk about such unpleasant subjects.'★

(*c*) A doctor comforts his patient: 'You have a very serious disease. Of ten persons who catch it only one survives. It is lucky you came to me, for I have recently had nine patients with this disease and they all died of it.'

(*d*) Dialogue in a film by Claude Berri:
'Sir, I would like to ask for your daughter's hand.
'Why not? You have already had the rest.'

(*e*) A marquis at the court of Louis XV unexpectedly returned from a journey and, on entering his wife's boudoir, found her in the arms of a bishop. After a moment's hesitation the marquis walked calmly to the window, leaned out and began going through the motions of blessing the people in the street.
'What are you doing?' cried the anguished wife.
'Monseigneur is performing my functions, so I am performing his.'

Is there a common pattern underlying these five stories? Starting with the last, we discover after a little reflection that the marquis's behaviour is both unexpected and perfectly logical – but of a logic not usually applied to this type of situation. It is the logic of the division of labour, governed by rules as old as human civilization. But we expected that his reactions would be governed by a different set of rules – the code of sexual morality. It is the sudden clash between these two mutually exclusive codes of rules – or associative contexts, or cognitive holons – which produces the comic effect. It compels us to perceive the situation in two self-consistent but incompatible frames of reference at the same time; it makes us function simultaneously on two different wave-lengths. While this unusual condition lasts, the event is not,

★This is a variant of Russell's anecdote in the Prologue.

as is normally the case, associated with a single frame of reference, but *bisociated* with two.

I have coined the term 'bisociation' to make a distinction between the routines of disciplined thinking within a single universe of discourse – on a single plane, as it were – and the creative types of mental activity which always operate on more than one plane. In humour, both the creation of a subtle joke and the *re-creative* act of perceiving the joke, involve the delightful mental jolt of a sudden leap from one plane or associative context to another.

Let us turn to our other examples. In the film dialogue, the daughter's 'hand' is perceived first in a metaphorical frame of reference, then suddenly in a literal, bodily context. The doctor thinks in terms of statistical probabilities, the rules of which are inapplicable to individual cases; and there is an added twist because, in contrast to what naive common sense suggests, the patient's odds of survival are unaffected by whatever happened before, and are still one against ten. This is one of the profound paradoxes of the theory of probability; the mathematical joke implies a riddle.

The widowed lady who looks upon death as 'eternal bliss' and at the same time 'an unpleasant subject', epitomizes the common human predicament of living in the 'divided house of faith and reason'. Here again the simple joke carries unconscious overtones and undertones, audible to the inner ear alone.

The masochist under the shower who punishes himself by depriving himself of his daily punishment is governed by rules which are a *reversal* of those of normal logic. (We can also construct a pattern where *both* frames of reference are reversed: 'A sadist is a person who is kind to a masochist.') However, the joker does not really believe that the masochist takes his hot shower as a punishment; he only pretends to believe it. *Irony* is the satirist's most effective weapon; it pretends to accept the opponent's ways of reasoning in order to expose their implicit absurdity or viciousness.

Thus the common pattern underlying these stories is *the perceiving of a situation or idea in two self-consistent but mutually incompatible frames of reference or associative contexts.* We might call it a collision between two mental holons, each governed by its own rule-book. This formula can be shown to have a general validity for all forms of humour and wit, some of which will be discussed below. But it covers only one aspect of humour – its *logical structure.* We must now turn to another fundamental aspect – the *emotional dynamics* which breathes life into that structure and makes us laugh, giggle or smile.

4

When a comedian tells a story, he deliberately sets out to create a certain tension in his listeners, which mounts as the narrative progresses. But it never reaches its expected climax. The punch-line or *pointe* acts as a verbal guillotine which cuts across the logical development of the story; it debunks our dramatic expectations; the tension we felt becomes suddenly redundant and is exploded in laughter, like water gushing from a punctured pipe. To put it differently, laughter disposes of emotive excitations which have become pointless and must somehow be worked off along physiological channels of least resistance; and the function of the 'luxury reflex' is to provide these channels.

A glance at a caricature by Hogarth or Rowlandson, showing the brutal merriment of people in a tavern, makes one realize at once that they are working off their surplus of adrenalin by contracting their face muscles into grimaces, slapping their thighs, and exhaling in explosive puffs through the half-closed glottis. Their flushed faces reveal that the emotions disposed of through these tension-relieving safety valves are brutality, envy, sexual gloating. However, if one leafs through an album of *New Yorker* cartoons, coarse laughter yields to an amused and rare-fied smile: the ample flow of adrenalin has been distilled and crystallized into a grain of Attic salt. As we move across the spectrum of humour, from its coarse to its subtle forms, from practical joke to brain-teaser, from jibe to irony, from anecdote to epigram, the emotional climate shows a parallel transformation. The emotion discharged in coarse laughter is aggression robbed

of its purpose; the jokes small children enjoy are mostly scatological; adolescents of all ages gloat on vicarious sex; the sick joke
trades on repressed sadism, satire on righteous indignation. There
is a bewildering variety of moods involved in different forms of
humour, including mixed or contradictory feelings; but whatever
the mixture, it must contain a basic ingredient which is indispensable: an impulse, however faint, of aggression or apprehension. It may appear in the guise of malice, contempt, the
veiled cruelty of condescension, or merely an absence of sympathy with the victim of the joke – 'a momentary anaesthesia of
the heart', as Bergson put it. In the subtler types of humour the
aggressive tendency may be so faint that only careful analysis
will detect it, like the presence of salt in a well-prepared dish –
which, however, would be tasteless without it. Replace aggression
by sympathy, and the same situation – a drunk falling on his face –
will no longer be comic but pathetic, and evoke not laughter but
pity. It is the aggressive element, the detached malice of the comic
impersonator which turns pathos into bathos, tragedy into
travesty. Malice may be combined with affection in friendly
teasing – or when we don't know whether we shall laugh or
cry at the misadventures of Charlie Chaplin; and the aggressive
component in civilized humans may be sublimated or no longer
conscious. But in jokes which appeal to children and primitive
people, cruelty and boastful self-assertiveness are much in evidence. In 1961 a survey carried out among American children
aged eight to fifteen made the researchers conclude that 'mortifi-
cation or discomfort or hoaxing of others very readily caused
laughter, while a witty or funny remark often passed unnoticed'.[4]
Similar views are reflected in historically earlier forms and
theories of the comic. In Aristotle's view, laughter was intimately
related to ugliness and debasement. Cicero held that 'the province
of the ridiculous . . . lies in a certain baseness and deformity'.
Descartes believed that laughter was a manifestation of joy 'mixed
with surprise or hatred or sometimes with both'. In Francis Bacon's
list of the causes which give rise to laughter, the first place is
given to 'deformity'. One of the most frequently quoted utter-
ances on the subject is this definition in Hobbes's *Leviathan*:

The passion of laughter is nothing else but sudden glory arising from a sudden conception of some eminency in ourselves by comparison with the infirmity of others, or with our own formerly.

Translated into our terminology, laughter appears as a harmless outlet for a sudden overflow of the self-assertive tendency. However much the opinions of the theorists differ, on this one point nearly all of them agree: that the emotions discharged in laughter always contain an element of aggressiveness. But aggression and apprehension are twin phenomena; psychologists talk of 'aggressive–defensive impulses'. Accordingly, one of the typical situations in which laughter occurs is the moment of sudden cessation of fear caused by some imaginary danger. Rarely is the nature of laughter as an over-flow of redundant tensions more strikingly manifested than in the sudden change of expression on the small child's face from anxious apprehension to the happy laughter of relief. This seems to be unrelated to humour; yet at a closer look we find here the same logical structure as before: the wildly barking little dog was first perceived by the child in a context of danger, then as a tail-wagging puppy; the tension has suddenly become redundant, and spills over.

Kant realized that what causes laughter is 'the sudden transformation of a tense expectation into nothing'. Herbert Spencer took up the idea and attempted to formulate it in physiological terms: 'Emotions and sensations tend to generate bodily movements. . . . When consciousness is unawares transferred from great things to small', the 'liberated nerve force' will expend itself along channels of least resistance – the bodily motions of laughter. Freud incorporated Spencer's theory of humour into his own,* with special emphasis on the release of repressed emotions in laughter; he also attempted to explain why the excess energy should be worked off in that particular way:

According to the best of my knowledge, the grimaces and contortions of the corners of the mouth that characterise laughter appear first

*For a detailed analysis of Freud's and Bergson's theories of humour, see *Insight and Outlook*, Appendix II.

in the satisfied and over-satiated nurseling when he drowsily quits the breast. . . They are physical expressions of the determination to take no more nourishment, an 'enough' so to speak, or rather a 'more than enough'. . . This primal sense of pleasurable saturation may have provided the link between the smile – that basic phenomenon underlying laughter – and its subsequent connection with other pleasurable processes of de-tension.[5]

In other words, the muscle-contractions of the smile, as the earliest expressions of relief from tension, would thereafter serve as channels of least resistance. Similarly, the explosive exhalations of laughter seem designed to 'puff away' surplus tension, and the agitated gestures obviously serve the same function.

It may be objected that such massive reactions often seem quite out of proportion to the slight stimulations which provoke them. But we must bear in mind that laughter is a phenomenon of the trigger-releaser type, where a minute pull may open the tap for vast amounts of stored emotions, often derived from unconscious sources: repressed sadism, sexual tumescence, unavowed fear, even boredom: the explosive laughter of a class of schoolboys at some trivial incident is a measure of their pent-up resentment during a boring lecture. Another factor which may amplify the reaction out of all proportion to the comic stimulus is the social infectiousness which laughter shares with other emotive manifestations of group-behaviour.

Laughter or smiling may also be caused by stimulations which are not in themselves comic, but *signs* or *symbols* deputizing for well-established comic patterns: Chaplin's boots, Groucho Marx's cigar, catch-phrases or allusions to family jokes. To discover why we laugh requires on some occasions tracing back a long, involved thread of associations to its source. This task is further complicated by the fact that the effect of such comic symbols – on a cartoon or on the stage – appears to be instantaneous, without allowing time for the accumulation and subsequent discharge of 'expectations' and 'emotive tensions'. But here memory comes into play, acting as a storage battery whose charge can be sparked off at any time: the smile which greets Falstaff's appearance on the stage is derived from a mixture of memories and expectations. Besides, even if our reaction to a *New Yorker* cartoon appears to be instantaneous, there is always a process in time until we 'see the joke'; the cartoon has to tell a story, even if it is telescoped into a few seconds. All of which goes to show that to analyse humour is a task as delicate as analysing the chemical composition of a perfume with its multiple ingredients – some of which are never consciously perceived, while others, when sniffed in isolation, would make us wince.

5

I have discussed first the logical structure of humour; and then its emotional dynamics. Putting the two together, we may summarize the result as follows: the bisociation of a situation or idea with two mutually incompatible contexts, and the resulting abrupt transfer of the train of thoughts from one context to another, puts a sudden end to our 'tense expectations'; the accumulated emotion, deprived of its object, is left hanging in the air, and is discharged in laughter. When the marquis rushes to the window and starts blessing the people in the street, our intellect turns a somersault and enters with gusto into the new game; but the malicious erotic feelings which the start of the story has aroused cannot be fitted into the new context; deserted by the nimble intellect, it gushes out in laughter like air from a punctured tyre. To put it differently: *we laugh because our emotions have a greater inertia and persistence than our reasoning processes.* Affects are incapable of keeping step with reasoning; unlike reasoning, they cannot 'change direction' at a moment's notice. To the physiologist this is self-evident since our self-assertive emotions operate through the phylogenetically old, massive apparatus of the sympathetic nervous system and its allied hormones, acting on the whole body, while language and logic are confined to the neocortex at the roof of the brain. Common experience provides daily confirmation of this particular aspect of the dichotomy between the old and the new brain. We are literally 'poisoned' by our adrenal humours; it takes time to talk a person out of a mood; fear and anger show persistent after-effects long after their causes have been removed. If we could change our moods as quickly as we jump from one idea to another, we would be acrobats of emotion; but since we are not, our thoughts and emotions frequently become dissociated. It is emotion deserted by thought that is discharged in laughter. For emotion, owing to its greater mass-momentum, is, as we have seen, unable to follow the sudden switch of ideas to a different type of logic; it tends to persist in a straight line. Ariel leads Caliban on by the nose: she jumps on a branch, he crashes into the tree. Aldous Huxley once wrote:

We carry around with us a glandular system which was admirably well adapted to life in the Paleolithic times but it is not very well adapted to life now. Thus we tend to produce more adrenalin than is good for us, and we either suppress ourselves and turn destructive energies inwards or else we do not suppress ourselves and we start hitting people.[6]

A third alternative is to laugh at people. There are other outlets for tame aggression such as competitive sports or literary criticism; but they are acquired skills, whereas laughter is a gift of nature, included in our native equipment. The glands that control our emotions reflect conditions at a stage of evolution when the struggle for existence was more deadly than at present – and when the reaction to any strange sight or sound consisted in jumping, bristling, fighting or running. As security and comfort increased in the species, new outlets were needed for the disposal of emotions which could no longer be worked off through their original channels, and laughter is obviously one of them. But it could only emerge when reasoning had gained a degree of independence from the 'blind' urges of emotion. Below the human level, thinking and feeling appear to form an indivisible unity; not until thinking became gradually detached from feeling could man perceive his own emotion as redundant, confront his glandular 'humours' with a sense of humour, and make the smiling admission, 'I have been fooled.'

6

The foregoing discussion was intended to provide the tools for
dissecting and analysing any specimen of humour. The procedure
to be followed is to determine the nature of the two (or more)
frames of reference whose collision gives rise to the comic effect
– to discover the type of logic or 'rules of the game' which
govern each. In the more sophisticated type of joke the 'logic'
is implied and hidden; and the moment we state it in explicit
form, the joke is dead. Unavoidably, the section that follows will
be strewn with cadavers.

Max Eastman, in *The Enjoyment of Laughter*, remarked of a
laboured pun by Ogden Nash: 'It is not a pun but a punitive
expedition'. That goes for most puns, even for Milton's famous
lines about the Prophet Elijah's ravens – which were 'though
ravenous/taught to abstain from what they brought'; or Freud's
character, who calls the Christmas season the 'alcoholidays'. Most
puns strike one as atrocious, perhaps because they represent the
most primitive form of humour: two disparate strings of thought
tied together in an acoustic knot. But the very primitiveness of
such bisociations based on pure sound may account for the pun's
immense popularity with children and its prevalence in certain
types of mental disorder ('punning mania').

From the *play on sounds* – puns and Spoonerisms – an ascending
series leads to the *play on words* and so to the *play on ideas*. When
Groucho Marx says of a safari in Africa, 'We shot two bucks,
but that was all the money we had', the joke hinges on the two
meanings of the word 'buck'. It is moderately funny, but would
be even less so without the reference to Groucho, which evokes a
visual image instantly arousing a high voltage of expectations.
The story of the marquis and the bishop is clearly of a superior
type of humour, because it plays not on mere words, but on ideas.

It would be quite easy – and equally boring – to draw up a
list in which jokes and witticisms are classified according to the
nature of the frames of reference whose collision creates the
comic effect. We have already come across a few, such as meta-

phorical versus literal meaning (the daughter's 'hand'); professional versus common-sense logic (the statistically minded doctor); incompatible codes of behaviour (the marquis); confrontations of the trivial and the exalted ('eternal bliss'); trains of reasoning travelling happily joined together in opposite directions (the sadist who is kind to the masochist). The list could be extended indefinitely; in fact *any* two cognitive holons can be made to yield a comic effect of sorts by hooking them together and infusing a drop of malice into the concoction. The frames of reference may even be defined by such abstract concepts as 'time' and 'weather'; the absent-minded professor who tries to read the temperature from his watch or to tell the hour from the thermometer, is comic for the same reason as it would be to watch a game of ping-pong played with a football or a game of rugby played with a ping-pong ball. The variations are infinite, the formula remains the same.

Jokes and anecdotes have a single point of culmination. The literary forms of *sustained humour*, such as the picaresque novel, do not rely on a single effect but on a series of minor climaxes. The narrative moves along the line of intersection of contrasted planes – e.g., the fantasy world of Don Quixote and the cunning horse-sense of Sancho Panza – or is made to oscillate between them; as a result tension is continuously generated and discharged in mild amusement.

Comic verse thrives on the melodious union of incongruities – Carroll's 'cabbages and kings'; and particularly on the contrast between lofty form and flatfooted content. Certain metric forms like the hexameter or Alexandrine arouse expectations of pathos, of the heroic and exalted; to pour into these epic moulds some homely, trivial content – 'Beautiful soup, so rich and green/ Waiting in a hot tureen' – is an almost infallible comic device. The rolling dactyls of the first lines of a limerick which carry, instead of Hector or Achilles, a young lady from Niger for a ride, make her ridiculous even before the expected calamities befall her. Instead of a heroic mould, a soft lyrical one may also pay off: 'And what could be moister/Than the tears of an oyster?'

Another type of *incongruity between form and content* yields the bogus proverb: 'The rule is: jam tomorrow and jam yesterday – but never jam today.' Two contradictory statements have been telescoped into a line whose homely, admonitory sound conveys the impression of a popular adage. In a similar way, *nonsense verse* achieves its effect by pretending to make sense, by forcing the reader to project meaning into the phonetic pattern of the *jabberwocky*, as one interprets the ink blots in a Rorschach test.

Satire is a verbal caricature which shows us a deliberately distorted image of a person, institution or society. The traditional method of the caricaturist is to *exaggerate* those features which he considers to be characteristic of his victim's personality and to *simplify* by leaving out everything that is not relevant for his purpose. The satirist uses the same technique; and the features of society which he selects for magnification are of course those of which he disapproves. The result is a juxtaposition, in the reader's mind, of his habitual image of the world in which he moves, and its absurd reflection in the satirist's distorting mirror. The reader is thus made to recognize familiar features in the absurd, and absurdity in the familiar. Without this double vision the satire would be humourless. If the human Yahoos were really such evil-smelling monsters as Gulliver's Houyhnhnm hosts claim, the book would not be a satire but the statement of a deplorable truth. Straight invective is not satire; it must deliberately overshoot its mark.

A similar effect is achieved if, instead of exaggerating the objectionable features, the satirist projects them by means of the *allegory* on to a different background, such as an animal society. A succession of writers, from Aristophanes through Swift and Anatole France to George Orwell, have used this technique to focus attention on deformities of society which, blunted by habit, we take for granted.

7

The coarsest type of humour is the *practical joke*: pulling away the chair from under the dignitary's lowered bottom. The victim is perceived, first as a person of consequence, then suddenly as an inert body subject to the laws of physics: authority is debunked by gravity, mind by matter; man is degraded to a mechanism. Goose-stepping soldiers act like automatons, the pedant behaves like a mechanical robot, the Sergeant-Major attacked by diarrhoea or Hamlet getting the hiccoughs show man's lofty aspirations deflated by his all-too-solid flesh. A similar effect is produced by artefacts which masquerade as humans: Punch and Judy, Jack-in-the-Box, gadgets playing tricks on their masters as if with calculated malice.

In Henri Bergson's theory of laughter, this dualism of subtle mind and inert matter – he calls it 'the mechanical encrusted on the living' – is made to serve as an explanation of *all* varieties of the comic, whereas in the light of what has been said it applies only to one type of comic situation among many others.

From the bisociation of *man and machine*, there is only a step to the *man–animal* hybrid. Disney's creations behave as if they were human without losing their animal appearance. The caricaturist follows the reverse procedure by discovering horsey, mousey, piggish features in the human face.

This leads us to the comic devices of *imitation, impersonation and disguise*. The impersonator is perceived as himself and some-body else at the same time. If the result is slightly degrading – but only in that case – the spectator will laugh. The comedian impersonating a public personality, two pairs of trousers serving as the legs of the pantomime horse, men disguised as women and women as men – in each case the paired patterns reduce each other to absurdity.

The most aggressive form of impersonation is the *parody*, designed to deflate hollow pretence, to destroy illusion, and to undermine pathos by harping on the human weaknesses of the victim. Wigs falling off, speakers forgetting their lines, gestures remaining suspended in the air: the parodist's favourite points of attack are again situated on the line of intersection between the sublime and the trivial.

Playful behaviour in young animals and children is amusing because it is an unintentional parody of adult behaviour, which it imitates or anticipates. Young puppies are droll, because their helplessness, affection and puzzled expression make them appear more 'human' than full-grown dogs; because their ferocious growls strike one as impersonations of adult behaviour – like a child in a bowler hat; because the puppy's waddling, uncertain gait makes it a choice victim of nature's practical jokes; because its bodily disproportions, the huge padded paws, Falstaffian belly and wrinkled philosopher's brow give it the appearance of a caricature; and lastly because we are such very superior beings compared to a puppy. A fleeting smile can contain many logical ingredients and emotional spices.

Both Cicero and Francis Bacon regarded *deformity* as the most frequent cause of laughter. Renaissance princes collected dwarfs, hunchbacks and blackamoors for their merriment. As we have become too humane for that kind of fun, we are apt to forget that it requires a good deal of imagination and empathy to recognize in a midget a fellow-human who, though different in appearance, thinks and feels much as oneself does. In children this projective faculty is still rudimentary; they tend to mock people with a stammer or a limp, and laugh at the foreigner with an odd pronunciation. Similar attitudes are shown by tribal or parochial societies to any form of appearance or behaviour that deviates from their strict norms: the stranger is not really human, he only pretends to be 'like us'. The Greeks used the same word 'barbarous' for the foreigner and the stutterer: the uncouth, barking sounds the stranger uttered were considered a parody of human speech. Vestiges of this primitive attitude are still found in the curious fact that we accept a foreign accent with tolerance, but find the imitation of a foreign accent comic. We know that the imitator's mispronunciations are mere pretence; this knowledge makes sympathy unnecessary and enables us to be childishly cruel with a clean conscience.

Another source of innocent merriment occurs when *the part and the whole* change roles, and attention becomes focused on a detail torn out of the functional context on which its meaning depended. When the gramophone needle gets stuck, the soprano's voice keeps repeating the same word on the same quaver, which suddenly assumes a grotesquely independent life. The same happens when faulty orthography displaces attention from meaning to spelling, or when the beam of consciousness is directed at functions which otherwise are performed automatically – the paradox of the centipede. The self-conscious, awkward youth, who 'does not know what to do with his hands' is a victim of the same predicament.

Comedies used to be classified according to their reliance on situations, manners or characters. The logic of the last two need no further discussion; in the first, comic effects are contrived by making a situation participate simultaneously in two independent chains of events with different associative contexts, which intersect through coincidence, mistaken identity, or confusions of time and occasion. The coincidence on which they are hinged is the *deux ex machina* of both comedy and antique tragedy.

Why *tickling* should produce laughter remained an enigma in all earlier theories of the comic. Darwin was the first to point out that the innate response to tickling is squirming and straining to withdraw the tickled part – a defence-reaction designed to escape attacks on vulnerable areas such as the soles of the feet, armpits, belly and ribs. If a fly settles on the belly of a horse, it causes a ripple of muscle-contractions across the skin – the equivalent of squirming in the tickled child. But the horse does not laugh when tickled, and the child not always. It will laugh only – and this is the crux of the matter – when it perceives tickling as *a mock attack*, a caress in mildly aggressive disguise. For the same reason people laugh only when tickled by others, not when they tickle themselves.

Experiments in Yale on babies under one year old revealed the not very surprising fact that they laughed fifteen times more often when tickled by their mothers than when they were tickled by strangers; and when tickled by strangers they mostly cried. For the mock attack must be recognized as being only pretence, and with strangers one cannot be sure. Even with its own mother there is an ever-so-slight feeling of uncertainty and apprehension, the expression of which will alternate with laughter in the baby's behaviour; and it is precisely this element of tension between the tickles which is relieved in the laughter accompanying the squirm. The rule of the game is: 'Let me be just a little frightened so that I can enjoy the relief'.

Thus the tickler is impersonating an aggressor, but is simultaneously known not to be one; this is probably the first situation in life which makes the infant live on two planes at once – a delectable foretaste of being tickled by the horror comic.

Humour in the visual arts reflects the same logical structures as discussed before. Its most primitive form is the distorting mirror at the fun fair which reflects the human frame elongated into a column or compressed into the shape of a toad; it plays a practical joke on the victim who sees the image in the mirror both as his familiar self and a patient lump of plasticine that can be stretched and squeezed into any absurd form. But while the mirror distorts mechanically, *the caricaturist* does it selectively, by the same technique of exaggerating characteristic features and simplifying the rest, which the satirist employs. Like the satirist, the caricaturist reveals the absurd in the familiar; and like the satirist he must overshoot his mark. His malice is rendered harmless by our knowledge that the monstrous pot-bellies and bow-legs he draws are not *real*; real deformities are no longer comic, they arouse pity.

The artist, painting a stylized portrait, also uses the technique of selection, exaggeration and simplification; but his attitude to the model is dominated by positive empathy instead of negative malice; and the features he selects for emphasis differ accordingly. In some character-studies by Leonardo, Hogarth or Daumier the passions reflected are so violent, the grimaces so ferocious, that it is impossible to tell whether they were meant as portraits or caricatures. If you feel that such distortions of the human face are not really possible, that Daumier merely *pretended* that they exist, then you are absolved from horror and pity and can laugh at his grotesques. But if you think that this is indeed what Daumier saw in those de-humanized faces, then you feel that you are looking at a work of art.

Humour in music is a subject to be approached with diffidence, because the language of music ultimately eludes translation into verbal symbols. All one can do is to point at some analogies: a 'rude' noise, such as the blast of a trumpet inserted into a passage

where it does not belong, has the effect of a practical joke; a
singer or an instrument out of tune produces a similar reaction;
the imitation of animal sounds, vocally or instrumentally,
exploits the technique of impersonation; a nocturne by Chopin
transposed into hot jazz, or a simple street song performed in the
style of the Valkyrie is a marriage of incompatibles. These are
primitive devices corresponding to the lowest levels of humour;
higher up we come across compositions like Ravel's *La Valse* – an
affectionate parody of the sentimental *Wiener Walzer*; or Haydn's
Surprise Symphony or the mock-heroics of Kodály's folk opera,
Hári János. But in comic opera it is almost impossible to sort out
how much of the comic effect is derived from the book, how
much from the music; and the highest forms of musical
humour, the unexpected delights of a light-hearted scherzo by
Mozart, defy verbal analysis – or else this would have to be so
specialized and technical as to defeat its purpose. Although a
'witty' musical passage, which springs a surprise on the audience
and cheats it of its 'tense expectations', certainly has the emotion-
relieving effect which tends to produce laughter, a concert audience may occasionally smile, but will hardly ever laugh; which
goes to show that the emotions evoked by musical humour are
of a subtler kind than those of the verbal and visual variety.

8

The criteria which determine whether a humorous offering will
be judged good, bad or indifferent, are of course partly a matter
of period taste and personal preference, partly dependent on the
style and technique of the humorist. It would seem that these
criteria can be summed up under three main headings: (*a*) originality, (*b*) emphasis, (*c*) economy.

The merits of *originality* are self-evident; it provides the essential
element of surprise, which cuts across our expectations. But true
originality is not very often met either in humour or in other
forms of art. One common substitute for it is to increase the
tension of the audience by various techniques of suggestive
emphasis. The clown's domain is the rich, coarse type of humour;

he piles it on; he appeals to sadistic, sexual, scatalogical impulses; one of his favourite tricks is repetition of the same situation, the same key-phrase. This diminishes the effect of surprise, but helps in drawing emotion into the familiar channel – more and more liquid is being pumped into the punctured pipeline.

Emphasis on local colour and ethnic peculiarities – as in Scottish, Jewish, Cockney stories – is a further means to channel emotion into familiar tracks. The Scotsman or Cockney must of course be caricatures if the comic purpose is to be achieved – in other words, exaggeration and simplification once more appear as indispensable tools to provide emphasis.

In the higher forms of humour, however, emphasis tends to yield to the opposite kind of virtue: *economy*. Economy, in humour and art, does not mean mechanical brevity, but the implicit hint instead of the explicit statement – the oblique allusion in lieu of the frontal attack. The old-fashioned *Punch* cartoon featuring the British lion and the Russian bear 'rubs it in'; the *New Yorker* cartoon poses a riddle which the reader must solve by an imaginative effort in order to 'see the joke'.

In humour, as in other forms of art, emphasis and economy are complementary techniques. The first forces the offering down the consumer's throat; the second tantalizes, to whet his appetite.

9

Earlier theories – including even Bergson's and Freud's – have treated humour as an isolated phenomenon, without attempting to throw light on the intimate connections between the comic and the tragic, between laughter and crying, between artistic inspiration, comic inventiveness and scientific discovery. Yet (as we shall see) these three domains of creative activity form a continuum with no sharp boundaries between wit and ingenuity, nor between the art of discovery and the discoveries of art.

It has been said, for instance, that scientific discovery consists in seeing an analogy which nobody has seen before. When, in the Song of Songs, Solomon compared the Shulamite's neck to a tower of ivory, he saw an analogy which nobody had seen before;

when William Harvey perceived in the exposed heart of a fish a messy kind of mechanical pump, he did the same; and when the caricaturist draws a nose like a cucumber, he again does just that. In fact, all the bisociative patterns discussed above, which constitute the 'grammar' of humour, can also enter the service of art or discovery, as the case may be. The pun has its equivalent in the rhyme, but also in the problems which confront the philologist. The clash between incompatible codes of behaviour may yield comedy, tragedy or new psychological insights. The dualism of mind and inert matter is exploited by the practical joker, but also provides one of the eternal themes of literature: man as a marionette on strings, manipulated by gods or chromosomes. The man–beast dichotomy is reflected by Donald Duck, but also in Kafka's *Metamorphosis* and the psychologist's rat-experiments. The caricature corresponds not only to the artist's character-portrait, but also to the scientist's diagrams and charts, which emphasize the relevant features and leave out the rest.

The conscious and unconscious processes underlying creativity are essentially combinatorial activities – the bringing together of previously separate areas of knowledge and experience. The scientist's purpose is to achieve *synthesis*; the artist aims at a *juxtaposition* of the familiar and the eternal; the humorist's game is to contrive a *collision*. And as their motivations differ, so do the emotional responses evoked by each type of creativity: discovery satisfies the 'exploratory drive'; art induces emotional catharsis through the 'oceanic feeling'; humour incites malice and provides a harmless outlet for it. Laughter can be described as the 'Haha reaction'; the discoverer's Eureka cry as the 'Aha! reaction'; and the delight of the aesthetic experience as the 'Ah . . . reaction'. But the transitions from one to the other are continuous: witticism blends into epigram, caricature into portrait; and whether one considers architecture, medicine, chess or cookery, there is no clear frontier where the realm of science ends and that of art begins. Comedy and tragedy, laughter and weeping, mark the extremes of a *continuous spectrum*.

SUMMARY

Humour provides a back-door entry to the domain of creativity because it is *the only example of a complex intellectual stimulus releasing a simple bodily response* – the laughter reflex.

To describe the unitary pattern underlying all varieties of humour I have proposed the term 'bisociation' – perceiving a situation or event in two mutually exclusive associative contexts. The result is an abrupt transfer of the train of consciousness to a different track, governed by a different logic or 'rule of the game'. This intellectual jolt deflates our expectations; the emotions they aroused have suddenly become redundant, and are flushed out along channels of least resistance in laughter.

The emotions thus involved, however complex, always contain a dominant element of the self-assertive, aggressive–defensive tendencies. They are based on the ancient adrenal–sympathetic branch of the nervous system – the old brain – and have a much stronger momentum and persistence than the subtle and devious processes of cortical reasoning, with which they are unable to keep step. It is emotion deserted by thought that is discharged, harmlessly, in laughter. But this luxury reflex could only arise in a creature whose reasoning has gained a degree of independence from its biological drives, enabling him to perceive his own emotions as redundant – to realize that he has been fooled. The person who laughs is the opposite of the fanatic whose reason has been blinded by emotion – and who fools himself.

After applying the theory to various types of the comic – from physical tickling to social satire – I discussed the criteria of styles and techniques in humour: *originality* or unexpectedness; *emphasis* through selection, exaggeration and simplification; and its reverse: *economy* or implicitness which forces the audience to make a re-creative effort.

Lastly, the brief cross–references to creativity in science and art at the end of this chapter may serve as an introduction to the sections that follow.

VII

THE ART OF DISCOVERY

I

Creativity in science could be described as the art of putting two and two together to make five. In other words, it consists in combining previously unrelated mental structures in such a way that you get more out of the emergent whole than you have put in. This apparent bit of magic derives from the fact that the whole is not merely the sum of its parts, but an expression of the relations between its parts; and that each new synthesis leads to the emergence of new patterns of relations – more complex cognitive holons on higher levels of the mental hierarchy.

Let me give a few brief examples selected from the numerous case-histories of scientific discoveries described in *The Sleepwalkers, The Act of Creation*, etc.

The motions of the tides were known to man from time immemorial. So were the motions of the moon. But the idea to connect the two, the idea that the tides were due to the attraction of the moon, was proclaimed for the first time by the German astronomer Johannes Kepler in the seventeenth century. By putting two and two together, he opened up the infinite vista of modern astronomy.

Lodestones – magnets – were known to the ancient Greeks as a curiosity of nature. In the Middle Ages they were used for two purposes: as mariner's compasses and as a means to attract an estranged wife back to her husband. Also well-known were the curious properties of amber which, when rubbed, acquired the power of attracting flimsy objects. The Greek for amber is *elektron*, but Greek science was no more interested in the freak phenomena of electricity than modern science is in telepathy. Nor were the Middle Ages. For some two thousand years magnetism and electricity were regarded as separate phenomena, as unrelated to each other as the tides and the moon. In 1820 Hans Christian Oersted discovered that an electric current flowing through a wire deflected a magnetic compass which happened to be lying on the table. At that historic moment the two hitherto separate contexts began to fuse into an emergent synthesis: electromagnetism – thus creating a kind of chain-reaction which is still continuing. At successive stages of it electricity and magnetism merged with radiant light, chemistry merged with physics, the humble *elektron* became an orbiting planet within the solar system of the atom, and ultimately energy and matter became unified in Einstein's single, sinister equation, $E = mc^2$.

If we go back to the beginnings of the scientific quest, there is an ancient tradition according to which Pythagoras discovered the secrets of musical harmony while watching some blacksmiths at work on his native island of Samos, and noticing that iron bars of different lengths gave out sounds of different pitch under the strokes of the hammer. This spontaneous amalgamation of arithmetic and music was probably the starting-point of physics.

From the Pythagoreans, who mathematized the harmony of the spheres, to their modern heirs, who combined space and time into a single continuum, the pattern is always the same: the discoveries of science do not create something out of nothing; they combine, relate and integrate already existing but previously separate ideas, facts, associative contexts – mental holons. This act of cross-fertilization – or self-fertilization within a single brain – appears to be the essence of creativity, and to justify the term 'bisociation'. We have seen how the humorist bisociates mutually incompatible mental structures in order to produce a *collision*. The scientist, on the other hand, aims at synthesis, at the *integration* of previously unrelated ideas. The Latin *cogito* comes from *coagitare*, to shake together. Bisociation in humour consists of the sudden shaking together of incompatible elements which briefly collide, then separate again. Bisociation in science means combining hitherto unrelated cognitive holons in such a way that a new level is added to the hierarchy of knowledge, which contains the previously separate structures as its members.

However, we have seen that the two domains are continuous, without a sharp boundary: each subtle witticism is a malicious discovery, and vice versa, many great discoveries of science have been greeted with howls of laughter, precisely because they seemed to represent a marriage of incompatibles – until the marriage bore fruit and the apparent incompatibility turned out to derive from prejudice. What looked like a collision ended in fusion: witticism is paradox stated, discovery is paradox resolved. Even Galileo treated Kepler's theory of the tides as a bad joke, and one can easily imagine a contemporary caricaturist drawing a fat-faced moon sucking up the earth's oceans through a straw. But the step from the sublime to the ridiculous is reversible: the satires of Swift and Orwell carry deeper lessons than a whole library of works on social science.

As we travel from the coarse toward the sophisticated types of humour, and then continue across the fluid boundary into the centre panel of the triptych on p. 110, we come across such hybrid cases as brain-twisters, logical paradoxes, mathematical games. The conundrums about Achilles and the Tortoise and about the Cretan Liar have for two millennia tickled philosophers and spurred logicians to creative efforts. The listener's task has been transformed from 'seeing the joke' into 'solving the problem'. And when he succeeds, he no longer roars with laughter as at the clown's antics; in the course of our journey laughter has gradually shaded into an amused, then an admiring smile: the emotional climate has changed from the Haha reaction into the Aha reaction.

2

The term 'Aha experience' was coined by *Gestalt* psychologists to indicate the euphoria which follows the moment of truth, the flash of illumination when the bits of the puzzle click into place – or, in our terms, when the bisociated contexts fuse in a new synthesis. The emotion exploding in coarse laughter is aggression robbed of its purpose; the tension ebbing away in the Aha reaction after the penny has dropped is mainly derived from a challenge to intellectual curiosity, the urge to explore and understand.

That urge is not confined to laboratory researchers. In recent years biologists have been led to recognize the existence of a primary instinct, the 'exploratory drive', which is as basic as the instincts of hunger and sex, and can occasionally be even more powerful. Countless experimental zoologists – starting with Darwin himself* – have shown that curiosity is an innate drive in rats, birds, dolphins, chimpanzees and men. It is the driving power which makes the laboratory rat find its way through the experimental maze without reward or punishment, and even defy punishment by traversing electrified grids instead of turning back. It makes the child take the new toy to pieces 'to see what's inside', and it is the prime mover behind human exploration and research.

The exploratory drive may of course combine with other drives such as hunger or sex. The pure scientist's proverbially 'detached' and 'disinterested' quest – his self-transcending absorption in the mysteries of nature – is in fact often combined with ambition, competitiveness, vanity. But these self-assertive tendencies must be restrained and highly sublimated to find fulfilment in the – mostly meagre – rewards for his slow and patient labours. There are, after all, more direct methods of asserting one's ego than the study of spiral nebulae.

But while the exploratory drive may be adulterated by ambition and vanity, in its purest form, the quest is its own reward.

'Were I to hold the truth in my hand', Emerson wrote, 'I would let it go for the positive joy of seeking.' In a classic experiment, Wolfgang Köhler's chimpanzee, Sultan, discovered after many unsuccessful efforts to rake in a banana placed outside his cage with a stick that was too short, that he could do it by fitting two hollow sticks together. His new discovery 'pleased him so immensely' that he kept repeating the trick and forgot to eat the banana.

However, subjective vanity apart, the self-assertive tendencies

*See *The Act of Creation*, Book Two, Ch. VIII.

also enter on a deeper level into the scientist's motivation. 'I am', wrote Freud, 'not really a man of science . . . but a *conquistador* . . . with the curiosity, the boldness, and the tenacity that belong to that type of person.' The exploratory drive aims at understanding nature, the conquistadorial element at mastering nature (including human nature). Excepting perhaps pure mathematics, every variety of the scientific quest has this dual motivation, although they need not be equally conscious in the individual scientist's mind. Knowledge can beget humility or power. The archetypes of the opposite tendencies are Prometheus and Pythagoras – one stealing the fire of the gods, the other listening to the harmony of the spheres. Freud's confession can be contrasted with the statements of many scientific geniuses that the only purpose of their labours was to lift a fraction of the veil covering the mysteries of nature, and their only motivation a feeling of awe and wonder. 'Men were first led to the study of natural philosophy,' wrote Aristotle, 'as indeed they are today, by wonder.' Maxwell's earliest memory was 'lying on the grass, looking at the sun, and *wondering*'. Einstein – the humblest of all – struck the same chord when he wrote that whoever is devoid of the capacity to wonder at the cosmic mystery, 'whoever remains unmoved, whoever cannot contemplate, or know the deep shudder of the soul in enchantment, might just as well be dead for he has already closed his eyes on life'. He could not foresee, when he discovered the wondrous equation which unified matter and energy, that it would turn into black magic.

Thus the ubiquitous polarity of the self-asserting and self-transcending tendencies is strikingly displayed in the domain of scientific creativity. Discovery may be called the emotionally neutral art – not because the scientist is devoid of emotion, but because his labours require a delicately balanced and sublimated blend of motivations, where the drives to exploration and domination are in equilibrium. For the same reason he is assigned the central panel of the triptych, between the jester who, exercising his wit at the expense of others, is primarily dominated by self-asserting malice, and the artist, whose creative work depends on the self-transcending power of his imagination.

The symbolic topology of the triptych seems further justified by the nature of the Aha reaction. It combines the explosive discharge of tension, epitomized in the Eureka cry which is akin to the Haha reaction, with the cathartic Ah . . . reaction – that 'deep shudder of enchantment' of which Einstein speaks, which is closely related to the artist's experience of beauty and the mystic's 'oceanic feeling'. The Eureka cry reflects the con-quistadorial, the Ah . . . reaction the mystic element in the hybrid motivation of the scientist's quest.

We can now continue the journey across the triptych into the third panel, where the emotional climate is dominated by the Ah . . . reaction.

VIII

THE DISCOVERIES OF ART

I

Laughing and weeping, aroused by comedy and tragedy, mark
the two extremes of a continuous spectrum. Both provide channels for the overflow of emotions; both are 'luxury reflexes'
without apparent utility. This much they have in common; in
every other respect they are direct opposites.

Although weeping is neither an uncommon nor a trivial
phenomenon, academic psychology has almost totally ignored it.
There are no theories of weeping comparable to Bergson's or
Freud's treatises on laughter; and the theory put forward in *The
Act of Creation* is the only one mentioned in Hilgard and Atkinson's standard textbook of psychology for American college
students.*

As a preliminary step, we must make a distinction between
weeping and crying: it is a peculiarity of the English language
to treat them as synonymous. *Weeping* has two basic reflex
characteristics: the secretion of tears and a specific way of breathing. *Crying* is the emission of sounds signalling distress or protest.
It may be combined with or alternate with weeping, but should

---

*From Hilgard and Atkinson, *Introduction to Psychology* (4th ed., 1967), Ch. 7
'Emotion', sub-section 'Weeping': 'Laughter and tears are often close together,
and although we associate laughter with joy and tears with sadness, there are also
tears of joy. The writer Arthur Koestler has noted the failure in text-books of
psychology to treat weeping, and he has attempted to supply this lack by an
analysis of his own. He notes five kinds of situations in which weeping accompanies
motivated behaviour.' The text-book then briefly mentions five such situations –
raptness, mourning, relief, sympathy, self-pity – and concludes: 'These illustrations show how emotions provide a kind of commentary on ongoing motivated
behaviour. The weeping is neither a drive nor an incentive, but it is a sign that
something motivationally important is occurring.'
And that's all that students of psychology are taught about weeping.

not be confused with it. Crying is a form of communication, weeping is a private affair. And we are talking, of course, of *spontaneous* weeping, not of the contrived sobs of stagecraft, public or private.

Let us compare the physiological processes involved in laughter and weeping. Laughter is triggered by the adrenal–sympathetic branch of the autonomic nervous system, weeping by the para-sympathetic branch. The first, as we have seen, serves to energize the body, tensing it for action; the second has the opposite effect: it lowers blood pressure, neutralizes excesses of blood-sugar, facilitates the elimination of body-waste and generally tends towards quietude and catharsis – literally the 'purging' of tensions.

This physiological contrast is clearly reflected in the visible manifestations of laughter and weeping. The laugher's eyes sparkle, the corners are wrinkled, but brow and cheeks are taut and smooth, which lends the face an expression of radiance; the lips are parted, the corners lifted. In weeping, the eyes are 'blinded by tears', they lose their focus and lustre; the features seem to crumble; even when weeping for joy or in aesthetic rapture, the transfigured face reflects a serene languidness.

A similar contrast is noticeable in bodily postures and motions. In laughter the head is thrown back by a vigorous contraction of the muscles in the neck; the person who weeps 'lets the head droop' (into the hands, on the table or on somebody's shoulder). Laughter contracts the muscles and begets agitated movements; in weeping the muscles go flabby, the shoulders slump forward, the whole posture reflects a 'letting go'.

The pattern of respiration in laughter consists of long, deep intakes of air, followed by bursts of explosive exhalatory puffs – ha-ha-ha! In weeping the process is reversed: short, gasping inhalations – sobs – are followed by long, sighing exhalations – a-a-h, ah. . . .

These manifest contrasts between laughter and weeping, and their dependence on two different branches of the autonomic nervous system, are in keeping with their origin in opposite types of emotion. The Haha reaction is triggered by the self-assertive, the Ah . . . reaction by the self-transcending emotions.

The first half of this statement should by now be obvious, the second requires some further comment.

2

In *The Act of Creation* I discussed in detail various situations which may lead to an overflow of tears – mourning, pity, helplessness, awe, religious or aesthetic rapture, etc. Only the last is directly relevant to our subject, but it is worth noting that *all* eye-moistening emotions have a basic element in common which is altruistic, i.e., self-transcending – a longing to enter into a quasi-symbiotic communion with a person, living or dead, or some higher entity which may be Nature, or a form of Art, or a mystic experience. These 'participatory' emotions are, as we have seen, subjective manifestations of the integrative tendency, reflecting the human holon's partness – its dependence on, and commitment to, some more comprehensive unit on a higher level of the hierarchy which transcends the narrow confines of the self. Listening to the organist playing in an empty cathedral, or looking at the stars on a summer night, may cause a welling-up of emotions which moisten the eyes, accompanied by an expansion of consciousness, which becomes quasi-depersonalized and – if the experience is very intense – leads into 'the oceanic feeling of limitless extension and oneness with the universe'* – the Ah . . . reaction in its purest form.

Ordinary mortals rarely ascend to such mystic heights, but they are at least familiar with the foothills. The self-transcending emotions have an extensive scale of intensity and a wide range of variety; they may be joyous or sad, tragic or lyrical. 'Weeping for joy' and 'weeping in sorrow' reflect the relative nature of the hedonic tone superimposed on all emotions.

A further contrast between the Haha and the Ah . . . reactions is worth underlining. In laughter, we saw, tension is suddenly exploded; in weeping it is gradually drained away, without debunking expectation, without breaking the continuity of mood;

*Romain Rolland describing the character of religious experience in a letter to Freud – who regretfully professed never to have felt anything of the sort.[1]

in the Ah . . . reaction *emotion and reason remain united*. Moreover, the self-transcending emotions do not tend towards bodily action, but towards passive quiescence. Respiration and pulse are slowed down; 'entrancement' is a step towards the trance-like states induced by contemplative mystics; the emotion is of a quality that cannot be consummated by any specific voluntary act. To be 'overwhelmed' by awe and wonder, 'enraptured' by a smile, 'entranced' by beauty – each of these words expresses passive surrender. The surplus of emotion cannot be worked off by any purposeful muscular activity, it can only be consummated in *internal* – visceral and glandular – processes (cf. above, Chapter III).

Finally some additional facts about the autonomic nervous system are pertinent to our theme. In strongly emotional or pathological conditions, the mutually antagonistic, i.e., equilibrating action of the two divisions (sympathetic and parasympathetic) no longer prevails; instead they may mutually *reinforce* each other, as in the sexual act; or over-excitation of one division may lead to a temporary *rebound* or over-compensatory 'answering effect' by the other;[2] lastly, the parasympathetic may act as a *catalyst* that triggers its antagonist into action.[3]*

The first of these three possibilities is relevant to our emotional state in listening to a Wagner opera, where relaxed, cathartic feelings seem to be paradoxically combined with euphoric arousal. The second possibility is reflected in 'emotional hangovers' of one kind or another. The third possibility is the most relevant to our theme: it shows in concrete physiological terms how one type of emotional reaction can act as a catalyst for its opposite – as self-transcending identification with the hero on the screen releases vicarious aggressiveness against the villain; as identification with a group or creed releases the savagery of mob-behaviour.

3

I have discussed the basic motivation of the creative scientist: the exploratory drive. Yet every great artist also has an element of

*See Appendix III.

the explorer in him: the poet does not 'manipulate words' (as the behaviourists would have it), he explores the emotive and descriptive potentialities of language; the painter is engaged, throughout his life, in learning to see (and in teaching others to see the world the way he does). Thus the creative drive has its unitary biological source, but it can be canalized into a variety of directions.

This is the first point to retain, if we wish to overcome the deplorable split into the 'two cultures' – unknown to the Renaissance as it was to antiquity – and to reaffirm the continuity between the panels of the triptych. Needless to say, continuity does not mean uniformity; it means the gradual shading, without breaks or dividing lines, of one colour of the rainbow into another.

The horizontal lines across the triptych of creativity are meant to indicate the continuity of some typical combinatorial patterns – some basic bisociative processes which are found in all three panels. These patterns are *trivalent* – they can enter the service of humour, discovery or art. Let me illustrate this by a few more examples, in addition to those already mentioned earlier.

We have seen, for example, that the caricaturists' cartoon, the scientist's diagram, and the artist's portrait employ the same bisociative technique of superimposing selective grids on the optical appearance. Yet in the language of behaviourist psychology we would have to say that Cézanne, glancing at a landscape, receives a 'stimulus', to which he responds by putting a dab of paint on the canvas – and that is all there is to it. In reality, perceiving the landscape and re-creating it are two activities which take place simultaneously on two different planes, in two different environments. The stimulus comes from a large, three-dimensional environment, the distant landscape. The response acts on a different environment, a small rectangular canvas. The two are governed by different rules of organization: an isolated brush-stroke on the canvas does not represent an isolated detail in the landscape. There is no point-to-point correspondence between the two planes; they are bisociated as wholes in the artist's creation and in the beholder's eye.

The creation of a work of art involves a series of processes which happen virtually all at the same time and cannot be rendered in verbal terms without suffering impoverishment and distortion. The artist, as the scientist, is engaged in projecting his vision of reality into a particular medium, whether the medium is paint, marble, or words, or mathematical equations. But the product of his efforts can never be an exact representation or copy of reality, even if he naively hopes to achieve one. In the first place, he has to come to terms with the peculiarities and limitations of his chosen medium. But in the second place, his own perception and world-view also have their own peculiarities and limitations imposed by the implicit conventions of his period or school and by his individual temperament. These lend coherence to his vision, but also tend to freeze into fixed formulae, stereotypes, verbal and visual clichés. The originality of genius, in art as in science, consists in a shift of attention to aspects of reality previously ignored, discovering hidden connections, seeing familiar objects or events in a new light.

In the discussion which followed a lecture at an American university on the theme of the present chapter, one of the 'resident painters' remarked angrily: 'I do not "bisociate". I sit down, look at the model and paint it.'

In a sense he was right. He had found his 'style', his visual vocabulary, some years earlier and was content to use it, with minor variations, to express everything he had to say. The erstwhile creative process had become stabilized into a skilled routine. It would be foolish to underestimate the achievements of which skilled routine is capable. whether in the chemical laboratory or in the painter's studio. But technical virtuosity is one thing, creative originality another; and we are only concerned here with the latter.

4

The trinity of caricature – diagram – stylized portrait provides one of the horizontal connecting lines across the three panels of the triptych. Some other such trivalent patterns have already been mentioned earlier. Thus the bisociation of *sound and meaning* in its humblest form yields the pun. Yet the *rhyme* is nothing but a glorified pun, where sound lends resonance to meaning; while for the anthropologist and linguist, sound provides effective clues to meaning. Likewise, when *rhythm* and *metre* invade meaning, they may produce a Shakespeare sonnet or a limerick; while in the central panel the study of rhythmic pulsations plays a vital role, from alpha waves to systole and diastole – the iambi and trochee of life. No wonder that metric verse carries echoes of the shaman's tom-tom and, to quote Yeats, 'lulls the mind into a waking trance'.

The triune character of other bisociative combinations appears almost over-obvious once one has realized the underlying principle and perceives the three domains of creativity as a continuum. Thus the tracing of *hidden analogies* yields the poetic metaphor, scientific discovery or comic simile, according to the explorer's motivation. The dichotomies of mind and matter, of spiritual being and/or hairless ape, yield endless variations for scientific, artistic or comic treatment.

Less obvious is the trivalent role of *illusion*. The actor or impersonator on the stage is two people at the same time. If the result is *degrading* – Hamlet getting the hiccups in the middle of his monologue – illusion is debunked and the spectator will laugh. If he is led to *identify* with the hero, he will experience the particular state of split-mindedness known as the magic of the stage. But beside the parodist and the actor there is a third type of impersonator who purposefully employs the human faculty of being oneself and someone else at the same time: the therapist or healer, who projects himself into the patient's mind and at the same time acts as a wise magician or father-figure. Empathy – *Einfühlung* – is a nice, sober term for the rather mysterious process of entering into a kind of mental symbiosis with other selves, of stepping out of one's skin, as it were, and putting oneself into the skin of the other. Empathy is the source of our intuitive understanding – more direct than language – of how the other thinks and feels; it is the starting-point of the science and art of medical diagnosis and psychiatry. The medicine man, ancient and modern, has a two-way relationship with the patient: he is trying to feel what the patient feels, and at the same time he is acting the part of one endowed with divine guidance, magic powers, secret knowledge. The tragedian creates illusion; the comedian debunks illusion; the therapist uses it for a definite purpose.

Coincidence may be described as the chance encounter of two unrelated causal chains which – miraculously it seems – merge into a significant event. It provides the neatest paradigm of the bisociation of previously separate contexts, engineered by fate. Coincidences are puns of destiny. In the pun, two strings of thought are tangled into an acoustic knot; in the coincidental happening two strings of events are knitted together by invisible hands.

Moreover, coincidence may serve as a classic example of the trivalence of bisociative patterns, as it is conspicuously represented on each of the three panels. It is the mainstay of the type of *comedy*, or farce, which relies on ambiguous situations created by the intersection of two independent series of events so that the situation can be interpreted – and misinterpreted – in the light of either one or the other, resulting in mistaken identity or confusion of time and occasion. In the classic *tragedy* apparent chance-coincidences are the *deus ex machina* by which the gods interfere in the destiny of man – Oedipus is trapped into murdering his father and marrying his mother by mistaken identity. Lastly, lucky hazards – the gifts of *serendipity* – play a conspicuous part in the history of scientific discoveries.

On a higher level of the triptych, however, the pattern undergoes a subtle change. The comedy of situations yields to the comedy of manners, which no longer relies for its effects on coincidence, but on the clash of *incompatible codes* of reasoning or conduct, as a result of which the hypocrisy or absurdity of one or both rule-books is exploded. Modern drama shows a similar change; destiny no longer acts from the outside, but from inside the personae; they are no longer marionettes on strings, manipulated by the gods, but victims of their own foolish and conflicting passions: 'the fault, dear Brutus, is not in our stars but in ourselves'.

Drama thrives on *conflict*, and so does the novel. The nature of the conflict may be explicitly stated or merely implied; but an element of it must be present, otherwise the characters would be gliding through a frictionless universe. The conflict may be fought out in the divided heart of a single character; or between two or more persons; or between man and his fate. Conflict between personalities may be due to a contrast in ideas or temperaments, systems of values or codes of conduct – as in the comedy. But while in the comedy the collision results in malicious debunking, conflict can attain the dignity of tragedy, if the audience is led to accept the attitudes of both antagonists as valid, each within its own frame of reference. If the author succeeds in this, the conflict will be projected into the spectator's – or reader's – mind and experienced as a clash between two simultaneous and incompatible identifications. 'We make out of our quarrels with others rhetoric, but out of our quarrels with ourselves poetry,' wrote Yeats. The comedian makes us laugh at the expense of the victim; the tragedian makes us suffer as his accomplice; the former appeals to the self-assertive, the latter to the self-transcending emotions. In between the two, in the emotionally 'neutral' zone, the psychologist, anthropologist and sociologist are engaged in *resolving* the conflicts by analysing the factors which gave rise to it.

5

One basic bisociation remains to be briefly discussed: the confrontation between the tragic and the trivial.

With due respect to Shakespeare's 'All the world's a stage', one might say that the ordinary mortal's life is played on two alternating stages, situated on two different levels – let us call them the trivial plane and the tragic plane of existence. Most of the time we bustle about on the trivial plane; but on some special occasions, when confronted with death or engulfed in the oceanic feeling, we seem to fall through a stage-trap or man-hole and are transferred to the tragic or absolute plane. Then all at once our daily routines appear as shallow, trifling vanities. But once safely back on the trivial plane we dismiss the experiences of the other as phantasms of overstrung nerves.

The highest form of human creativity is the endeavour to bridge the gap between the two planes. Both the artist and the scientist are gifted – or cursed – with the faculty of perceiving the trivial events of everyday experience *sub specie aeternitatis*, in the light of eternity; and conversely to express the absolute in human terms, to reflect it in a concrete image. Our ordinary mortal has neither the intellectual nor the emotional equipment to live for more than brief transition periods on the tragic plane. The Infinite is too inhuman and elusive to cope with unless it is made to blend itself with the tangible world of the finite. The existentialist's Absolute becomes emotionally effective only if it is bisociated with something concrete – dovetailed into the familiar. This is what both scientist and artist are aiming at, though not always consciously. By bridging the gap between the two planes, the cosmic mystery becomes humanized, drawn into the orbit of man, while his humdrum experiences are transformed, surrounded by a halo of mystery and wonder.

Needless to say, not all novels are 'problem novels', subjecting the reader to a sustained barrage of existential conundrums. But indirectly and implicitly every great work of art has some bearing on man's ultimate problems. Even a humble daisy has a root, and a work of art, however lighthearted or serene, is ultimately nourished through its delicate capillaries by the archetypal sub-strata of experience.

By living on both planes at once, the creative artist or scientist is able to catch an occasional glimpse of eternity looking through the window of time. Whether it is a mediaeval stained-glass window or Newton's formula of universal gravity, is a matter of temperament and taste.

6

In the previous sections I discussed the continuity of the domains of humour, discovery and art; the emotional climate in each of the three domains and its derivation from the basic polarity of emotions; lastly the 'horizontal lines' across the triptych-model, indicating the structural affinities between the bisociative patterns of creative activity in the three domains. We must now have a closer look at the psychology of the creative act itself.

All coherent thinking and acting is governed by 'rules of the game', although we are mostly unaware of being controlled by them. In the artificial conditions of the psychological laboratory the rules are explicitly spelt out by the experimenter; for instance: 'name opposites'. Then the experimenter says 'dark' and the subject promptly answers 'light'. But if the rule is 'synonyms', the subject will respond with 'black' or 'night' or 'shadow'. Note that though the rule is fixed, it leaves the subject a choice of several answers, even in this simple game. To talk, as behaviourists do, of stimuli and responses forming a chain in a vacuum is meaningless: what response a particular stimulus will evoke depends (a) on the fixed rules of the game and (b) on the flexible strategies which the rules permit, guided by past experience, temperament and other factors.

But the games we play in everyday life are more complex than those in the laboratory, where the rules are laid down by explicit order. In the normal routines of thinking and talking the rules exercise their control implicitly, from way below the level of conscious awareness. Not only the codes of grammar and syntax operate hidden in the gaps between the words, but also the codes of commonsense logic and of those more complex mental structures which we call 'frames of perception' or 'associative contexts', and which include our built-in, axiomatic prejudices and emotional inclinations. Even if consciously bent on defining the rules which govern our thinking, we find it extremely difficult to do so and have to enlist the help of specialists – linguists, semanticists, psychiatrists, and so forth. We play the games of life, obeying rule-books written in invisible ink or a secret code. But there are problem-situations where playing the game is not enough, and only creative originality points the way out of the trap.

In *The Act of Creation* I proposed the term 'matrix' as a unifying formula to refer to these cognitive structures – that is, to all mental habits, routines and skills governed by an invariant code (which may be explicit or implicit), but capable of varied strategies in attacking a problem or task. In other words, 'matrices' are mental holons and display all the characteristics of holons discussed in previous chapters. They are controlled by canonical rules, but guided by feedbacks from the outer and inner environment; they range from pedantic rigidity to flexible adaptability – within the limits permitted by the code; they are ordered into 'vertical', abstractive hierarchies which interlace in 'horizontal' associative networks and cross-references (cf. 'arborization and reticulation', Chapter I).

When life confronts us with a problem or task, it will be dealt with according to the same set of rules which enabled us to deal with similar situations in our past experience. It would be foolish to belittle the value of such law-abiding routines. They lend coherence and stability to behaviour, and structured order to reasoning. But when the difficulty or novelty of the task exceeds a critical limit, these routines are no longer adequate to cope with it. The world is on the move, and new situations arise, posing questions and offering challenges which cannot be met within the conventional frames of reference, the established rule-books. In science, such situations arise under the impact of new data which shake the foundations of well-established theories. The challenge is often self-imposed by the insatiable exploratory drive, which prompts the original mind to ask questions which nobody has asked before and to feel frustrated by dusty answers. In the artist's case, the challenge is a more or less permanent one, arising out of the limitations of his medium of expression, his urge to escape from the constraints and distortions imposed by the conventional styles and techniques of his time, his ever-hopeful struggle to express the inexpressible.

When the mind is at the end of its tether it can – on rare occasions – show itself capable of surprisingly original, quasi-acrobatic feats, which lead to revolutionary breakthroughs in science or art and open new vistas, a radically changed outlook. But every revolution has a destructive as well as a constructive aspect. When we speak of a 'revolutionary' discovery in science or of revolutionary changes in artistic style, we imply the destructive aspect.* The destruction is wrought by jettisoning previously sacrosanct doctrines and seemingly self-evident axioms of thought, cemented into our mental habits. This is what enables us to distinguish between creative originality and diligent routine. A problem solved or a task accomplished in accordance with established rules of the game leaves the matrix of the skill intact – unharmed and possibly even enriched by the experience. Creative originality, on the other hand, always involves unlearning and re-learning, undoing and re-doing. It involves the breaking up of petrified mental structures, discarding matrices which have outlived their usefulness, and reassembling others in a new synthesis – in other words, it is a complex operation of dissociation and bisociation, involving several levels of the mental holarchy.

All the biographical evidence[4] indicates that such a radical re-shuffling operation requires the intervention of mental processes beneath the surface of conscious reasoning, in the twilight zones of awareness. In the decisive phase of the creative process the rational controls are relaxed and the creative person's mind seems to *regress* from disciplined thinking to less specialized, more fluid ways of mentation. A frequent form of this is the retreat from articulate verbal thinking to vague, visual imagery. There is a naive popular belief that scientists arrive at their discoveries by reasoning in strictly rational, precise, verbal terms. The evidence mentioned indicates that they do nothing of the sort. In 1945, Jacques Hadamard's famous inquiry[5] among American mathematicians to find out their working methods produced the striking conclusion that nearly all of them (with only two exceptions) tackled their problems neither in verbal terms nor by algebraic symbols, but relied on visual imagery of a vague, hazy nature. Einstein was among them; he wrote: 'The

*cf. Sir Karl Popper: 'In order that a new theory should constitute a discovery or a step forward it should conflict with its predecessor; that is to say, it should lead to at least some conflicting results. But this means, from a logical point of view, that it should contradict its predecessor: it should overthrow it. In this sense, progress in science – or at least striking progress – is always revolutionary.'[6]

words of the language as they are written or spoken do not seem
to play any role in my mechanism of thought . . . which relies
on more or less clear images of a visual and some of a muscular
type . . . It also seems to me that what you call full consciousness
is a limit-case which can never be fully accomplished because
consciousness is a narrow thing.'[7]

Most of the creative scientists, who have described their
working methods, seem to have been visualizers who shared
Woodworth's opinion: 'Often we have to get away from speech
to think clearly.' Verbal reasoning occupies the latest and highest
level in the mental hierarchy, but it can degenerate into
pedantic rigidity which erects a screen between the thinker and
reality. Creativity often starts where language ends, that is, by
regressing to pre-verbal and seemingly pre-rational levels of
mental activity, which may in some respects be comparable to
the dream, but closer perhaps to the transitory states between
sleep and full wakefulness.

Such regression implies a temporary suspension of the 'rules
of the game' which control our reasoning routines; the mind in
labour is momentarily liberated from the tyranny of rigid, over-
precise schemata, their built-in prejudices and hidden axioms;
it is led to un-learn and acquire a new innocence of the eye and
fluidity of thought, which enable it to discover hidden analogies
and reckless combinations of ideas which would be unacceptable
in the sober, wide-awake state. The biographies of great scientists
provide countless examples of this phenomenon; their virtually
unanimous emphasis on spontaneous intuitions and hunches of
unknown origin suggests that there always are large chunks of
irrationality embedded in the creative process – not only in art,
where we take it for granted, but in the exact sciences as well.

In earlier books[8] I have ventured some guesses as to how this
unconscious guidance works – how a temporary regression to
less sophisticated mental levels can produce the happy combination of ideas, the focal bisociation, which produces the solution
of the problem. It is a common experience on awaking from sleep
to try to hang on to the remembrance of a dream which is running
away, like sand through a sieve, out of conscious reach. One may

call this phenomenon 'oneirolysis' – from oneiros, dream, plus lysis, dissolution. The dream itself, while it lasts (and to some extent also the drowsy daydream) drifts effortlessly from one scenario to another, in a freewheeling manner, indifferent to the rules of logic and the conventional limitations of space, time or cause; it establishes bizarre connections and churns out analogies between cabbages and kings which disintegrate when the sleeper awakes and which he cannot describe in precise verbal terms – except by saying that something reminded him of something, but he no longer knows what or why. Now in the throes of the creative obsession, when all levels of the mental hierarchy, including the unconscious strata, are saturated with the problem, the familiar phenomenon of oneirolysis may be reversed into a kind of oneirosynthesis, in which those vaguely sensed connections form a nascent analogy. It may be a hazy, tentative affair, like Einstein's 'images of a visual or muscular type', or Faraday's 'lines of force' surrounding magnets which he saw in vivid hallucinations; and its shape may be changing from camel to weasel like Hamlet's cloud. The unconscious reaches of fertile minds must be teeming with such nascent analogies, hidden affinities, and the cloudy 'forms of things unknown'. But we must also remember that clouds form and dissolve again; and cloudbursts are rare events.

7

The French have an expression for which I can find no English equivalent: reculer pour mieux sauter – draw back to take a running jump. The process I have been discussing follows a similar pattern: a temporary regression to more primitive and uninhibited levels of ideation, followed by the creative forward leap. Disintegration and reintegration, dissociation and bisociation reflect the same pattern. Cogitation in the creative sense is co-agitation, the shaking together of the previously separate; but the fully conscious, rational mind is not the best cocktail shaker. It is invaluable in our daily routines, but the revolutionary breakthroughs in science and art always represent some variation of reculer pour mieux sauter.

We might call it an archetypal pattern, for it has its close equivalents in other fields. Thus psychotherapy, from shamanism to our day, has always relied on that particular kind of undoing–redoing process which Ernst Kris called 'regression in the service of the ego'. The neurotic, with his compulsions, phobias and elaborate defence mechanisms, is governed by eccentric but rigid 'rules of the game'. The therapist's aim is to induce a temporary regression, to make him retrace his steps to the point where things went wrong, and to come up metamorphosed, reborn.

The same pattern is reflected in the death and resurrection (or 'withdrawal and return') motif in mythology. Joseph is thrown into a well, Jonah is reborn out of the belly of the whale, Jesus is resurrected from the tomb.

Lastly, as we shall see later, *reculer pour mieux sauter*, draw-back-to-leap, plays a crucial part not only in mental creativity, but also in the creative evolution of higher life-forms. We shall see that biological evolution may be described as a series of escapes from the blind alleys of stagnation, over-specialization and maladjustment, by an undoing and re-forming process which is basically analogous to the phenomena of mental evolution and in some respects foreshadows them. But before moving on towards those wider vistas, there are still some loose ends to be tied up relating to creativity in science and art.

8

In the previous sections I have been at pains to stress that the artist and scientist do not inhabit separate universes, merely different regions of a continuous spectrum – a rainbow stretching from the infra-red of poetry to the ultra-violet of physics, with many intermediate ranges – such hybrid vocations as architecture, photography, chess-playing, cooking, psychiatry, science fiction or the potter's craft. But to avoid over-simplification, after emphasizing the affinities, I must briefly discuss the differences – some apparent, some real – between the opposite ends of the continuum.

The most obvious difference seems to lie in the nature of the criteria by which we judge scientific and artistic achievement. One of the imaginary barriers between the two is the popular belief that the scientist, unlike the artist, is in a position to attain to 'objective truth' by submitting theories to experimental tests. In fact, experimental evidence can confirm certain expectations based on a theory, but it cannot confirm the theory itself. The same set of experimental data can often be interpreted in more than one way – which is why the history of science echoes with as many venomous controversies as the history of literary criticism. Thus we again have a series of continuous gradations from the relatively objective methods of testing a scientific theory by experiment to the relatively subjective criteria of aesthetic value; but the emphasis is on 'relative'. In fact the progress of science is strewn, like an ancient desert trail, with the bleached skeletons of discarded theories which once seemed to possess eternal life. The history of art shows equally agonizing reappraisals of accepted values, criteria of relevance, styles of representation. In the course of the last two centuries, European literature went through the rise and fall of classicism; romanticism; naturalism; surrealism; and Dada; the socially conscious novel; existentialism; the *nouveau roman*. In the history of painting, the changes were even more drastic. But the same zig-zag course characterizes the progression of science, whether you turn to the history of physiology and medicine (not to mention psychology); or evolutionary biology; or the abrupt changes of outlook in the 'hard-core' science of physics from the Aristotelian to the Newtonian to the Einsteinian conception of the universe. The data may be 'hard', like the contours of a Rorschach blot, but what you read into them is another matter. There is of course a considerable difference in the degree of precision and objectivity, between the methods of judging a theorem in physics and a work of art. But, to say it once more, the difference is a matter of degrees, and there are continuous transitions between them.

We must also remember that the testing and judging of a discovery comes *after* the act; whereas the decisive moment in the creative act itself is for the scientist, as it is for the artist, a leap into the dark, into the twilight zones of consciousness, where both are equally dependent on their fallible intuitions. False inspirations and crank theories are as abundant in the history of science as bad works of art; yet they command in the victim's mind the same forceful conviction, the same euphoria, as the happy finds which are *post factum* proven right.* In this respect the scientist is in no better position than the artist: while in the throes of the creative process, guidance by truth is as uncertain and subjective as guidance by beauty. And some of the greatest scientists have confessed that at the crucial moment when taking the plunge, they were not guided by logic, but by a sense of beauty that they were unable to define.

A virgin by Botticelli, and a mathematical theorem by Poincaré, do not betray any similarity between the motivations and aspirations of their respective creators. Yet it was Poincaré himself who wrote that what guided him in his unconscious gropings towards the 'happy combinations which yield new discoveries' was 'the feeling of mathematical beauty, of the harmony of number, of forms, of geometric elegance. This is a true aesthetic feeling that all mathematicians know.' The greatest living English physicist, Paul Dirac, went éven further with his famous pronouncement: 'It is more important to have beauty in one's equations than to have them fit experiment.' It was a shocking thing to say, but he got the Nobel Prize nevertheless.

And vice versa, painters, sculptors and architects have always been guided, and often obsessed, by scientific or pseudo-scientific theories: the Golden Section of the Greeks; the geometry of perspective and foreshortening; Dürer's and Leonardo's 'ultimate laws of perfect proportion'; Cézanne's doctrine that all natural form can be reduced to spheres, cylinders and cones, and so forth. The counterpart of the mathematician's apology which puts beauty before logical method is Seurat's pronouncement:

---

*To quote Nobel laureate Albert Szent-Györgyi, discoverer of Vitamin C: 'There is but one safe way to avoid mistakes: to do nothing or, at least, to avoid doing something new . . . The unknown lends an insecure foothold and venturing out into it, one can hope for no more than that the possible failure will be an honourable one.'⁹

'They see poetry in what I have done. No, I apply my method, and that is all there is to it.'

Thus both sides recognize the continuity of the triptych: the scientist by confessing his dependence on intuitive hunches which guide his theorizing, while the artist values, or overvalues, the abstract theories which impose discipline on his intuitions. The two factors complement each other; the relative proportions in which they combine depend foremost on the medium in which their creative drive finds its expression.

Similar considerations apply to the rules of harmony and counterpoint, the theoretical aspects of music; and, of course, to literature. The novelist, the poet or playwright do not create in a vacuum; their world-view is influenced – whether they realize it or not – by the philosophical and scientific climate of their time. John Donne was a mystic, but he instantly realized the significance of Galileo's telescope:

> Man has weav'd out a net, and this net throwne
> Upon the Heavens, and now they are his owne.

Newton had a comparable impact; so of course had Darwin, Marx, Frazer of *The Golden Bough*, Freud or Einstein.

Keats' *Ode on a Grecian Urn* ends with the famous lines:

> Beauty is truth, truth beauty – that is all
> Ye know on earth, and all ye need to know.

This is certainly a poetic exaggeration, but also a touching profession of faith in the essential unity of the two cultures, artificially separated by the quirks in our educational and social system. In the unprejudiced mind, any original scientific discovery gives rise to aesthetic satisfaction, because the solution of a vexing problem creates harmony out of dissonance; and vice versa, the experience of beauty can only arise if the intellect endorses the validity of the operation – whatever its nature – designed to elicit the experience. Intellectual illumination and emotional catharsis are the twin rewards of the act of creation, and its re-creative echo in the beholder. The first constitutes the moment of truth, the Aha reaction, the second provides the Ah . . . reaction of the aesthetic experience. The two are complementary aspects of an indivisible process.

9

One more apparently fundamental difference between the history of science and the history of art remains to be discussed.

In Solzhenitsyn's novel *The First Circle* some prisoners are having an argument about the progress of science. One of them, Gleb Nerzhin, exclaims in a passionate outburst:

'Progress! Who wants progress? That's just what I like about art – the fact that there can't be any "progress" in it.'

He then discusses the tremendous advances in technology during the previous century and concludes with the taunt: 'But has there been any advance on *Anna Karenina*?'

The opposite attitude was taken by Sartre in his essay 'What is Literature?', where he compared novels to bananas which you can enjoy only while they are fresh. *Anna Karenina*, in this view, must have rotted long ago.

Solzhenitsyn's hero reflects the traditional view that science progresses in a cumulative manner, brick upon brick, the way a tower is built, whereas art is timeless, a playing of fresh variations on eternal themes. To a limited extent and in a relative sense, this conventional view is of course justified. In the great discoveries of science, the bisociation of previously separate contexts (electricity and magnetism, matter and energy, etc.) results in a new synthesis, which in its turn will merge with others on a higher, emergent level of the hierarchy. The evolution of art does not, generally, show this overall pattern. The frames of perception which enter into the artist's creative process are chosen for their sensuous qualities and emotive potential; his bisociative act consists in their *juxtaposition* rather than an intellectual *fusion* to which, by their very nature, they do not readily lend themselves.

But once again, this difference is relative, not absolute. If you accept Gleb Nerzhin's view *in toto*, then it is pointless to search for objective criteria of 'progress' in literature, painting or music; art, then, does not evolve, it merely formulates and reformulates the same archetypal experiences in the costumes and styles of the period; and although the vocabulary is subject to changes – including the visual vocabulary of the painter – the statement contained in a great work of art remains valid and unmarked by time's arrow, untouched by the vulgar march of progress.

But at a closer look this view turns out to be historically untenable. For one thing, there are periods in which a given art-form shows a definite, cumulative evolution, comparable to scientific progress. To quote our leading art historian, Sir Ernst Gombrich:

In antiquity the discussion of painting and sculpture inevitably centred on [the] imitation [of nature] – mimesis. Indeed it may be said that the progress of art towards that goal was to the ancient what the progress of technology is to the modern: the model of progress as such. Thus Pliny told the history of sculpture and painting as the history of inventions, assigning definite achievements in the rendering of nature to individual artists: the painter Polygnotus was the first to represent people with open mouth and with teeth, the sculptor Pythagoras was the first to render nerves and veins, the painter Nikias was concerned with light and shade. The history of these years [*ca.* 550 to 350 B.C.] as it is reflected in Pliny or Quintilian was handed down like an epic of conquest, a story of inventions. . . In the Renaissance it was Vasari who applied this technique to the history of the arts of Italy from the thirteenth to the sixteenth century. Vasari never fails to pay tribute to those artists of the past who made a distinct contribution, as he saw it, to the mastery of representation. 'Art rose from humble beginnings to the summit of perfection' [Vasari says] because such natural geniuses as Giotto blazed the trail and others were thus enabled to build on their achievements.[10]

'If I could see further than others,' said Newton, 'it is because I stood on the shoulders of giants.' Leonardo said much the same. 'It is a wretched pupil', he wrote, 'who does not surpass his master.' Dürer and others expressed similar opinions. What they evidently meant was that during the period of explosive development which started with Giotto around the year 1300, each successive generation of painters had discovered new tricks and techniques – foreshortening, perspective, the treatment of light, colour and texture, the capture of movement and facial expression – inventions which the pupil could take over from the master and use as his baseline for new departures.

As for literature, it need hardly be emphasized that the various schools and fashions of the past were not static, but evolved during their limited life-span toward greater refinement and technical perfection – or decadence. We take it for granted that today's physicists know more about the atom than Democritus; but then Joyce's *Ulysses* also knows more about human nature than Homer's *Odysseus*. On a shorter time-scale, even films no more than twenty years old appear now – exceptions always granted – surprisingly dated: obvious, over-acted, over-explicit. There is hardly a writer, past or present, who did not or does not sincerely believe his style and technique of writing to be closer to reality, intellectually and emotionally, than those of the past. Let us face it: our reverence for Homer or Goethe is sweetened by a dash of condescension not unlike our attitude to infant prodigies: how clever they were for their age!

Thus we can safely reject as a gross over-simplification Gleb Nerzhin's view that science is cumulative like a brick-layer's work, while art is timeless, a dance of coloured balls on the jets of a fountain. The history of art, too, shows cumulative progress – in certain periods, though not in others. In the history of European painting, for instance, there are two outstanding periods in which we find rapid, sustained, cumulative progress in representing Nature, almost as tangible as the progress in engineering. The first stretches roughly from the middle of the sixth to the middle of the fourth century B.C., the second from the beginning of the fourteenth to the middle of the sixteenth century. Each lasted for about six to eight generations, in the course of which each giant did indeed stand on the shoulders of his predecessors, and could take in a wider view. It would of course be silly to say that these were the *only* periods of cumulative progress. But it is neverthe-less true that in between these periods of rapid evolution there are much longer stretches of stagnation or decline. Besides, there are the lone giants, who seem to appear from nowhere and cannot be fitted into any neat pyramid of acrobats balancing on each other's shoulders.

The conclusion seems to be obvious. Our museums and libraries demonstrate that there *is* a cumulative progression in every art-form – in a limited sense, in a limited direction, during limited periods. But these short, luminous trails sooner or later peter out in twilight and confusion, and the search for a new departure in a new direction is on.

However, contrary to popular belief, the evolution of science does not show a more coherent picture. Only during the last three hundred years has its advance been continuous and cumula-tive; but those unfamiliar with the history of science – and they include the majority of scientists – tend to fall into the mistaken belief that the acquisition of knowledge has always been a neat and tidy ascent on a straight path towards the ultimate peak.

In fact, neither science nor art has evolved in a continuous way. Whitehead once remarked that Europe in the year 1500 knew less than Archimedes who died in 212 B.C. In retrospect there was only one step separating Archimedes from Galileo, Aristarchus of Samos (who fathered the heliocentric system) from Copernicus. But that step took nearly two thousand years to be made. During that long period, science was hibernating. After the three short glorious centuries of Greek science, roughly coinciding with the cumulative period of Greek art, comes a period of suspended animation about six times as long; then a new furious awakening, so far only about ten generations old.

Progress, then, in science as in art, is neither steady nor absolute, but – to say it again – a progression in a limited sense during limited periods in limited directions; not along a steady curve, but in a jagged, jerky, zigzag line.

A Chinese proverb says that there is a time for fishing and a time for drying the nets. If you take a kind of bird's-eye view of the history of any branch of science, you will find a rhythmic alternation between long periods of relatively peaceful evolution and shorter bursts of revolutionary change. Only in the peaceful periods which follow after a major breakthrough is the progress of science continuous and cumulative in the strict sense. It is a period of consolidating the newly conquered frontiers, of verifying, assimilating, elaborating and extending the new synthesis: a time for drying the nets. It may last a few years or several generations; but sooner or later the emergence of new empirical data, or a change in the philosophical climate, leads to stagnation, a hardening of the matrix into a closed system, the rise of a new orthodoxy. This produces a crisis, a period of fertile anarchy in which rival theories proliferate – until the new synthesis is achieved and the cycle starts again; but this time aiming in a different direction, along different parameters, asking a different kind of question.

It is thus possible to detect a recurrent pattern in the evolution of both science and art. As a rule the cycle starts with a passionate rebellion against and rejection of the previously dominant school or style with a subsequent breakthrough towards new frontiers: call this *phase one*. The *second phase* in the cycle has a climate of optimism and euphoria; on the footsteps of the giants who spearheaded the advance, their more pedestrian followers and imitators move into the newly opened territories to explore and exploit its rich potentials. This, as said before, is the phase *par excellence* of cumulative progress in elaborating and perfecting new insights and techniques in research, and new styles in art. The *third phase* brings saturation, followed by frustration and deadlock. The *fourth* and last phase is a time of crisis and doubt – epitomized in John Donne's complaint on the fall of Aristotelian cosmology: ' 'Tis all in pieces, all coherence gone.' But it is also a time of wild experimentation (Fauvism and Dada and its equivalents in science) and of creative anarchy – *reculer pour mieux sauter* – which prepares and incubates the next revolution, initiating a new departure – and so the cycle starts again.

This recurrent pattern is in some respects analogous to the successive stages in the process of individual discovery, according to the schema proposed by Helmholtz and Graham Wallas:

conscious preparation – unconscious incubation – illumination – verification and consolidation. But while the individual's process of discovery is concluded at the last of these stages, on the historical scale the last stage of one cycle shades into the first stage of the next.

A more recent theory which has strong affinities with the conception of historic cycles first developed in *The Act of Creation* and summarized above is Thomas Kuhn's much-quoted essay *The Structure of Scientific Revolutions*. Kuhn calls the cumulative phases of the cycle 'normal science' and refers to the revolutionary breakthroughs as 'paradigm changes'. In spite of the different terminology, there are some striking similarities between Kuhn's schema and the one proposed in *The Act of Creation*, though they were developed independently from each other. Both represent radical departures from George Sarton's venerable theory which asserts that the history of science is the only history which displays cumulative progress, and that, accordingly, the progress of science is the only yardstick by which we can measure the progress of mankind.

In fact, however, as we have seen, the progress of science on the charts of history does not appear as a continuously ascending curve, but as a zigzag line, not unlike the history of art. This does not mean, of course, that there is no advance; only that both are advancing on an unpredictable, often erratic course.

In the course of the last hundred years, history has accelerated like a rocket taking off, and has produced new discoveries at a breath-taking rate – but also more crises, about-turns and undoing-redoings than ever before. This is in evidence in all branches of science and art – in painting and literature, physics and brain-research, genetics and cosmology. In every field the demolition squads were as feverishly active as the construction workers, but we see only what the latter built and tend to forget the once proud citadels of orthodoxy that were destroyed. No doubt in the next few decades we shall witness even more spectacular feats of undoing–redoing. Some speculative hunches on this subject will be found in later chapters.

PART THREE

Creative Evolution

IX

CRUMBLING CITADELS

I

One of the crumbling citadels of orthodoxy mentioned at the end of the previous chapter is the neo-Darwinian theory of evolution (which also goes by the name of 'synthetic theory'). The situation was summed up by Professor W. H. Thorpe when he wrote of 'an undercurrent of thought in the minds of perhaps hundreds of biologists over the last twenty-five years' who reject the neo-Darwinian dogma.* The contradictions and tautologies of the synthetic theory have actually been known even longer, as a kind of open secret, and yet the dogma has been and still is strenuously defended by the academic community, with the penalty of discreet but effective ostracism for heretics. The reason for this paradox seems to be twofold: firstly, commitment to a scientific theory can be as charged with emotion as a religious credo – a subject much in evidence throughout the history of science; secondly, the absence of a coherent alternative to neo-Darwinism makes many biologists feel that a bad theory is better than no theory at all. Whether this is to be regarded as good scientific strategy is a matter of opinion.

The essence of the theory is perhaps easiest to convey by drawing a parallel between neo-Darwinism in biology and behaviourism in psychology. Both derived their inspiration from the same *Zeitgeist* of reductionist philosophy which prevailed during the first half of our century. Behaviourism was founded by John Broadus Watson just before the First World War, and made its sensational impact mainly by proclaiming that 'consciousness' and 'mind' are empty words with no basis in reality. Half a century

*It was this remark of Thorpe's which sparked off the 'Beyond Reductionism' symposium (cf. Ch. I).

later, Professor Skinner of Harvard University – probably
the most influential academic psychologist of our time – continued
to proclaim the same views in even more extreme form. In
Skinner's standard textbook *Science and Human Behaviour*, the
hopeful student of psychology is told from the very outset that
'mind', 'ideas', etc., are non-existent entities, 'invented to provide
spurious explanations. . . . Since mental or psychic events are
asserted to lack the dimensions of physical science, we have an
additional reason for rejecting them.'[1] (By the same logic, we
may reject the reality of radio waves, because they consist of
vibrations in a vacuum devoid of any physical properties.)

I have often found it difficult to convince non-academic friends
that this patently absurd doctrine still dominates academic
psychology. As a recent critic wrote:

It is an interesting exercise to sit down and try to be conscious of what
it means to say that consciousness does not exist. History has not
recorded whether or not this feat was attempted by the early behaviourists. But it has recorded elsewhere and in large the enormous
influence which the doctrine that consciousness does not exist has had
on psychology in this century.[2]

We are now approaching a vital issue towards which behaviourism and neo-Darwinism show strikingly similar attitudes.
It concerns their views of the driving forces behind biological
evolution on the one hand, and cultural evolution on the other.
Take cultural evolution first. How can scientific discovery and
artistic originality be explained in the mindless universe of the
behaviourist? Here is Watson's answer – and let me point out
that the quote which follows is the *only* passage in his book in
which creativity is mentioned (Watson's italics):

One natural question often raised is, how do we ever get new verbal
creations such as a poem or a brilliant essay? *The answer is that we get
them by manipulating words, shifting them about until a new pattern is hit
upon.* . . How do you suppose Patou builds a new gown? Has he any
'picture in his mind' of what the gown is to look like when it is finished?
He has not. . . He calls his model in, picks up a new piece of silk, throws

it around her, he pulls it in here, he pulls it out there... He manipulates the material until it takes on the semblance of a dress... Not until the new creation aroused admiration and commendation, both his own and others, would manipulation be complete – the equivalent of the rat's finding food... The painter plies his trade in the same way, nor can the poet boast of any other method.[3]

The two points to retain here are (a) that the solution is 'hit upon' *by chance* after many random attempts, and (b) that it is retained because it has been *rewarded* by approval.

Thirty years after Watson's book was published, Skinner drew the same conclusions about the way scientific discoveries are made – though by that time behaviourism had developed its own esoteric jargon:

The result of solving a problem is the appearance of a solution in the form of a response... The appearance of the response in his [the human individual's] behaviour is no more surprising than the appearance of any response in the behaviour of any organism.[4]

The 'organisms' to which he refers here are the experimental rats in the so-called Skinner box which behaviourists regard as the most effective means for the study of psychology.* The box is equipped with a food tray and a bar which can be pushed down like the lever of a slot machine, whereupon a food pellet drops into a tray. When a rat is placed into the box it will sooner or later 'hit upon' the lever with its paw by pure chance, and be automatically rewarded by a pellet; and it will sooner or later learn that to obtain a pellet it must press the bar. This experimental procedure is called 'operant conditioning'; pressing the bar is called 'emitting an operant response'; the food pellet is called a 'reinforcer'; withholding the pellet is a 'negative reinforcer'; the number of times the rat presses the bar in a given period of time is the 'rate of response', which is automatically recorded and plotted on charts. The purpose of these experiments is to enable

*Nothing in the ambitious titles of Skinner's *The Behaviour of Organisms* and *Science and Human Behaviour* indicates that the data in them are almost exclusively derived from conditioning experiments on rats and pigeons.

the behaviourist to realize his stated purpose: 'to measure, predict and control behaviour' – including human behaviour.

The details of behaviourist rat-lore do not concern us here;* the relevant point is again that the animal's discovery of the secret of the lever was due to pure *chance*, and that lever-pressing was added to its repertory of skills because it was 'reinforced' by *rewards*.

If we now turn to the Darwinian's answer to the question how man evolved out of a primordial blob of slime, we find that it is much the same as Watson's answer to the question how Patou transforms a piece of material into an elegant dress: 'He pulls it in here, he pulls it out there . . . he manipulates the material until it takes on the semblance of a dress.' Darwinian evolution is supposed to operate on the same principle, that is, by manipulating *at random* the organic raw material – putting a tail here, putting a pair of wings there – until a suitable pattern is hit upon, and *retained* owing to its fitness to survive.

In other words, behaviourism and neo-Darwinism, which both occupy key positions in the contemporary sciences of life, base their explanations of biological and cultural evolution on essentially the same model operating in two stages: the first step ruled by blind chance, the second by selective rewards. Thus biological evolution is the outcome of *nothing but* (a) random mutations (the monkey at the typewriter) (b) preserved by natural selection (which rewards fitness); and cultural progress is the result of *nothing but* (a) random tries preserved by (b) reinforcements (the stick and the carrot).

Biological Evolution	Cultural Evolution
(a) Chance mutations	Random tries
(b) Natural selection	Reinforcements

It is strange that no attention has been paid to this parallel. Perhaps the reason is that psychologists are not interested in evolution, and evolutionists are not interested in psychology.

*See *The Ghost in the Machine*, Ch. I–III and Appendix II.

Leaving (a) – the role of chance – to be discussed later, it has been shown a long time ago that both (b) concepts – 'reinforcement' and 'natural selection' – are devoid of any explanatory value. Take 'reinforcement' first, and listen once more to Professor Skinner:

The verbal stimulus 'come to dinner' is an occasion upon which going to a table and sitting down is usually reinforced by food. The stimulus comes to be effective in increasing the probability of that behaviour and is produced by the speaker because it does so.[5]

In case the reader should be in doubt, this is not a parody but a quote from Skinner's book *Verbal Behaviour*, published in 1957. He also informs his readers that 'a man talks to himself . . . because of the reinforcement he receives';[6] that thinking is in fact 'behaving which automatically affects the behaviour and is reinforcing because it does so';[7] that 'just as the musician plays and composes what he is reinforced by hearing, or as the artist paints what reinforces him visually, so the speaker engaged in verbal fantasy says what he is reinforced by hearing or writes what he is reinforced by reading',[8] and that the creative artist is 'controlled entirely by the contingencies of reinforcement'.[9]

In training the rat to press a lever in the box or to find its way through a maze, the term 'reinforcement' had a concrete meaning: by giving or witholding rewards the rat's behaviour could be effectively conditioned by the experimenter. But the behaviourists' heroic attempt to extrapolate from the Skinner box to the painter's studio, with 'reinforcement' as a *deus ex machina*, leads him, as we have seen, into hair-raising absurdities. Yet his philosophy compels him to try his best to show that human behaviour is *nothing but* a more sophisticated form of rat-behaviour. A last quotation from Skinner will drive the point home. The writer's 'verbal behaviour', he tells us, 'may reach over centuries or to thousands of listeners or readers at the same time. The writer may not be reinforced often or immediately, but his net reinforcement may be great.'[10]

What this means is, if anything, that every writer would like to write an immortal masterpiece. He persists in his efforts because of the reinforcement he receives, and reinforcement means whatever it is that makes him persist in his efforts.[11] As Chomsky[12] and others have pointed out, the concept of reinforcement is based on a tautology, and its explanatory value has been reduced to nil.

2

A similar fate is overtaking the Darwinian household concept of natural selection or the survival of the fittest – which, as we have seen, is the evolutionist's equivalent of the behaviourist's 'reinforcement'.

Once upon a time, it all looked so simple. Nature rewarded the fit with the carrot of survival and punished the unfit with the stick of extinction. The trouble only started when it came to defining 'fitness'. Are pygmies fitter than giants, brunettes fitter than blondes, left-handers fitter than right-handers? What exactly are the criteria of 'fitness'? The first answer that comes to mind is: the fittest are obviously those who survive longest. But when we talk about the evolution of *species*, the lifespan of individuals is irrelevant (it may be a day for some insects, a century for tortoises); what matters is *how many offspring* they produce in their life-time. Thus natural selection looks after the survival and reproduction of the fittest, and the fittest are those which have the highest rate of reproduction – we are caught in a circular argument which completely begs the question of what makes evolution evolve. This lethal flaw in the theory was recognized by leading evolutionists (Mayr, Simpson, Waddington, Haldane, etc.) several decades ago;[13] it was and is, as I said, an open secret. However, since no satisfactory alternative was in sight, the crumbling edifice had to be defended. Thus Sir Julian Huxley in 1953:

So far as we know, not only is Natural Selection inevitable, not only is it *an* effective agency of evolution, but it is *the* only effective agency of evolution. [Huxley's italics.][14]

Compare this *ex cathedra* pronouncement to the devastating comment by the late Professor Waddington (who was himself an eminent member of the neo-Darwinian establishment, but given to critical doubt):

Survival does not, of course, mean the bodily endurance of a single individual, outliving Methuselah. It implies, in its present-day inter-pretation, perpetuation as a source for future generations. That indivi-dual 'survives' best which leaves most offspring. Again, to speak of an animal as 'fittest' does not necessarily imply that it is strongest or most healthy or would win a beauty competition. Essentially it denotes nothing more than leaving most offspring. The general principle of natural selection, in fact, merely amounts to the statement that the individuals which leave most offspring are those which leave most off-spring. It is a tautology.[15]

Von Bertalanffy put it even more pointedly. Commenting on the orthodox theory, he remarked, 'It is hard to see why evolution has ever progressed beyond the rabbit, the herring, or even the bacterium which are unsurpassed in their reproductive capacities.'[16]

To avoid misunderstandings: no critic would of course deny that biological *misfits*, incapable of coping with life's demands, would be eliminated in the course of evolution. But the elimina-tion of deformity does not explain the evolution of higher forms. The action of a weedkiller is beneficial, but it does not explain the emergence of new plant species. It is a common fallacy among evolutionists to confuse the process of *elimination* of the unfit with the process of *evolution* towards some undefinable ideal of 'fitness'. The defenders of the synthetic theory could easily put an end to this confusion by replacing the discredited term 'natural selection' by 'selective elimination'. However, they only went as far as replacing the slogan 'survival of the fittest' by the less offensive 'differential reproduction' – but that, as we have just seen, provided no escape from the labyrinth of tautologies.

Nor did it help to resort to yet another synonym for fitness, namely, 'adaptability'. To cut a long story short, here is von Bertalanffy again:

. . . In my opinion, there is no scintilla of scientific proof that evolution in the sense of progression from less to more complicated organisms had anything to do with better adaptation . . . or production of larger offspring. Adaptation is possible at any level. . . An amoeba, a worm, an insect or non-placental mammal are as well adapted as placentals; if they were not, they would have become extinct long ago.[17]

In other words, nobody questions the truism that a species can only survive if it is able to adapt to the environment, but there are *countless ways of adapting to one and the same environment*, and some of these ways are so incredibly tortuous and complicated that the term 'adaptation' becomes empty of meaning. Consider this example from Sir Alister Hardy's *The Living Stream*:

There are some kinds of orchids with flowers which mimic, in colour, shape and smell, the female form of certain insects and so offer sexual attraction to the males of these insect species; the excited spouses who come for the creative act, unwittingly, by carrying pollen, complete, instead, the sexual process for the flower![18]

Or, to quote von Bertalanffy yet again:

I for one . . . am still at a loss to understand why it is of selective advantage for the eels of Comacchio to travel perilously to the Sargasso sea, or why *Ascaris* has to migrate all around the host's body instead of comfortably settling in the intestine where it belongs; or what was the survival value of a multiple stomach for a cow when a horse, also vegetarian and of comparable size, does very well with a single stomach.[19]

And how does 'adaptation' explain the fantastic transformations of the caterpillar into a chrysalis – spinning itself into a cocoon, where it undergoes a complete transformation which involves the dissolution of the larval organs and tissues and their complete re-moulding into a winged adult? Books on natural history have innumerable examples of such far-fetched ways of 'making a living' as a species, but they are rarely mentioned in theoretical works on evolution, because they reveal too glaringly that the theory begs the vital questions. Thus 'adaptation', as a *deus ex machina* of 'natural selection', shares the fate of its precursors, 'survival of the fittest' and 'differential reproduction'.

3

According to the neo-Darwinian doctrine, the raw material on which the magic of natural selection operates is provided by random mutations, i.e., chemical changes in the genes, the carriers of heredity. These changes are triggered by radiations, noxious chemicals or excessive heat, and are 'random' in the sense of being completely unrelated to the animal's needs or welfare, or its natural environment: they are in the nature of accidents which interfere with the normal functioning of the delicately balanced organism. Accordingly, the vast majority of mutations have either damaging or trivial effects; but from time to time, so the theory goes, there is a lucky hit, which will be preserved by natural selection, because it happens to confer some small advantage on the bearer of the mutated gene; and given sufficient time, 'anything at all will turn up', as Sir Julian Huxley wrote. 'The hoary objection of the improbability of an eye or a hand or a brain being evolved by "blind chance" has lost its force' – because 'natural selection operating over stretches of geological time'[20] explains everything.

Compare this statement with the following by Waddington:

To suppose that the evolution of the wonderfully adapted biological mechanisms has depended only on a selection out of a haphazard set of variations, each produced by blind chance, is like suggesting that if we went on throwing bricks together into heaps, we should eventually be able to choose ourselves the most desirable house.[21]

Nevertheless, Jacques Monod (Nobel Prize, 1965) calls evolution a 'gigantic lottery'[22] or 'nature's roulette'[23] and concludes:

Chance alone is at the source of every innovation, of all creation in the biosphere. Pure chance, absolutely free but blind, at the very root of the stupendous edifice of evolution: this central concept of modern biology is no longer one among other conceivable hypotheses. It is today the *sole* conceivable hypothesis, the only one that squares with observed and tested fact. And nothing warrants the supposition – or the hope – that on this score our position is likely ever to be revised . . .[24]

The universe was not pregnant with life nor the biosphere with man. Our number came up in the Monte Carlo game.[25]

But the roulette analogy hides rather than indicates the fantastic improbability of any major evolutionary advance produced by chance mutations. For such an event to occur, it is not enough that a certain required number, say the 17, should come up on the roulette table – but that it should come up simultaneously on a dozen or so tables in the same establishment, followed by the 18, 19 and 20 simultaneously on all tables.

Let me illustrate this by a few examples. The first is very simple and trivial, involving only four roulette wheels. The giant panda has on its front limbs an added, sixth finger. This could be a typical case of a deformation caused by a deleterious chance mutation; it happens to be quite useful to the panda in manipulating bamboo shoots, but it would of course be a useless hindrance if it were not equipped with the requisite muscles, nerves and blood-supply. The chances that among all possible genetic mutations just those which produced the added bones, nerves, muscles and arteries occurred *simultaneously* and *independently* from each other are infinitesimally small. And yet in this case we have only four main factors – four roulette wheels at work. When it comes to such composite marvels as the vertebrate eye – that classic stumbling block of the Darwinian theory – with its retina, rods and cones, lens, iris, pupil and what have you, the odds against the harmonious evolution of its components by independent random mutations, i.e., by 'blind chance', becomes, *pace* Huxley, absurd. Darwin himself clearly realized this when, in 1860, he wrote to Asa Gray: 'I remember well the time when the thought of the eye made me cold all over.'[26] It still has that effect on the upholders of the doctrine, so they avoid discussing it, or resort to elaborate evasions.*

*For a summary of the problems posed by the evolution of the eye see, e.g. Grassé (1973), pp. 176–81 and Wolsky (1976), pp. 106 f.

Equally chilling is the idea that some ancestral reptiles became transformed into birds by the small, step-by-step changes caused by random mutations affecting different organs. In fact one gets goose-pimples at the mere thought of the number of Monod's roulette wheels which must be kept spinning to produce the simultaneous transformation of scales into feathers, solid bones into hollow tubes, the outgrowth of air sacs into various parts of the body, the development of the shoulder muscles and bones to athletic proportions, and so forth. And this re-casting of bodily structure is accompanied by basic changes in the internal systems, including excretion. Birds never spend a penny. Instead of diluting their nitrogenous waste in water, which is a heavy ballast, they excrete it from the kidneys in a semi-solid state through the cloaca. Then there is also the little matter of the transition, by 'blind chance', from the cold-blooded to the warm-blooded condition. There is no end to the specifications which have to be met to make our reptile airborne or to construct a camera eye out of living software.

To conclude this section, here is a less dramatic example of an evolutionary advance – the seemingly modest step which led to the transformation of the amphibian egg into the reptilian egg. I have described this process in *The Ghost in the Machine*, and am quoting it again, because its explanation by the Darwinian schema is not only vastly improbable, but logically impossible.

The vertebrates' conquest of dry land started with the evolution of reptiles from some primitive amphibian form. The amphibians reproduced in the water, and their young were aquatic. The decisive novelty of the reptiles was that, unlike amphibians, they laid their eggs on dry land; they no longer depended on the water and were free to roam over the continents. But the unborn reptile inside the egg still needed an aquatic environment: it had to have water or else it would dry up at an early stage. It also needed a lot of food: amphibians hatch as larvae who fend for themselves, whereas reptiles hatch fully developed. So the reptilian egg had to be provided with a large mass of yolk for food, and also with albumen – the white of egg – to provide the water. Neither the yolk by itself, nor the egg-white itself, would have had any selective value. Moreover, the egg-white needed a vessel

to contain it, otherwise its moisture would have evaporated. So there
had to be a shell made of a leathery or limey material, as part of the
evolutionary package-deal. But that is not the end of the story. The
reptilian embryo, because of this shell, could not get rid of its waste
products. The soft-shelled amphibian embryo had the whole pond as a
lavatory; the reptilian embryo had to be provided with a kind of
bladder. It is called the allantois, and is in some respects the forerunner
of the mammalian placenta. But this problem having been solved, the
embryo would still remain trapped inside its tough shell; it needed a
tool to get out. The embryos of some fishes and amphibians, whose
eggs are surrounded by a gelatinous membrane, have glands on their
snouts: when the time is ripe, they secrete a chemical which dissolves
the membrane. But embryos surrounded by a hard shell need a mechanical tool: thus snakes and lizards have a tooth transformed into a
kind of tin-opener, while birds have a caruncle – a hard outgrowth
near the tip of their beaks which serves the same purpose, and is later
shed by the adult animal.[27]

Now according to the Darwinian schema, all these changes
must have been gradual, each small step caused by a chance
mutation. But it is obvious that each step, however small,
required simultaneous, interdependent changes affecting *all* the
factors involved in the story. Thus the liquid store in the albumen
could not be kept in the egg without the hard shell. But the shell
would be useless, in fact murderous, without the allantois and
without the tin-opener. Each of these changes, if they had occurred alone, would have been harmful, and the organisms thus
affected would have been weeded out by natural selection (or
rather, as suggested above, by 'natural elimination'). You cannot
have an isolated mutation A, preserve it over an incalculable
number of generations until mutation B occurs in the same lineage
and so on to C and D. Each single mutation would be wiped off
the slate before it could be combined with all the others. They
are all interdependent within the organism – which is a functional
whole, and not a mosaic. The doctrine that the coming together of
all requisite changes was due to a series of coincidences is an
affront not only to common sense but to the basic principles of
scientific explanation. In a recently published major work,

Professor Pierre Grassé (who, for thirty years, held the chair for evolution at the Sorbonne without losing his Gallic wit) commented:

Where is the gambler, however obsessed with his passion, who would be crazy enough to bet on the roulette of random evolution? The creation, by grains of dust carried by the wind, of Dürer's *Melancholia* has a probability less infinitesimal than the construction of an eye through the mishaps which might befall the DNA molecule – mishaps which have *no connection whatsoever* with the future functions of the eye.

Daydreaming is permissible, but science should not succumb to it. [Grasse's italics][28]

4

When we talk about the evolution of species, we mostly have the emergence of new forms and physical structures in mind, as we see them displayed in museums of natural history. But evolution creates not only new shapes; it also creates new types of behaviour, new instinctual skills which are innate and hereditary. If the forces behind the emergence of new structures are obscure, those behind the evolution of innate skills are shrouded in total darkness. As Nobel laureate Niko Tinbergen lamented: 'The backward position of ethology is striking . . . A genetics of behaviour still has to be developed.'[29]

The reason for this is simple: neo-Darwinism does not possess the theoretical tools to tackle the problem. The only explanation it has to offer for the incredibly complex instinctual skills of animals is that these too are produced by random mutations somehow affecting the neural circuitry in the animal's brain and nervous system, which are then preserved by 'natural selection'. It would be a wholesome exercise for graduate students in biology to repeat this explanatory formula like a Sanskrit mantra while watching a spider constructing its web, a blue-tit shaping its nest, a badger constructing a dam, an oyster-catcher carrying its prey skyward and dropping it on a hard rock, the social activities in the welfare state of the honey-bee, and so on. One could fill a library with illustrations of the staggeringly complex patterns of instinctual activities of various species of animals which defy any explanation in terms of the Darwinian mantra. I shall quote one of the less well-known examples from Tinbergen:

A female of this species [the so-called digger wasp], when about to lay an egg, digs a hole, kills or paralyses a caterpillar, and carries it to the hole, where she stows it away after having deposited an egg on it (phase *a*). This done, she digs another hole, in which an egg is laid on a new caterpillar. In the meantime, the first egg has hatched and the larva has begun to consume its store of food. The mother wasp now turns her attention again to the first hole (phase *b*), to which she brings some more moth larvae; then she does the same in the second hole. She returns to the first hole for the third time to bring a final batch of six or seven caterpillars (phase *c*), after which she closes the hole and leaves it forever. In this way she works in turn at two or even three holes, each in a different phase of development. Baerends investigated the means by which the wasp brought the right amount of food to each hole. He found that the wasp visited all the holes each morning before leaving for the hunting grounds. By changing the contents of the hole and watching the subsequent behaviour of the wasp, he found that (1) by robbing a hole he could force the wasp to bring far more food than usual; and (2) by adding larvae to the hole's contents he could force her to bring less food than usual.[30]

But another wasp, *Eumenes amedei*, goes still one better. The somewhat gruesome description which follows is borrowed from *Darwin Retried* by Norman Macbeth:*

The egg is not laid upon or among the caterpillars, as in many allied species. These caterpillars are only partially paralysed, and can still move their claws and champ their jaws. Should one of them feel the nibblings of the tiny grub, it might writhe about and injure the grub. Both the egg and the grub must be protected, and to this end the egg is suspended by a tiny thread of silk fastened to the roof. The caterpillars may wriggle and writhe, but they cannot come near it.

*This brilliant treatise by a Harvard lawyer highlights the shortcomings and inconsistencies of the neo-Darwinian theory. Sir Karl Popper called it a 'most meritorious and really important contribution to the debate'.

When the grub emerges from the egg, it devours its eggshell, then spins for itself a tiny silken ribbon-sheath in which it is enfolded tail-uppermost and with head hanging down. In this retreat it is suspended above the pile of living food. It can lower itself far enough to nibble at the caterpillars. If they stir too violently it can withdraw into its silken sheath, wait until the commotion has subsided, then descend again to its meal. As the grub grows in size and strength, it becomes bolder; the silken retreat is no longer required; it can venture down and live at its ease among the remains of its food.[31]

At this point, I think, the mantra loses its hypnotic power even over pious neo-Darwinists. As Tinbergen said: 'A genetics of behaviour still has to be developed.' But the synthetic theory is unable to provide the tools for it.

5

How could a doctrine which in effect begged all the basic questions gain general acceptance among biologists and be considered as gospel truth by the public? (The same question might be asked about behaviourism.) Part of the answer is again found in von Bertalanffy:

I think the fact that a theory so vague, so insufficiently verifiable and so far from the criteria otherwise applied in 'hard 'science, has become a dogma, can only be explained on sociological grounds. Society and science have been so steeped in the ideas of mechanism, utilitarianism and the economic concept of free competition, that instead of God Selection was enthroned as ultimate reality.[32]

This is no doubt part of the answer, but other factors also enter into it. First, the theory contained a basic truth: the fossil record testified that evolution was a fact, that Darwin was right and Bishop Wilberforce was wrong, so Darwinism became something of a credo for all enlightened, progressive people, while the details of the theory could be left to the experts.

The experts, however, including Darwin himself, soon ran into trouble. There is a little-known episode in the early history of Darwinism which is pertinent to our theme.* In 1867, eight years after the publication of *The Origin of Species*, a professor of engineering at Edinburgh University, Fleeming Jenkin, published an article which amounted to a complete refutation of Darwin's theory.[33] Jenkin demonstrated, by an astonishingly simple logical deduction, that *no new species could ever arise from chance variations* by the mechanisms of heredity accepted at the time. For the theory of heredity, in Darwin's day, was based on the assumption that the native endowment of the newborn was an alloy or 'blend' of the characteristics of the parents, to which blend each parent contributed approximately one half. Darwin's own cousin, Francis Galton, gave a mathematical formulation to this 'law of ancestral inheritance', as it was called. Assuming now that an individual endowed with a useful chance variation (later to be called a random mutation) cropped up within the species, and mated with a normal partner (i.e., with one of the vast majority of the population), then their offspring would inherit only 50 per cent of the useful new characteristic, the grandchildren only 25 per cent, the great-grandchildren 12·5 per cent, and so on, until the hopeful novelty vanished like a drop in the ocean, long before natural selection had a chance to make it spread.

It is remarkable, as Sir Alister Hardy wrote,[34] that 'the great brains of the Victorian era' did not notice the basic logical fallacy which Jenkin pointed out. Darwin himself was so shaken that he inserted a whole new chapter in the sixth edition of *The Origin*, in which he resuscitated the Lamarckian theory of evolution through the inheritance of acquired characteristics which earlier he had described as 'a load of rubbish', and which is still anathema to Darwinists. As his letters to Wallace indicate, he saw no other way out.† But Darwin's followers ignored the master's relapse into the Lamarckian heresy (which, anyway, did not provide the

---

*The following is a condensed version of the account of this episode in *The Case of the Midwife Toad*, pp. 52 f.

†His son, Francis Darwin, later commented: 'It is not a little remarkable that the criticisms, which my father, as I believe, felt to be the most valuable ever made on his views, should have come, not from a professed naturalist but from a Professor of Engineering, Mr Fleeming Jenkin.'[35] Yet the sixth edition does not even mention his name.

required answers), and during the last decades of the nineteenth century Darwinism had run into a dead end – although the public was unaware of it. The leading English Darwinist at the time, William Bateson, wrote in retrospect: 'In the study of evolution progress had well-nigh stopped. The more vigorous, perhaps the more prudent, had left this field of science.'[36]

In the year 1900, however, by an unexpected and dramatic turn of events, the crisis was resolved – or so it seemed at the time; the clouds vanished, and Darwinism became transformed into neo-Darwinism.

This crucial event was the rediscovery of a paper called 'Experiments in Plant Hybridisation' by the Augustine monk Gregor Mendel, published in 1865, in the *Proceedings of the Natural History Society of Brünn* (now Brno) in Moravia. Thirty-five years later, long after Mendel's death, this paper was unearthed almost simultaneously and independently, by three biologists in three different countries (Tschermak in Vienna, de Vries in Leyden, Correns in Berlin). Each had been searching the literature for some clue to indicate the way out of the cul-de-sac, and each saw immediately the significance of Mendel's hybrid garden peas – which, like Newton's apple, were to become an integral part of science-lore. Mendel's experiments showed that the 'units of heredity' – later to be called genes – which determined the colour, size, and other features of his plants, did not 'blend' and thus become diluted; they were rather like hard, stable marbles which combined into a variety of mosaic patterns, but preserved their identity and were transmitted unchanged and intact to subsequent generations – even though the effect of 'recessive' genes was masked if they were paired with 'dominant' ones.

Here, at long last, was the answer to Jenkin's crucial objection. For it could now be assumed that whenever a chance mutation occurred it would not be whittled away through blendings, but would be preserved in successive generations and thus give 'natural selection' a chance to pick and choose.

Now everything was falling into place. Every single factor determining a hereditary trait was contained in a Mendelian gene, and every gene had its allotted place in the chromosomes in the cell-nucleus, like beads on a string. Evolution no longer had any secrets – or so it seemed. Bateson, instantly cured of his despair when he read Mendel's paper in a railway carriage, gave his youngest son the name Gregory, in honour of the Bohemian monk. 'Only those', he wrote twenty years later, 'who remember the utter darkness before the Mendelian dawn, can appreciate what happened.'[36]

The details of Mendelism do not concern us here, only its impact on the theory of evolution. It turned out to be decisive.

Bateson was the first to show that Mendel's laws of inheritance applied to plant and animal alike. He experimented on poultry; but the favourite experimental subject of the new science of genetics was the small fruit-fly *Drosophila melanogaster*, which propagates very fast and has only four pairs of chromosomes. This made it possible to apply statistical methods to the study of hereditary variations among large populations of the fly caused by spontaneous or artificially induced mutations (by irradiation, heat, etc.). In its own limited field, the science of genetics was immensely successful, and still is. But it took a long time for the more thoughtful among its practitioners to realize that their labours, while providing new insights into the mechanisms of minor hereditary *variations*, had little or no relevance to the basic problem of *evolution*: the origin and why and how of the major steps up the evolutionary ladder, the emergence of higher life-forms and new life-styles. In the words of Pierre Grassé who, let us remember, held the chair of evolution for thirty years at the Sorbonne (italics in the original):

Variation is one thing, evolution quite another: this cannot be emphasised strongly enough . . .[37]

Let us repeat it once more: mutations do not provide an explanation for the nature or temporal order of the phenomena of evolution; they do not create evolutionary novelties; they cannot account for the precise fitting together of the parts of an organ, and the mutual co-ordination of organs . . .[38]

Mutations provide change, but not progress . . .[39]

The repertory of mutations, or *mutation-spectrum* of a species has nothing to do with evolution. The '*Jordanons*' (equivalents of mutations) of the whitlow grass (*Erophila verna*); of the wild pansy (*Viola tricolor*); of the Plantains (Plantago); of the candytuft (Iberis), which add up to a rich and well-catalogued assortment, are the irrefutable proof of it. When all is said, *Erophila verna*, *Viola tricolor*, etc., despite their numerous mutations, do not evolve. *This is a fact*.

The various races of dogs, and of all the other domesticated animals, represent merely the mutation spectrum of the species, manipulated by artificial selection. The same applies to garden plants. Nothing in all this amounts to an evolution.[40]

Nor, we may add, do Mendel's garden peas or the geneticist's fruit flies have any real bearing on 'evolution by natural selection'. Mendel's observations referred to such single traits as yellow seeds or green seeds, purple flowers or white flowers, etc., which were dependent on a single gene and were 'trivial' in the sense that they did not have any evolutionary significance. Similarly, all the mutations observed or induced in more than half a century of experimentation with *Drosophila* were either deleterious or trivial – variations in the pattern of bristles on the fly's body, in the colour of the eyes, etc. Such isolated features which do not interact or interfere with the functioning of the organism as a whole, can indeed be safely left to the roulette wheel. In fact none of the mutations observed in millions of *Drosophila* have produced offspring showing any evolutionary advantage.

Once more the Darwinian theory, in spite of the invigorating injection of Mendelism, had come to a dead end. Bateson, who had been the first in England to greet the 'Mendelian dawn', was also among the first to express his disillusionment. Two years before his death in 1926, he told his son Gregory that it was a mistake to have committed his life to Mendelism, that this was a blind alley which would not throw any light on the differentiation of species, nor on evolution in general.[41]

Even earlier he wrote in *Problems of Genetics*:

The many converging lines of evidence point so clearly to the central fact of the origin of the forms of life by an evolutionary process that we are compelled to accept this deduction, but as to almost all the essential features . . . we have to confess an ignorance nearly total. The

transformation of masses of population by imperceptible steps guided
by selection is, as most of us now see, so inapplicable to the facts,
whether of variation or of specificity, that we can only marvel both at
the want of penetration displayed by the advocates of such a proposition, and at the forensic skill by which it was made to appear acceptable
even for a time.[42]

Bateson coined the term 'genetics' and occupied the first
university chair devoted to the new field in Cambridge. Wilhelm
Johannsen, the Danish pioneer of neo-Darwinism, coined the
term 'gene'. By 1923 he, too, realized that all the experimental
evidence spoke against the theory: 'The Problem of Species,
Evolution, does not seem to be approached seriously through
Mendelism nor through the related modern experiences in
mutations.'[43]

Yet the upholders of the theory, steeped in the mechanistic
tradition, were apparently unable to see that random mutations
of single factors – 'atoms' of heredity – were irrelevant to the
central problem of evolutionary progress, which requires simultaneous, coordinated changes of all the relevant components in the
structure and function of the organic holarchy. The geneticists'
obsession with the bristles of the fruit-fly, and the behaviourists'
obsession with the lever-pressing of the rat, show a more than
superficial analogy: both derive from a reductionist philosophy
which regards the living creature as a collection of elementary
bits of heredity (Mendelian genes) or bits of behaviour (conditioned reflexes or operant responses).

6

I have quoted some voices of dissent coming from biologists in
eminent academic positions. There have been many others, just
as critical of the orthodox doctrine, though not always as out-
spoken – and their number is steadily growing. Although these
criticisms have made numerous breaches in the walls, the citadel
still stands – mainly, as said before, because nobody has a satisfactory alternative to offer. The history of science shows that a

well-established theory can take a lot of battering and get itself into a tangle of contradictions – the fourth phase of 'Crisis and Doubt' in the historic cycle* and yet still be upheld by the establishment until a breakthrough occurs, initiating a new departure, and the start of a new cycle.

But that event is not yet in sight. In the meantime, the educated public continues to believe that Darwin has provided all the relevant answers by the magic formula of random mutation plus natural selection – quite unaware of the fact that random mutations turned out to be irrelevant and natural selection a tautology.

Towards the end of the last century Samuel Butler, another disenchanted Darwinian, wrote in his *Notebooks*:

I attacked the foundations of morality in *Erewhon*, and nobody cared two straws. I tore open the wounds of my Redeemer as he hung upon the Cross in *The Fair Haven*, and people rather liked it. But when I attacked Mr Darwin they were up in arms in a moment.[44]

Nearly a century later, the emotional reactions to such *lèse majesté* are still much the same.

7

In the 1950s a new popular symbol was added to Newton's apple and Mendel's peas: the double helix. The unravelling of the chemical structure of DNA, the nucleic acid in the chromosomes, carrier of the 'hereditary blueprint', was in itself a remarkable achievement and focused attention on the new field of molecular biology or molecular genetics. At first it looked – as had been the case with Mendel's laws – like a heavenly gift to neo-Darwinism, but it soon turned out to be more of a Trojan horse: the new insights gained into the infinitely complex bio-chemistry underlying the 'strategy of the genes' finally demolished the naively simplistic model of Mendelian genetics.

In the earlier versions of the model, the chromosomes were represented as the keyboard of a grand piano with millions of

*See above, Ch. VIII, 9.

keys.* The fertilized egg had the whole keyboard at its disposal. As the embryo developed and each cell became differentiated, most of its keyboard was sealed off by 'scotch tape' and only those keys remained operative which served the cell's specialized functions. The 'scotch tape' is called in the language of genetics a 'repressor'. The agent which strikes the key which activates the gene at the required time is an inducer or 'operator'. A mutated gene is a key which has got out of tune. On some occasions, when quite a lot of keys have gone quite a lot out of tune, the result, we were asked to believe, was a wonderful new melody – a reptile transformed into a bird, or a monkey into a man.† Somewhere along the line the theory had obviously gone wrong.

The point where it went wrong was, as we have seen, the atomistic concept of the gene. At the time when genetics got into its stride, the nineteenth-century type of atomism was being abandoned by physicists, but was still in full bloom in the life sciences: reflexes were atoms of behaviour, and genes were atomic units of heredity. A certain gene was responsible for straight or curly hair, another for haemophilia; and the organism was represented as a mosaic composed of these elementary units. But by the middle of our century these rigidly atomistic concepts of Mendelian genetics had been considerably softened up – and had actually become fluid. It was realized that a single gene may affect a wide range of different characteristics (pleiotropy). And vice versa, a great number of genes may interact with each other to produce a single characteristic (polygeny). Some trivial feature, such as the colour of the iris, may depend on a single gene, but

---

*See above, Ch. I, 9.

†This may sound like a malicious caricature of the theory. However, I used this musical simile for the first time in *The Ghost in the Machine* (1967) and three years later Monod himself endorsed it, as it were: 'Even today,' he wrote,[45] 'a good many distinguished minds seem unable to accept or even to understand that from a source of noise natural selection alone and unaided could have drawn all the music of the biosphere.'

Another metaphor, approved by geneticists, compares mutations (during replication of the chromosomes) to copying errors committed by careless typists.[46] Grassé commented: 'The monks of the Middle Ages made copying errors which altered and corrupted the texts which they had to reproduce. Who would dare to pretend that these mistakes constitute the works?'[47]

the hereditary configuration of all important features of the organism depends on the totality of genes – the gene complex or 'genome' as a whole. Thus by 1957 one could read statements like the following in respectable biology textbooks:

All genes in the total inherited message tend to act together as an integrated whole in the control of development . . . It is easy to fall into the habit of thinking that an organism has a set number of characteristics with one gene controlling each character. This is quite incorrect. The experimental evidence indicates clearly that genes never work altogether separately. Organisms are not patchworks with one gene controlling each of the patches. They are integrated wholes, whose development is controlled by the entire set of genes acting co-operatively.[48]

This is a far cry from the earlier versions of the theory. In those early days of genetics, a gene could be 'dominant' or 'recessive', and that was about all there was to know about it. But with the advent of molecular biology, phenomena of previously undreamt-of complexity entered into the model (just as in subatomic physics), so that more and more terms had to be coined and added to the vocabulary: repressor genes, with co-repressors and apo-repressors; modifier genes, switch genes, operator genes which activate other genes, 'cistrons' and 'operons' (Monod) which constitute sub-systems of interacting genes (we might call them 'genetic holons'), and even genes which regulate the rate of mutations in genes. While the activities of the chromosomes had originally been conceived like the unfolding of a linear sequence as on a tape-recorder, it should have gradually become apparent that the genetic controls in the cells of the developing embryo operate as a *self-regulating micro-hierarchy*, equipped with feedback devices from a hierarchy of environments* which surrounds each and every cell.

Such a holarchy – unlike a recording tape or a 'blueprint' – must be conceived of as a stable, flexible affair. Yet it must to a large extent be self-regulating and capable of self-repair. It must

*See above, Ch. I, 9.

not only protect the growing embryo against the hazards and buffetings to which it is exposed, but also protect the species against the evolutionary hazards of phylogeny – the random mutations occurring in its own chromosomal genes.

The conception of a 'genetic micro-hierarchy'* is still regarded with scepticism or hostility among the hard core of the defenders of the synthetic theory – mainly, perhaps, because its acceptance would lead to a basic revaluation of our notions of the evolutionary process – as will be seen in subsequent chapters.

8

Unlike the current metaphor of the 'genetic blueprint' which gives the impression of a fixed topological map to be mechanically copied, the concept of a 'genetic hierarchy' implies that the selective and regulative controls in the organism operate on several levels.

The lowest levels are concerned with *eliminating* harmful variations in the genetic material; the higher levels with *co-ordinating* the effects of acceptable changes. The mystery, as we shall see, lies in the operation of the higher levels – the coordination (or orchestration) of those changes which transform the amphibian egg into a reptilian egg, and a reptile into a bird. But first, I must say a few words about the operation of the lower levels.

Several biologists (among them von Bertalanffy, Darlington, Spurway, Lima-de-Faria and, more recently, Monod) have suggested that the evolutionary screening process – the action of the 'selective weedkiller' – might start inside the organism, on the level of the molecular chemistry of the genome itself. Mutations are alterations in the sequence of the chemical units in the chromosomes (the four letters of the genetic alphabet); they have been compared to the copying errors of mediaeval monks which corrupted the antique texts.[49] The concept of 'internal selection' launched by the biologists just quoted, implies that there is a

---

*A term first proposed, as far as I know, by L. L. Whyte.

hierarchy of correctors and proof readers at work to eliminate the misprints. In the orthodox theory, natural selection is entirely governed by the pressures of the *external* environment, which kills off the unfit and blesses the fit with abundant progeny. In the light of the foregoing, however, any chromosomal change, whatever its cause, must pass the tests of *internal* selection for physical, chemical and biological fitness before being let loose as an evolutionary novelty. Thus the concept of a genetic micro-hierarchy imposes strict limitations on the range and evolutionary impact of random mutations and *reduces the importance of the chance factor to a minimum.* The proverbial monkey at the type-writer works in fact on a very sophisticated machine which the manufacturers have programmed to print only words which convey meaning and to erase nonsense syllables automatically.* Thus the hierarchic model at least enables us to get rid of the monkey-typist and of Monod's roulette wheel. It does not answer the ultimate question who or what programmed that prodigious typewriter, but it puts the question mark where it properly belongs and enables us to approach the problem step by step as we move on to higher levels of the genetic hierarchy.

The next step leads us to the remarkable powers of regeneration and self-healing which reside in the gene-complex as a whole, or a substantial sub-assembly of it. These powers are demonstrated by experimental embryology; we remember (p. 41) that if, in the early stages of development of the newt embryo, the tissue which would normally develop into its tail, is transplanted into the position of a future leg, that tissue will grow not into a tail, but into a leg. Such magic is not confined to ontogeny; it can also be observed in phylogeny. I have given one example among many in *The Ghost in the Machine*:

The fruit-fly has a mutant gene which is recessive, i.e., when paired with a normal gene, has no discernible effect . . . But if two of these mutant genes are paired in the fertilized egg, the offspring will be an

*This metaphor is almost literally applicable to mistakes made in the protein manufacture in micro-organisms due to 'nonsense syllables' appearing in the RNA.[50]

eyeless fly. If now a pure stock of eyeless flies is made to inbreed, then the whole stock will have only the 'eyeless' mutant gene ... Nevertheless, within a few generations, *flies appear in the inbred 'eyeless' stock with eyes that are perfectly normal.* The traditional explanation of this remarkable phenomenon is that the other members of the gene-complex have been 'reshuffled and re-combined in such a way that they deputise for the missing normal eye-forming gene'.[51]

But no biologist has been so perverse as to suggest that the new eyes evolved by pure chance, thus repeating in a few generations an evolutionary process which took millions of years. Nor does the concept of natural selection provide the slightest help. The re-combination of genes to deputize for the missing gene must have been coordinated according to some overall plan, or set of rules, governing the action of the gene-complex as a whole. It is this coordinating activity, originating at the apex of the genetic hierarchy which ensures *both* the genetic stability of species over millions of years, and their evolutionary modifications along biologically acceptable lines. *The central problem of evolutionary theory is how this vital coordinating activity is carried out.* This is where the big question mark comes in. The metaphor has shifted from the croupier at the roulette wheel to the conductor directing his orchestra.

This shift was already foreshadowed by some of the founding fathers of neo-Darwinism who became dissenters, such as Bateson and Johannsen. The latter (who, we remember, coined the term 'gene') wrote that after all the minute effects of Mendelian mutations had been taken into consideration, there would still remain 'a great central something' which contained the clue to the enigma.[52]

Waddington had an ambivalent attitude to the official theory; I have quoted him poking fun at evolution-by-chance-mutation; on the other hand, he wanted to avoid a complete break with the Darwinian doctrine. As a way out of the dilemma, he proposed in a much-quoted broadcast lecture that in the evolution of a complex organ, such as the human eye, a chance mutation may 'affect the whole organ in a harmonious way'. This implies that the mutation affecting a single component – say, the lens – acts merely as a trigger on a complex pre-set system which has been programmed to react 'in a harmonious way' (our 'programmed typewriter'); and that this programming is also inherited, i.e., represented on a higher level of the genetic hierarchy. Moreover, the harmonious evolution of seemingly unrelated organs (i.e., the wings, air-sacs and digestive system of birds) is coordinated at an even higher level – the 'great central something' at the apex of the hierarchy.

Jacques Monod was confronted with the same dilemma. His brave attempt in *Chance and Necessity* to defend the beleaguered citadel could be compared to Custer's Last Stand. Though he keeps repeating that 'chance alone is at the source of all creation in the biosphere', etc., he is compelled by the evidence derived from his own field to acknowledge the existence of the 'great central something' by postulating a second basic principle of evolution besides chance, which he calls *teleonomy* (his italics):

One of the fundamental characteristics common to all living beings without exception [is] that of being *objects endowed with a purpose or project*, which at the same time they exhibit in their structure and carry out through their performances . . .[53]

The cornerstone of the scientific method is . . . the *systematic* denial that 'true' knowledge can be got at by interpreting phenomena in terms of final causes – that is to say, of 'purpose'. . . Objectivity nevertheless obliges us to recognize the teleonomic character of living organisms, to admit that in their structure and performance they act projectively – realise and pursue a purpose . . .[54]

But what, one might ask, is the difference between Monod's 'teleonomy' and the good old Aristotelian teleology, defined by the *Concise Oxford Dictionary* as the 'doctrine of final causes, view that developments are due to the purpose or design that is served by them'? And even more shockingly, does not the passage quoted remind one of the Lamarckian heresy, according to which evolution is nature's reponse to the organisms' needs? Grassé commented:

The Darwinians have coined the words pseudo-teleology and tele-onomy to refer to final causes whose existence at the same time they deny. They say that the appearances are deceptive, that the constituents of life are all products of chance; and that what we take for finality* is nothing but the ordering of haphazard building blocks by natural selection . . . As a matter of fact, the terms pseudo-teleology and tele-onomy pay tribute to finality, as hypocrisy pays homage to virtue . . .[55]

Yet Jacques Monod was not a hypocrite. He was brilliant in his specialized field, but disarmingly naive concerning the theoretical implications of it – what his compatriots call a *terrible generalisateur*. This, of course, applies to many of his eminent colleagues in the neo-Darwinian establishment. Guided – perhaps unconsciously – by the maxim that a bad theory is better than no theory, they are unable or unwilling to realize that the citadel they are defending lies in ruins.

---

*'Finality': principle of final cause, i.e., purpose viewed as operative in the universe. 'Teleology': view that developments are due to the purpose or design served by them (*Concise Oxford Dictionary*).

X

LAMARCK REVISITED

I

Genetic atomism is dead. As dead as the atomism of nineteenth-century physics, which regarded atoms as hard little indivisible marbles. The living organism is not a mosaic, where each bit is governed by a separate gene, and evolution does not proceed by replacing individual bits in a haphazard fashion until, lo and behold, the image of a fish is replaced by that of an amphibian. In *The Ghost in the Machine* I compared the present crisis in evolutionary theory with the falling apart of medieval cosmology. The pages that follow carry the argument one step further.

2

In his *Evolution Old and New*, published in 1879, Samuel Butler wrote: 'Lamarck has been so systematically laughed at that it amounts to little less than philosophical suicide for anyone to stand up on his behalf.' Nearly half a century later, Paul Kammerer, the most brilliant Lamarckian of his time, was driven into bodily suicide by the laughter and hostility of his fellow biologists.* At the time of writing, another fifty years later, Lamarckism is still an emotional minefield, which academics may enter only at the risk of having their reputations and careers blown to bits.†

The explosive core of the argument was – and still is – a seemingly innocuous postulate: 'the inheritance of acquired

---

**The Case of the Midwife Toad* is an account of his life and the controversy surrounding his work.

†In France there is more tolerance in thsi respect; after all, Lamarck **was** French, Darwin British.

characteristics', which Lamarck formulated at the beginning of the nineteenth century, in his *Philosophie Zoologique*. The term 'acquired characteristics' refers to improvements in physique, skills, or ways of life, which individuals acquire through their efforts to cope with the environment and to exploit the opportunities it offers; in other words, progressive changes *which correspond to the vital needs of the species* and which – here's the rub – are transmitted, according to Lamarck, from parents to offspring through the channels of heredity. Successive generations would thus benefit from the struggles and exertions of their forebears by direct bodily inheritance (and not only indirectly through imitative learning from their elders).

Some early Lamarckians actually believed that a blacksmith's son would be born with stronger than average biceps, without having to develop them by repeating his father's efforts all over again, and that a concert pianist's offspring would inherit some of his father's acquired skill. But neo-Lamarckians abandoned these naive views a long time ago; they hold that only biologically vital characteristics which are acquired in response to intense and persistent pressures of the environment *over many generations* become eventually hereditary, that is, incorporated into the gene-complex. In spite of this qualification, the essence of Lamarckism is the belief that the efforts of the parents are not entirely wasted, that some of the benefits derived from their experiences and labours are transmitted to their offspring, and that this is the principal active cause of evolution 'from amoeba to man'.

Thus in the Lamarckian view, evolution is a *cumulative* process, the outcome of the purposeful striving of living organisms (not very different from Monod's teleonomy), whereas in the neo-Darwinian view evolution is an *accidental* process, in the course of which the parents can transmit through the channels of heredity only what they have inherited themselves, plus some (mostly harmful) aberrations in the genetic material. Thus from the point of view of the offspring, the struggles and achievements of their ancestors were wasted, and amounted, in the words of *Ecclesiastes*, to mere 'vanity and chasing the wind'. The two contrasting attitudes can be summed up by two quotations: the first is from Kammerer, the Lamarckian:

It is not merciless selection that shapes and perfects the machinery of life; it is not the desperate struggle for survival alone which governs the world, but rather out of its own strength everything that has been created strives upwards towards light and the joy of life, burying only that which is useless in the graveyard of selection.[1]

The second quotation is from Simpson of Harvard, an eminent neo-Darwinian:

It does seem that the problem [of evolution] is now essentially solved and that the mechanism of adaptation is known. It turns out to be basically materialistic, with no sign of purpose as a working variable in life history . . . Man is the result of a purposeless and materialistic process . . .[2]

It is not surprising that such diametrically opposed attitudes became fraught with emotion, comparable to the theological disputes of the past. As Sir J. A. Thomson wrote in 1908:

The question as to the transmissibility of characters acquired during life by the body of the parent . . . is much more than a technical problem for biologists. Our decision in regard to it affects not only our whole theory of organic evolution, but even our every-day conduct. The question should be of interest to the parent, the physician, the teacher, the moralist, and the social reformer – in short, to us all.[3]

It is not only of historical interest that Darwin himself remained all his life half a Darwinist and half a Lamarckist. In his *The Variation of Animals and Plants under Domestication*, published in 1868, and in his notebooks, he gave a whole series of spurious examples of the inheritance of acquired characteristics: 'the cat had its tail cut off at Shrewsbury, and its kittens had all short tails', or 'a man losing part of his little finger and all his sons being born with deformed little fingers', and many similar old wives' tales in which he earnestly believed; and in 1875, towards the end of his life, he wrote to Galton that each year he found himself more compelled to revert to the inheritance of acquired characteristics because chance variations and natural selection alone were apparently insufficient to explain the phenomena of evolution. The examples he quoted were no doubt apocryphal, but they prove that if Lamarckism was 'a disreputable ancient superstition' (as Professor Darlington called it), Darwin himself shared it.[4] And so did Herbert Spencer, the great apostle of Darwinism, who wrote in his *Principles of Biology* (1893):

Close contemplation of the facts impresses me more strongly than ever with the two alternatives – *either there has been inheritance of acquired characters, or there has been no evolution* [italics in the original].[5]

Thus in that early period it was possible, and even usual among evolutionists, to be both a Lamarckian and a Darwinian at the same time. With the advent of neo-Darwinism this peaceful co-existence came to an end, Lamarck was excommunicated, and the eclecticism of the early evolutionists was transformed into an attitude of sectarian intolerance.

The ostensible cause of the schism was a doctrine, propounded in 1885, three years after Darwin's death, by the German zoologist August Weismann – the doctrine of the 'continuity and unalterability of the germ-plasm'. Weismann's 'germ-plasm' is the carrier of the hereditary endowment (today called the 'genetic blueprint'); it is located in the sex-cells – sperm and ovum – which are set aside at an early stage in the development of the embryo, isolated from the soma-cells that will give rise to the rest of the body; and is transmitted to the next generation along the 'continuous germ-tract', unaltered and unaffected by anything that happened to the transient individuals which harboured the immortal plasm in their ovaries and testicles. The doctrine that no 'acquired characteristic' can penetrate the barrier protecting the germ-plasm and alter the hereditary endowment became an integral part of the neo-Darwinist creed, and still is – brought up to date in Crick and Watson's provocatively named 'central dogma'. It tells us that the DNA chains of heredity in the chromosomes are kept in splendid isolation from the rest of the body, that they are potentially immortal molecular structures, protected from the hazards of life, and passed on, unaltered, from generation to generation, *ad infinitum*, unless some nasty radiation intervenes. It is a depressing doctrine, whether true or not. The indications are that it is not.

Neo-Darwinism did indeed carry the nineteenth-century brand of materialism to its extreme limits by proclaiming the evolution of man to be the result of 'a purposeless materialistic process', ruled by 'blind chance'. And therein, precisely, lay its perverse philosophical attraction – in its uncompromising rejection of any trace of purpose in the manifestations of life; in its grim determination to reduce ethical values and mental phenomena to the elementary laws of physics; and to brand those aspects of biology which cannot be thus reduced, as unworthy of scientific attention.

How this metaphysical bias influenced and distorted scientific methodology is illustrated by a hilarious episode rarely mentioned in the textbooks. In order to prove his doctrine that the 'germ-plasm' remained unaffected by acquired characteristics, Weismann amputated the tails of twenty-two successive generations of rats to see whether eventually a tail-less rat would be born. No such rat was born, so Lamarck was refuted. However, as one unrepentant Lamarckian remarked, Weismann might as well have studied the inheritance of a wooden leg. For Lamarck's thesis was that only such acquired characteristics become inheritable which an animal develops as a result of its natural, vital needs – and having its tail chopped off can hardly be called a vital need of the rat.

3

Neither Weismann, nor anybody else, has been able to disprove Lamarckian inheritance, because of the inherent difficulty of proving a negative: the Lamarckians could always argue, with perfect justification, that evolution works on an incomparably larger time-scale than a research team, however patient. This was admitted even by staunch Darwinians, such as J. B. S. Haldane:

It must be remembered that however many experiments fail, it is always possible that the effects of acquired characters . . . may be impressed on a species at a rate not susceptible to experimental verification, yet rapid enough to be of importance in geological time.[6]

It is rather amusing to note that Sir Julian Huxley, as we have seen, used exactly the same argument in defence of Darwinian inheritance against its critics: the ' "hoary objection" of the improbability of an eye or a hand or a brain being evolved by blind chance has "lost its force" because natural selection is "operating over the stretches of geological time".'[7]

While it was thus impossible to *disprove* either the Darwinian or the Lamarckian theory by experiment, it turned out to be equally impossible to *prove* either of them. On the Lamarckian side, the great Pavlov in Leningrad and MacDougall at Harvard attempted to show that the results of conditioning in mice and rats were inherited – and failed to do so.* On the other hand, the patient labours of the Darwinian geneticists on thousands of generations of *Drosophila* have also failed to produce any evolutionary improvement. As far as the direct experimental evidence is concerned, the two sides might have called it quits.

If the neo–Darwinians nevertheless carried the day – for the time being – the reason was, apart from metaphysical bias, that they were apparently able to offer 'modern', scientific explanations of some aspects of the evolutionary process, which the Lamarckians were unable to do. The discovery of Mendel's laws, the statistical approach to genetics, and lastly the 'breaking of the genetic code', each looked at first like an added confirmation of Darwin's prophetic foresight (forgetting his own lapses into Lamarckism). The mechanism of evolution which he had proposed may have been crude, in need of modifications and refinements; but the Lamarckians could not offer any mechanism at all in keeping with modern biochemistry. Random mutations in the chromosomes, triggered by radioactivity or noxious chemicals, were *prima facie*

*Perhaps closest to such proof came Kammerer's controversial experiments, described in *The Case of the Midwife Toad* and J. McConnell's experiments on *Planaria*.[8]

scientifically acceptable as a base for natural selection. But no acceptable hypothesis was forthcoming to explain how an acquired bodily or mental feature could alter the 'genetic blueprint', contained in the micro-structure of the chromosomes. So once more the principle prevailed that a bad theory is better than no theory, and Lamarckism acquired the stigma of a 'disreputable superstition' because it postulated a principle in nature without being able to offer a mechanism, in terms of contemporary science, to account for it.

This situation, however, has many precedents in the history of science. When Kepler suggested that the tides were caused by the attraction of the moon, even Galileo dismissed the idea as an 'occult fancy' because there was no conceivable mechanism which could explain action-at-a-distance. Later on, some of Newton's most eminent contemporaries rejected universal gravity because it meant, in his own words, 'grappling with ghost fingers at distant objects' and thus contradicted the laws of mechanics. *Mutatis mutandum*, Lamarckism was rejected because the proposition that the experiences acquired by the living organism could influence the structure of its hereditary chromosomes contradicted the laws of genetics summed up in the 'central dogma'.

In actual fact the central dogma succumbed in less than twenty years after its proclamation under the weight of rapidly accumulating new evidence. On 25 June 1970, the *New Scientist* (which does not go in for sensational headlines) announced: 'Biology's Central Dogma Turned Topsy-Turvy' and *The Times* Science Report followed suit: 'Big Reverse for Dogma of Biology'.[9] The experimental work, which overturned the central dogma (and which six years later was rewarded by a Nobel Prize)* is too technical to be detailed here; suffice it to say that it established beyond dispute that in certain bacteria the 'hereditary blueprint' can be altered by the incorporation of agents of external origin (viruses), which may have harmful or benign effects.[10] Or, as Grassé summed it up:

---

*Shared by Temin, Baltimore and Dulbecco

These results demonstrate that there exists a molecular mechanism which, in certain circumstances, supplies information from outside to the organism and inserts this information into the organism's genetic code. This is of immense importance to evolutionists.[11]

It is indeed. This is why I called molecular genetics a Trojan Horse inside the citadel.

It would, of course, be silly to jump to the conclusion that because viruses can produce hereditary changes in a cell, therefore continued piano practice by the parents will make them beget musical prodigies. Nevertheless, the discoveries of molecular genetics in the course of the last decade have finally demolished Weismann's doctrine of the 'unalterability of the germ-tract' and modified its modern version, the 'central dogma'. Taken in conjunction with the criticisms discussed earlier on, they may signal the beginning of the end of neo-Darwinism as represented in contemporary textbooks. Darwinian selection no doubt plays a part in the evolutionary process, but only a subordinate part (comparable to the action of the selective weedkiller) and there is a growing realization that there must be other principles and forces at work on the vast canvas of evolutionary phenomena. In other words, the evidence indicates that evolution is the combined result of a whole range of causative factors – some known, others dimly guessed, yet others so far completely unknown.

4

In *The Case of the Midwife Toad* I suggested that within that wide range of causative factors a 'modest niche might be found for a kind of modified "mini-Lamarckism" as an explanation for some limited and rare evolutionary phenomena'.[12] In the light of recent developments I am no longer sure that the niche must be so modest, and the phenomena so rare. It would of course be absurd to revert to the naive version of Lamarckism which Darwin himself embraced. As said before, Lamarckism only makes sense if the inheritability of acquired characteristics is confined to such bodily features and skills which organisms acquire in response to persistent pressures and challenges of the environment over many generations.

This limitation is essential, and the reasons for it can be explained by a simple analogy. Our sense organs for sight and hearing act like narrow slits or filters which admit only a very limited frequency range of electro-magnetic and sound waves. But even this reduced input is too much for us to cope with. Our minds would cease to function if we had to attend to each of the millions of stimuli which – in William James's classic phrase – constantly bombard our receptor organs in a 'blooming, buzzing confusion'. Thus the nervous system and the brain itself function as a multilevelled hierarchy of filtering and classifying devices, which eliminate a large proportion of the input as irrelevant 'noise', and assemble the relevant information into coherent patterns before it is presented to consciousness.* A typical example of this filtering-and-synthesizing process is what psychologists call the 'cocktail-party phenomenon' – our remarkable ability to isolate and attend to a single voice from the medley of sounds impinging on the ear-drum.

Now what the Weismann doctrine, or the central dogma, really amounts to is the postulate that a comparable filtering apparatus must protect the hereditary blueprint in the germ-cells against the 'buzzing confusion' of biochemical intrusions which otherwise would play havoc with the continuity and stability of the species. But that does not necessarily exclude the possibility that some very persistent and vital acquisitions, made by generation after generation, may not gradually seep through the filter and become hereditary. There are, at any rate, some classical examples, quoted over and over again in the literature, which seem to cry out for a Lamarckian explanation because Darwinism has none to offer:

There is, for example, the hoary problem why the skin on the soles of our feet is so much thicker than elsewhere. If the thickening occurred *after* birth, as a result of pressure and friction, there would be no problem. But the skin of the sole is already thickened *in the embryo* which

*cf. Ch. I, 13.

has never walked, bare-foot or otherwise. A similar, even more striking phenomenon are the horny callosities on the African warthog's forelimbs, on which the animal leans while feeding; on the knees of camels; and, oddest of all, the two bulbous thickenings on the ostrich's undercarriage, one fore, one aft, on which that ungainly bird squats. All these callosities make their appearance, as the skin on our feet does, *in the embryo. They are inherited characteristics.* But is it conceivable that these callosities should have evolved by chance mutations just exactly where the animal needed them? Or must we assume that there is a causal, Lamarckian connection between the animal's need to protect these vulnerable spots and the genetic mutation which satisfies that need?[13]

These examples, and many others which are too technical to be cited here, have been bandied about by Lamarckians ever since the controversy started; and the Darwinians, unable to offer a satisfactory explanation, consistently evaded the issue, or – on Samuel Butler's phrase – kept 'ostrichizing' the evidence. A century after Butler, these evasive tactics still prevail.*

It is admittedly difficult to see how an acquired callosity could conceivably produce a change in the chromosomes. But, as Waddington himself pointed out in an earlier book,[14] 'even if improbable, such processes would not be theoretically inexplicable. It must be for experiment to decide whether they happen or not'. He even produced a 'speculative model' to show a possible way how changes in the activities of body-cells could affect the gene-activities in germ-cells by means of adaptive enzymes. As he wrote, the model was 'intended only to suggest that it may be unsafe to consider that the occurrence of directed non-random mutations related to the environment can be ruled out of court a priori'.[15]

---

*The interested reader will find a recent example of it in the discussion which took place at the Alpbach Symposium after Professor Waddington's paper 'The Theory of Evolution Today', when the hoary tale of the ostrich and the warthog was brought up again by the present writer.[16] It was particularly interesting to note that although Waddington was, as we have seen, highly critical of the synthetic theory, he instantly rallied to its defence when it was attacked from outside.

5

It has been known for a long time that the 'Weismann barrier' which supposedly isolates the reproductive cells, the carriers of heredity, from the rest of the body, does not apply to plants; nor to lowly animals such as flatworms and hydra, which can regenerate a whole individual, including its reproductive organs, from virtually any segment of their bodies. Ultimately, biologists will have to face the choice of clinging to the dogma of the 'impenetrable wall' protecting the 'unalterable germ-tract' from the rest of the world, and ascribing all evolutionary alterations of it to pure chance – or admitting that the wall is porous, a system of fine-meshed filters which permits only selected, vital information to penetrate into the inner sanctum of heredity in the germ-cells. Molecular genetics does not tell us – as yet – how this is achieved; but it is a new science in constant flux and it does not exclude *a priori* the possibility of a phylogenetic memory for vital and recurrent experiences encoded in the chromosomes. How else but through some process of phylogenetic learning and memory-formation could the complex inherited skills of building a bird's nest or weaving a spider's web have arisen? The official theory, as we have seen, has no explanation for the genetics of such inherited virtuosity.

To recapitulate: one can draw an analogy between the filtering apparatus which operates in the nervous system to protect the mind from irrelevant stimuli, and the genetic micro-hierarchy which protects the hereditary endowment against harmful chance mutations, and coordinates the effects of useful ones. We can now extend the analogy and suggest that there is also a Lamarckian micro-hierarchy at work in the process of evolution, which prevents acquired characteristics from interfering with the hereditary blueprint – except for those select few which respond to some vital need of the species, originating in sustained pressures by the environment over many generations – like the thickened skin on the soles of the human embryo. We would thus have a quasi-Darwinian micro-hierarchy, mainly responsible for the immensely rich *variations* on the same level of the evolutionary ladder, and a quasi-Lamarckian micro-hierarchy, mainly responsible for the *evolution* to higher levels. And there are no doubt still other causative factors at work, beyond our present horizon.

Only a fool could deny the revolutionary impact of Darwinism on the outlook of the nineteenth century, when – as one biologist put it,[17] the educated public was faced with the alternative 'for Darwin or against evolution'. But the narrow sectarianism of the neo-Darwinists of our own age is an altogether different matter; and in the not-too-distant future biologists may well wonder what kind of benightedness it was that held their elders in its thrall. This prognosis is shared by some of the critics I have quoted, and perhaps by the majority of the younger generation. It is certainly significant that even in the Introduction, written by an eminent entomologist, to the Everyman Library's Centenary Edition of Darwin's *The Origin of Species*, we can hear a note of sharp dissent from the orthodox attitude:

This situation, where scientific men rally to the defence of a doctrine they are unable to define scientifically, much less demonstrate with scientific rigour, attempting to maintain its credit with the public by the suppression of criticism and the elimination of difficulties, is abnormal and undesirable in science.[18]

It is perhaps significant that in later Everyman editions of *The Origin of Species* this introduction no longer appears.

XI

STRATEGIES AND PURPOSE IN EVOLUTION

I

In Chapter I, 10 I mentioned the classic example of the forelimbs of vertebrates which, whether they serve reptiles, birds, whales or man, show the same basic design of bones, muscles, nerves, etc., and are accordingly called homologous organs. The functions of legs, wings and flippers are quite different, yet they all are variations on a single theme – strategic modifications of a pre-existing structure: the forelimb of the common reptilian ancestor. Once Nature has 'taken out a patent' on a vital organ, she sticks to it, and that organ becomes a stable evolutionary holon. Its basic design seems to be governed by a fixed *evolutionary canon*; while its adaptation to swimming, walking, or flying is a matter of evolution's flexible *strategy*.

This principle is readily applicable to all levels of the evolutionary hierarchy, from the sub-cellular level to the primate brain. The same four chemical bases in the chromosomal nucleic acid – DNA – constitute the four-letter alphabet of the genetic codes throughout the animal kingdom; the same 'make' of organelles function in their cells; the same chemical fuel – ATP – provides their energy; the same contractile proteins serve the motions of the amoeba and of human muscles. Animals and plants are made of homologous molecules, organelles, and even more complex homologous sub-structures. They are the stable holons in the evolutionary flux, the nodes on the tree of life.

The theories of evolution discussed in previous pages are primarily concerned with the nature of evolutionary *strategies* (Darwinian, Lamarckian, etc.) which made the higher forms of life branch out of the roots at the base of the hierarchy. But dazzled by the prodigious *variety* of plants and animals, biologists were inclined to pay less attention to the *uniformity* of those basic units – reflected in the phenomena of homology – and the *limitations* which it imposed on all existing and possible forms of life on this planet. After all, the basic uniformity of the organelles which constitute the living cell is itself derived from the limitations imposed by the basic chemistry of organic matter such as amino-acids, proteins, enzymes. On a higher level, the genetic micro-hierarchies impose further constraints on hereditary variations. Still further up the 'great central something' regulates – in ways unknown to us – the 'harmonious coordination' of genetic changes. Their combined effect is the evolutionary canon, which permits a great amount of variations, but only in limited directions *on a limited number of themes*. Evolution is not a free-for-all but – to revert to our formula – a game with fixed rules and flexible strategies, played over thousands of millennia.

To illustrate these somewhat abstract considerations, I shall once more use the example of the Australian marsupials, which I used in *The Ghost in the Machine*.* I called them an enigma wrapped in a puzzle. The enigma is shown by the drawings on p. 208. The puzzle is why evolutionists refuse to see the problems that it poses.

2

The class mammalia has two main sub-classes:† marsupials and placentals. They have evolved, independently from each other, from a common ancestry (the now extinct therapsids, or mammal-like reptiles). The marsupial embryo is expelled from the womb in a very immature state of development and is reared in an elastic pouch attached to the mother's belly. A newborn kangaroo is a half-finished job: about an inch long, naked, blind, its hind-legs no more than embryonic buds. One might speculate whether the human infant, more developed but still helpless at birth,

*The section that follows is a compressed version of *The Ghost in the Machine*, pp. 143–6.

†Not counting the nearly extinct egg-laying mammals, such as the duck-billed platypus.

would be better off in a maternal pouch; one is also reminded of African or Japanese women carrying their infants strapped to their backs. But whether the marsupial method is better or worse than the placental, the point is that they differ. Pouch and placenta might be called variations in strategy within the general schema of mammalian reproduction.

The two lines split up, as already said, at the very beginning of mammalian evolution some time before Australia became separated from the Asiatic mainland in the late Cretacean. The marsupials (who had branched out from the common ancestral type earlier than the placentals) got into Australia before it was cut off; the placentals did not. So the two lines evolved in complete separation for about a hundred million years. The enigma is why so many animals in the Australian fauna, produced by the independent evolutionary line of the marsupials, look so startlingly like their opposite numbers among placentals. The drawings on p. 208 show on the left side three specimens of marsupials, on the right the corresponding placentals. It is as if two artists who have never met and never shared the same model, had drawn parallel series of almost identical portraits.

When Australia became an island, the only mammalian immigrants who had managed to get there in time were tiny, mouse-like, pouched animals, perhaps not unlike the still extant yellow-footed pouched mouse, but even more primitive. And yet these archaic creatures, confined to their island continent, branched out and gave rise to pouched versions of our placental moles, ant-eaters, flying squirrels, cats, wolves, lions, and so on – each like a somewhat clumsy copy of its placental namesake. Why, if evolution were a free-for-all, why did Australia not produce some entirely different species of animals, like the bug-eyed monsters of science fiction? The only moderately unorthodox creation of that isolated island in a hundred million years are the kangaroos and wallabies; the rest of the fauna consists of rather inferior duplicates of more efficient placental types – variations on a limited number of themes, within the repertory of the evolutionary canon.

The only explanation for this enigma which the official theory

(a)

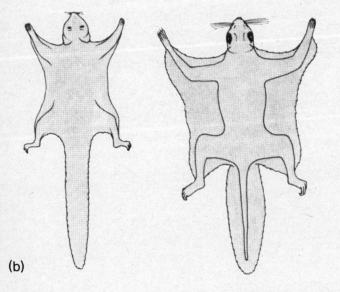

(b)

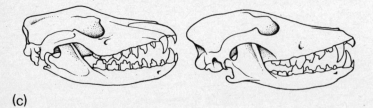

(c)

(a) Marsupial jerboa and placental jerboa (b) Marsupial flying phalanger and placental flying squirrel. (c) Skull of Tasmanian wolf and skull of placental wolf (after Hardy).

has to offer is summed up in the following quotation from an authoritative textbook:

Tasmanian [i.e., marsupial] and true wolves are both running predators, preying on other animals of about the same size and habits. Adaptive similarity [i.e., adaptation to similar environments] involves similarity also of structure and function. The mechanism of such evolution is natural selection.[1]

And G. G. Simpson, the leading Harvard authority on evolution discussing the same problem, concludes that the explanation is 'selection of random mutations'.[2]

This is question-begging on a truly heroic scale. We are asked to believe that the vague phrase 'preying on animals of approximately the same size and habits' – which can be applied to hundreds of different species – provides a sufficient explanation for the emergence of the nearly identical skulls shown on p. 208. Even the evolution of a single species of wolf by random mutation plus selection presents, as we have seen, insurmountable difficulties. To *duplicate* this process independently on island and mainland would mean squaring a miracle. The puzzle remains why the Darwinians are not puzzled – or pretend not to be.*

3

The Australian *Doppelgängers* lend strong support to the hypothesis that there are unitary laws underlying evolutionary diversity, which permit virtually unlimited variations on a limited number of themes. They include, on the lower levels of the hierarchy, macromolecules, organelles and cells which represent evolutionary holons; higher up, homologous organs such as the vertebrate forelimbs, lungs, and gills, not to mention eyes equipped with lenses – which have evolved, independently from each other, several times in evolutionary lines as far apart as molluscs, spiders and vertebrates. Still higher up we have to

*Various terms have been invented to describe this phenomenon such as 'convergence', 'parallelism', 'homeoplasy', but these are purely descriptive, without explanatory value.

include in the list the more or less standardized vertebrate types exemplified by the drawings. The 'more or less' we can ascribe to variations in evolutionary strategy in a changing environment; but their standardization we can only explain by rules built into the genetic micro-hierarchies which confine evolutionary advances to certain main avenues, and filter out the rest.

This conception of 'archetypal forms' goes back to the German transcendentalists of the eighteenth century, including Goethe (and eventually to Plato); but it was revived by a number of modern evolutionists who toyed with the idea of 'internal selection' without spelling out its profound implications.* Thus Helen Spurway concluded from the universal recurrence of homologous forms that the organism has only 'a restricted mutation spectrum' which 'determines its possibilities of evolution'.[3] Other biologists have talked of 'organic laws co-determining evolution', 'moulding influences guiding evolutionary change along certain avenues';[4] while Waddington reverted to 'the notion of archetypes . . . the idea, that is, that there are only a certain number of basic patterns which organic form can assume'.[5] What they are implying (without saying it in as many words) is that, given the conditions on our particular planet, its gravity and temperature; the composition of its atmosphere, oceans and soil; the nature of available energies and raw materials, life from its inception in the first blob of living slime could only evolve *in a limited number of directions in a limited number of ways*. But this in turn implies that just as the basic pattern of the twin wolves was foreshadowed, or present *in potentia*, in their common ancestry, so the mammal-like reptile creature must have been potentially present in the ancestral chordate – and so on back to the ancestral protist, and tne first self-replicating strand of nucleic acid.

This seems to be the inevitable conclusion derived from the phenomena of homology – which Sir Alister Hardy has called 'absolutely fundamental to what we are talking about when we speak of evolution'.[6] If this line of argument is correct, it puts an

*See above, Ch. IX, 7. For an excellent short critical discussion see L. L. Whyte's *Internal Factors in Evolution* and W. H. Thorpe's review of the book in *Nature*, 14 May, 1966.

end to the monsters of science fiction as possible forms of life on earth – or on other planets similar to it. But it does not mean the opposite either: it emphatically does *not* mean a rigidly predetermined universe which unwinds like a mechanical clockwork. It means – to revert to one of the *leit-motifs* of this book – that the evolution of life is a splendid game played according to fixed rules which limit its possibilities but leave sufficient scope for virtually limitless variations. The rules are inherent in the basic structure of living matter, the variations are derived from flexible strategies which take advantage of the opportunities offered by the former.

In other words, evolution is neither a free-for-all dependent on chance alone, nor the execution of a rigidly predetermined computer programme. It could be compared to musical composition of the classical type, whose possibilities are limited by the rules of harmony and the structure of the diatonic scales – which nevertheless permit an inexhaustible number of original creations. Or it could be compared to a game of chess, obeying fixed rules with equally inexhaustible variations. And lastly – to quote from *The Ghost in the Machine* –

. . . the vast number of existing animal species (about one million) and the small number of major classes (about fifty) and of major phyla or divisions (about ten), could be compared with the vast number of works of literature and the small number of basic themes or plots. All works of literature are variations on a limited number of *leitmotivs*, derived from man's archetypal experiences and conflicts, but adapted each time to a new environment – the costumes, conventions and language of the period. Not even Shakespeare could invent an original plot. Goethe quoted with approval the Italian dramatist Carlo Gozzi,* according to whom there are only thirty-six tragic situations. Goethe himself thought that there were probably even less; but their exact number is a well-kept secret among writers of fiction. A work of literature is constructed out of thematic holons.[7]

But there is still plenty of scope left for the writer to make what he can out of Gozzi's meagre list of thirty-six themes.

*Author of *Turandot* and many other successful works.

And there is plenty of scope for evolutionary strategies to make the best of the limited possibilities inherent in the physico-chemical structure of living matter as it exists on earth – and presumably on other planets where conditions are similar to those on earth. We shall return to this speculative subject later on.

4

It may be objected that to talk of the 'strategy of evolution' means falling into the trap of anthropomorphism – attributing human motivations to nature. In fact the approach suggested here should rather be called 'biomorphic', because it is based on the purposeful aspects inherent in the phenomena of life, as opposed to the 'robotomorphic' approach of reductionism. Science ought not to be afraid of applying the terms 'purpose' and 'strategy' to evolution; they do not imply that there is a divine Strategist at work. Yet it is precisely this unjustified fear that has muddied the controversy and landed the orthodox theorists in a morass of contradictions. To quote once more a representative spokesman, Professor G. G. Simpson, evolution '. . . turns out to be basically materialistic, with no sign of purpose . . . and with any possible Purposer pushed back to the incomprehensible position of First Cause . . . Man is the result of a purposeless and materialistic process that did not have him in mind. He was not planned.'[8]

Here the logical fallacy, based on a spurious alternative, is explicitly revealed: evolution is *either* purposeless *or* there must be a divine Purposer at work. One wonders how it comes to pass that naturalists, once they specialize in genetics, become so blind to nature that they fail to see purposiveness as a fundamental characteristic of life which does not require the postulate of a Purposer because it is inherent in the concept of life itself; or – to quote Sinnott – because purpose is 'the directive activity shown by individual organisms that distinguishes living things from inanimate objects'.[9] The term 'purposiveness', applied to a living organism, means goal-directed instead of random activity; flexible strategies to attain a goal instead of rigid, mechanized responses; adapting to the environment, but on the organism's own terms, often in rather fanciful ways like the orchid or the butterfly; and adapting the environment to its own needs. Or, as the Nobel laureate H. J. Muller wrote: 'Purpose is not imported into nature, and need not be puzzled over as a strange or divine something else that gets inside and makes life go . . . it is simply implicit in the fact of biological organization.'[10]

Thus it has now become more or less respectable to talk of purpose or directiveness in *ontogeny*, that is, the individual's development during its life-history; but it is still considered heretical to apply the same terms to *phylogeny*, that is, the history of evolution. Ontogeny is purposive, phylogeny blind; ontogeny is guided by memory and learning, phylogeny is unaffected by either of them. Yet we have seen that the more thoughtful among the neo-Darwinians feel increasingly unhappy about this artificially created chasm, and have started to build bridges across it – such as Monod's 'teleonomy', or the concept of genetic micro-hierarchies which filter and coordinate hereditary changes. Simpson himself, in spite of his dogmatism, was led to realize that phylogeny is an abstraction unless regarded as a sequence of ontogenies, and that 'the course of evolution is through changes of ontogenies'. But if ontogenies are purposeful, it is difficult to see why their summation should be purposeless – unless we subscribe to the Weismann–Crick dogma of the 'unalterable germ-track' (which would be the only example found in nature of a biological process devoid of feedback).

Thus the hoary conundrum about the Purposer behind the purpose can be laid to rest. The Purposer is each and every individual organism from the inception of life, which struggled and strove to make the best of its limited possibilities; and the sum total of these ontogenies reflects the active striving of living matter towards the optimal realization of the planet's evolutionary potential.

5

The emphasis in the last paragraph was on 'active striving'. When orthodox evolutionists talk of 'adaptations', they mean –

as behaviourists do when they talk of 'responses' – a basically passive process, entirely controlled by 'the contingencies of the environment'. This may suit their philosophy, but is certainly not in keeping with the evidence which shows, in G. E. Coghill's phrase, that 'the organism acts on the environment before it reacts to it'.[11] Almost from the moment a creature is hatched or born, it lashes out at the environment, be it liquid or solid, with cilia, flagellae, or muscles; it swims, crawls, glides, pulsates; it kicks, yelps, breathes, feeds on the environment. It does not merely adapt to the environment but adapts the environment to its own needs – it eats and drinks its environment, fights and mates with it, burrows and builds in it; it does not merely 'respond' to the environment, but asks questions by exploring it. Let us remember (Chapter VII, 2) that the 'exploratory drive' is a primary instinct, as basic as hunger and sex, and can occasionally prove even more powerful then these. Countless naturalists, starting with Darwin himself, have shown that curiosity is an instinctual urge in rats, birds, dolphins, monkeys, etc.; and we have seen that it is the main driving force which motivates artists and scientists alike. Thus the exploratory drive is a dominant factor in man's mental evolution; and it has been suggested, by Hardy and others, that it may also be a dominant factor in biological evolution. In this view, evolutionary progress is based on the *initiative* of some enterprising individuals in the species, who discover a new method of feeding, or self-protection, or some new skill which, spreading by imitation, is incorporated into the species's way of life. To illustrate the process, Hardy cites as an example, one of 'Darwin's finches' on the Galapagos islands, *C. pallidus.* This remarkable bird pecks holes or crevices into the bark of trees, and 'having excavated, it picks up a cactus spine or twig, one or two inches long, and holding it lengthwise in its beak, pokes it up the crack, dropping the twig to seize the insect as it emerges. . . . Sometimes the bird carries a spine or twig about with it, poking into cracks and crannies as it searches one tree after another.'[12]

After describing a number of similar examples, Hardy suggests that the main causative factor of evolutionary progress is *not* the selective pressure of the environment, but the initiative of the living organism – 'the restless, exploring and perceiving animal that discovers new ways of living . . . It is adaptations which are due to the animal's behaviour, to its restless exploration of its surroundings, to its initiative, that distinguish the main diverging lines of evolution . . . giving the lines of runners, climbers, burrowers, swimmers and conquerors of the air.'[13]

One might call this the 'progress-by-initiative' theory of evolution. The pioneers of the species initiate a new habit, a change in behaviour, which spreads through the population and is copied by successive generations – until a lucky chance-mutation transforms it into a hereditary instinct. Thus the process is initiated by the animal, and the lucky mutation comes only afterwards, as a kind of genetic endorsement which incorporates the new skill into the genetic blueprint. The role of chance has been further reduced; the monkey at the typewriter needs only to go on trying until he hits a pre-specified key.

When I wrote *The Ghost in the Machine* I found this theory rather attractive, but on second thoughts it reveals a crucial flaw, in still relying – though to a lesser extent than the orthodox theory – on random mutations to achieve the fantastically complex changes in the nervous system that are needed in order to insert a new habit or skill into the organism's native equipment. The emphasis on initiative, on the active role of the exploring animal remains attractive, but the basic riddle of the ostrich's callosities or the spider's architectural brilliance is left unsolved. From a methodological point of view it seems preferable to assume that the insect-hunting skill of Darwin's finch became impressed on its chromosomes by some unknown process *because it was useful* – that is, by Lamarckian inheritance – instead of invoking once more the Darwinian mantra.

6

Evolution, as seen through human eyes, appears as a shockingly wasteful process. Biologists take it for granted that for every one of the existing one million species, hundreds must have perished in the past; and those lines which have survived seem to have become stagnant, their evolution having come to a standstill in the far-distant past. The principal cause of both extinction and stagnation appears to have been over-specialization with its concomitant loss of adaptability to changes in the environment. Julian Huxley has compared evolution to a maze with an '. . . enormous number of blind alleys with a very occasional path to progress . . . All reptilian lines were blind alleys save two – one which was transformed into birds, and another which became the mamals. Of the bird stock, all lines came to a dead end; of the mammals all but one – the one which became man.'[14]

The human paradigm of over-specialization is the pedant, the slave of habit, whose thinking and behaviour move in rigid grooves – a predestined victim of any unexpected calamity. His equivalent in the animal kingdom is the pathetic koala bear, which specializes in feeding on the leaves of a particular variety of eucalyptus tree and on nothing else; and which has hook-like claws, ideally suited for clinging to the bark of the tree – and for nothing else. All orthodoxies tend to breed human koalas.

One line of escape from the maze of blind alleys is of particular relevance to our theme: a phenomenon which goes under the name of 'paedomorphosis'. It was described by Garstang in the 1920s, and taken up by several biologists;* but although the existence of the phenomenon is generally accepted, it made little impact on the orthodox theory and is rarely mentioned in the textbooks. It indicates that at certain critical stages evolution can *retrace its steps*, as it were, along the path which led to the dead end and make a fresh start in a new, more promising direction. The crucial event in this process is the appearance at the foetal, larval or juvenile stage of some useful evolutionary novelty which is carried over into the adult stage of the organism's progeny. The following example will show what is meant:

There is fairly good evidence in favour of the hypothesis that the chordates – and thus we, the vertebrates – are descended from the larval

*Among them Hardy and de Beer in England, Koltsov and Takhtajan in the Soviet Union.[15]

stage of some primitive echinoderm, rather like the sea urchin or sea cucumber [echinoderm = 'prickly-skinned']. Now an adult sea cucumber would not be a very inspiring ancestor – it is a sluggish creature which looks like an ill-stuffed sausage with leathery skin, lying on the sea bottom. But its free-floating larva is a much more promising proposition: unlike the adult sea cucumber, the larva displays bilateral symmetry like a fish; it has a ciliary band – a forerunner of the nervous system – and some other sophisticated features not found in the adult animal. We must assume that the sedentary adult residing on the sea bottom had to rely on mobile larvae to spread the species far and wide in the ocean, as plants scatter their seeds in the wind; that the larvae, which had to fend for themselves, exposed to much stronger selective pressures than the adults, gradually became more fish-like; and that eventually they became sexually mature while still in the free-swimming, larval state – thus giving rise to a new type of animal which never settled on the bottom at all, and altogether eliminated the senile, sedentary cucumber stage from its life history.[16]

Now this lowering of the age of sexual maturity is a well-known evolutionary phenomenon called *neoteny*. It has two aspects: the animal starts to breed while still in a larval or juvenile stage; and it never reaches the fully adult stage, which is dropped off – eliminated from its life cycle ('terminal abbreviation'). Thus the ancestors' juvenile stages of development become the definite condition of their descendants, while the ancestors' mature characteristics have fallen by the roadside. What this amounts to is a process of 'juvenilization'* and de-specialization – a successful escape from a dead-end in the evolutionary maze. As J. Z. Young wrote, commenting on Garstang's views:

> The problem which remains is in fact not 'how have vertebrates been formed by sea-squirts?', but how have vertebrates eliminated the [adult] sea-squirt stage from their life history? It is wholly reasonable to consider that this has been accomplished by paedomorphis.[17]

Sir Gavin de Beer compared the process to the re-winding of a biological clock when evolution is in danger of running down and coming to a standstill: 'A race may become rejuvenated by

---

*A term proposed by Julian Huxley (1952), p. 532.

pushing the adult stage of its individuals off from the end of their ontogenies, and such a race may then radiate out in all directions.'[18]

The record from palaeontology and comparative anatomy does indeed suggest that this retracing of steps to escape from the blind alleys of over-specialization was repeated at each major evolutionary turning point. I have mentioned the evolution of the vertebrates from the larval stage of some primitive echino-derm. Hardy and Koltsov[19] have given numerous other examples and Takhtajan[20] has shown that paedomorphosis is also a common occurrence in the evolution of plant life. Insects have in all likelihood evolved from a millipede-like ancestor – not, however, from its adult form, whose structure is too specialized, but from its larval form. The conquest of the dry land was pioneered by amphibians whose ancestry can be traced back to some primitive type of lung-breathing fish, whereas the later lines of highly specialized gill-breathing fishes came to a dead end. The examples could be multiplied; but the most striking case of paedomor-phosis is the evolution of our own species.

Since Bolk's pioneering work, published in 1926, it is now generally accepted that the human adult resembles the embryo of an ape rather than an adult ape.

In both simian embryo and human adult, the ratio of the weight of the brain to total body weight is disproportionately high. In both, the closing of the sutures between the bones of the skull is retarded to permit the brain to expand. The back-to-front axis through man's head – i.e., the direction of his line of sight – is at right angles to his spinal column: a condition which, in apes and other mammals, is found only in the embryonic, not in the adult stage. The same applies to the angle between backbone and uro-genital canal – which may account for the singularity of the human way of copulating face to face. Other embryonic – or, to use Bolk's term, *foetalized* – characteris-tics in adult man are: the absence of brow-ridges; the scantiness and late appearance of body hair; pallor of the skin; retarded growth of the teeth, and a number of other features . . .[21]

The 'missing link' between ape and man will probably never be found – because it was an embryo.

7

Paedomorphosis – or juvenilization – thus appears to play an important part in the grand strategy of evolution. It involves a *retreat* from specialized adult forms to earlier, less committed and more plastic stages in the development of organisms – followed by a sudden advance in a new direction. It is as if the stream of life had momentarily reversed its course, flowing uphill for a while towards its original source; then opened up a new stream-bed – leaving the koala bear stranded on his tree like a discarded hypothesis. In other words, we are faced here with the same pattern of *reculer pour mieux sauter*, 'step back to leap', which we have encountered at the critical turning points in the evolution of science and art. Biological evolution is to a large extent a history of escapes from the blind alleys of over-specialization, the evolution of ideas a series of escapes from the tyranny of mental habits and stagnant routines. In biological evolution the escape is brought about by a retreat from the adult to a juvenile stage as the starting-point for the new line; in mental evolution by a temporary regression to more primitive and uninhibited modes of ideation, followed by the creative forward leap (the equivalent of a sudden burst of 'adaptive radiation'). Thus these two types of progress – the emergence of evolutionary novelties and the creation of cultural novelties – reflect the same undoing–redoing pattern and appear as analogous processes on different levels.

Neither biological evolution nor cultural progress follows a continuous curve. Neither of them is strictly cumulative in the sense of continuing to build where the previous generation had left off. Both progress in the zigzag fashion described in Chapter VIII. The advance of science is continuous only during those periods of consolidation and elaboration which follow a main breakthrough or 'paradigm-change'. Sooner or later, however, consolidation leads to increasing rigidity, orthodoxy, and so into the blind alley of over-specialization – the equivalent of the Irish elk or the koala bear. But the new theoretical structure which emerges from the breakthrough is not just added to the old edifice; it branches out from the point where the evolution of ideas has taken the wrong turn. The great revolutions in the history of science have a decidedly paedomorphic character. In the history of literature and art, the zigzag course is even more in evidence: we have seen how the periods of cumulative progress within a given 'school' or technique end inevitably in stagnation, mannerism or decadence, until the crisis is resolved by a revolutionary shift in sensibility, emphasis, style.

8

The analogy between biological and cultural evolution can be further substantiated if we turn our attention to one of the fundamental attributes of living organisms: their power of self-repair, and to the dramatic manifestation of that power in the phenomena of *regeneration* (which Needham called 'one of the more spectacular pieces of magic in the repertoire of living organisms').* It is as fundamental to life as the capacity for reproduction, and in some lower organisms which multiply by fission or budding, regeneration and reproduction are often indistinguishable. Thus if a flatworm is transversely cut into halves, the head part will grow a new tail, and the tail-end will grow a new head; even if cut into half a dozen slices, each will regenerate a complete animal. Flatworms, hydra, sea-squirts and starfish, all of which can regenerate a whole individual from a small fraction of the body, could be called biological holograms.

Higher up on the evolutionary ladder, amphibians are capable of regenerating a lost limb or organ; and once more the magic is performed according to the undoing–redoing formula; the tissue-cells near the amputation stump de-differentiate and *regress* to a quasi-embryonic state, then re-differentiate and re-specialize to form the regenerated structure.†

*See *Insight and Outlook*, Ch. x.; *The Ghost in the Machine* Ch. xiii.

†A classic case of such 'metaplasia' is the regeneration of the crystalline lens of the salamander eye: 'If the lens is carefully removed with fine instruments, it is replaced by a new lens that originates at the upper margin of the iris; the latter is the pigmented part of the eye, enclosing the pupil. The first change, following lens extirpation, is the disappearance of the pigment in the upper iris; that is, a

Now the replacement of a lost limb or eye-lens is a phenomenon of a different order from ordinary wound-healing. The *regenerative potential* of a species provides it with an added safety device in the service of survival – a method of self-repair which relies on the genetic plasticity of uncommitted embryonic cells. But it signifies more than a mere safety device, for we have just seen that the major evolutionary novelties were brought about by a similar retreat from adult to embryonic levels. Indeed, the major steps on the line of ascent which led up to our species could be described as a series of operations of *phylogenetic self-repair*: of escapes from blind alleys by the undoing and remoulding of maladapted structures.

As we continue our ascent toward the higher animals, from reptile to mammal, the power of regenerating bodily structures decreases, and is replaced by the increasing power of the brain and nervous system to reorganize the organism's pattern of behaviour. In the first half of this century, K. S. Lashley, in a series of classical experiments, demolished the notion of the nervous system as a rigid reflex-automaton. He demonstrated that brain tissues which in the rat normally serve a specialized function can, in certain circumstances, take over the function of other, injured brain tissues. For example, he taught his rats certain visual discrimination skills; when he removed their optical cortex, the skills were gone, as one would expect; but contrary to what one would expect, the mutilated rats were able to learn the task again. Some other brain area, not normally specializing in visual learning, must have taken over this function, deputizing for the lost area. Similar feats of what one might call meta-adaptations have been reported in insects, birds, chimpanzees, and so on.*

Lastly, in our own species, the ability to regenerate bodily structures is reduced to a minimum, but compensated by man's unique

---

process of de-differentiation. Next, the two tissue layers that comprise the iris separate and expand at the rim where they are continuous, and form a small vesicle. This vesicle grows downward to assume the normal position of a lens; eventually it becomes detached from the iris and differentiates into a typical lens.'[22]

*See *The Act of Creation*, Book II, Ch. III.

power to re-mould his patterns of thought and behaviour – to meet critical challenges by creative responses. And thus we have come full circle through biological evolution back to the various manifestations of human creativity, based on the undoing-redoing pattern, which runs as a *leit-motif* from paedomorphosis to the revolutionary turning points in science and art; to the mental regeneration at which the regressive techniques in psychotherapy are aimed; and finally to the archetypes of death-and-resurrection, withdrawal-and-return which recur in all mythologies.

9

One of the basic doctrines of the nineteenth-century mechanistic world-view was Clausius' famous 'Second Law of Thermodynamics'. It asserted that the universe was running down towards its final dissolution because its energy is being steadily, inexorably dissipated into the random motion of molecules, until it ends up as a single, amorphous bubble of gas with a uniform temperature just above absolute zero: cosmos dissolving into chaos.

Only fairly recently did science begin to recover from the hypnotic effect of this gloomy vision, by realizing that the Second Law applies only in the special case of so-called 'closed systems' (such as a gas enclosed in a perfectly insulated container), whereas all living organisms are 'open systems' which maintain their complex structure and function by continuously drawing materials and energy from their environment. Instead of 'running down' like a mechanical clockwork that dissipates its energy through friction, a living organism is constantly building 'up' more complex substances from the substances it feeds on, more complex forms of energy from the energies it absorbs, and more complex patterns of information – perceptions, knowledge, stored memories – from the input of its sensory receptors.

But although the facts were there for everyone to see, orthodox evolutionists were reluctant to accept their theoretical implications. The idea that living organisms, in contrast to machines, were primarily *active*, and not merely *reactive*; that instead of passively adapting to their environment they were, to quote Judson Herrick, 'creating in the sense that new patterns of structure and behaviour are constantly fabricated' – such ideas were profoundly distasteful to Darwinians, behaviourists and reductionists in general.[23] That the venerated Second Law, which had been so useful in physics, did not apply to living matter, and was in a sense *reversed* in living matter, was indeed hard to accept by an orthodoxy still convinced that all phenomena of life could ultimately be reduced to the laws of physics.

It was in fact a physicist, not a biologist, the Nobel laureate Erwin Schrödinger, who put an end to the tyranny of the Second Law with his celebrated dictum: 'What an organism feeds on is negative entropy.'[24] Now *entropy* is the term for degraded energy which has been dissipated by friction and other wasteful processes, and cannot be retrieved; in other words, it is a measure of energy gone to waste. The Second Law can be expressed by saying that the entropy of a closed system tends to increase towards a maximum when all of its energy will have been dissipated into the chaotic motions of gas molecules; so if our universe is a closed system, it must eventually 'unwind' itself from cosmos into chaos. Entropy became a key-concept of physics – its alias for Thanatos; it even found its way into Freud's concept of the death-wish (see Chapter II).

'Negative entropy' (or 'negentropy') is thus a somewhat perverse way of referring to the power of living organisms to 'build up' instead of running down, to create complex structures out of simpler elements, integrated patterns out of shapelessness, order out of disorder. The same irrepressible building-up tendency is manifested in the progress of evolution, the emergence of new levels of complexity in the organismic hierarchy and new methods of functional coordination, resulting in greater independence from, and mastery of, the environment.

A few pages earlier, I referred to 'the active striving of living matter towards the optimal realization of the planet's evolutionary potential'. In a similar vein, the veteran biologist and Nobel prize winner Albert Szent – Györgyi proposed to replace 'negentropy', and its negative connotations, by the positive term *syntropy*,

which he defines as an 'innate drive in living matter to perfect
itself'. He also called attention to its equivalent on the psychological level as 'a drive towards synthesis, towards growth,
towards wholeness and self-perfection'.[25]

What all this amounts to is, frankly speaking, a revival of
vitalism, which the reductionist orthodoxy had branded as a dark
superstition. The origin of the concept dates back to Aristotle's
entelechy, the vital principle or function which turns mere substance into a living organism and at the same time strives towards
perfection. Since Aristotle, the concept of a vital force which
infuses life into inanimate substance was taken up by various
authors in various guises: Galen's and Kepler's *facultas formatrix*;
Galvani's 'life force', Leibniz's 'monads'; Goethe's *Gestaltung*,
Bergson's *élan vital*. At the beginning of our century, the term
entelechy was adopted by the German biologist Hans Driesch,
whose classic experiments in embryology and regeneration convinced him that these phenomena cannot be explained by the
laws of physics and chemistry alone, while the opposite school of
'mechanists' claimed that they could be so explained. Owing to
the rapid advances in biochemistry, vitalism kept losing ground
as an unnecessary hypothesis with a mystical flavour – until the
pendulum started to swing in the opposite direction. Schrödinger's revolutionary concept of negentropy, published in 1944,
which found such universal acclaim, reintroduced vitalism
through the back door, as it were.* But it should be called *neo-
vitalism*, to distinguish it from its pre-scientific forerunners. Its
basic message has been summed up with admirable simplicity
by Szent-Györgyi (who can hardly be accused of an unscientific
attitude):

If elementary particles are put together to form an atomic nucleus,
something new is created which can no longer be described in terms of
elementary particles. The same happens over again if you surround

---

*Other terms were coined which amounted to reinstating vitalism in a respec-
table disguise: thus the German biologist Woltereck proposed 'anamorphosis' for
the trend in nature towards the emergence of more and more complex forms,
while L. L. Whyte called it the 'morphic principle'.

this nucleus by electrons and build an atom, when you put atoms together to form a molecule, etc. Inanimate nature stops at the low level of organization of simple molecules. But living systems go on and combine molecules to form macromolecules, macromolecules to form organelles (such as nuclei, mitochondria, chloroplasts, ribosomes or membranes) and eventually put all these together to form the greatest wonder of creation, a cell with its astounding inner regulations. Then it goes on putting cells together to form 'higher organisms' and increasingly more complex individuals, of which you are an example. At every step new, more complex and subtle qualities are created, and so in the end we are faced with properties which have no parallel in the inanimate world, though the basic rules remain unchanged.[26]

By the 'basic rules' he means the laws of physics and chemistry which retain their validity in the realm of biological phenomena but are insufficient to explain them, because they 'have no parallel in the inanimate world'. Hence the postulate of syntropy (or negentropy or *élan vital*) as an 'innate drive in living matter to perfect itself' – or towards an optimal actualization of its evolutionary potential.

In the present theory this 'innate drive' derives from the 'integrative tendency'. It is more specific than the terms I have just quoted, because it is inherent in the conception of hierarchic order, and manifested on every level, from the symbiosis of organelles within the cell, to ecological systems and human societies. Its opponent, the self-asserting tendency, is equally ubiquitous on every level. It provides a clue to the puzzling conservativeness of the evolutionary process as reflected in the phenomena of homology, the stability of species, and the slow rate of change, the survival of 'living fossils' (also known as 'persistent types'); and lastly, when not held in check by the integrative tendency, in the blind alleys of stagnation and over-specialization. For we have seen (Chapter II, 4) that the self-assertive tendency is indeed conservative, intent on preserving and asserting the individuality of the holon '. . . in the here and now of existing conditions, whereas the integrative tendency has the dual function of co-ordinating the constituent parts of a system in its existing state, *and* of generating new levels of organization in evoloving hierarchies – whether biological, social, or cognitive. Thus the self-assertive tendency is oriented towards the present, concerned with self-maintenance, whereas the integrative tendency may be said to work both for the present and towards the future.'

Evolution has been compared to a journey from an unknown origin towards an unknown destination, a sailing along a vast ocean; but we can at least chart the route which carried us from the sea-cucumber stage to the conquest of the moon; and there is no denying that there is a wind which makes the sails move. But whether we say that the wind, coming from the distant past, pushes the boat along, or whether we say that it drags us along into the future, is a matter of choice. The purposiveness of all vital processes, the strategy of the genes and the power of the exploratory drive in animal and man, all seem to indicate that the pull of the future is as real as the pressure of the past. Causality and finality are complementary principles in the sciences of life; if you take out finality and purpose you have taken the life out of biology as well as psychology.*

If this be called vitalism, I have no objection, and shall quote in reply a profound remark by that arch-vitalist, Henri Bergson:

The vitalist principle may indeed not explain much, but it is at least a sort of label affixed to our ignorance, so as to remind us of this occasionally, while mechanism invites us to ignore that ignorance.

But the last word in this chapter belongs to Professor Grassé:

The joint efforts of paleontology and of a molecular biology purged of dogmatism, ought to lead eventually to the discovery of the precise mechanism o evolution – but possibly without revealing to us the causes which determine the direction of evolutionary lineages, and the purposefulness of structures, functions and vital cycles. It seems possible that confronted with these problems, biology is reduced to helplessness and must hand over to metaphysics. [27]

---

*Even the elusive Waddington, in one of his later books, argued in favour of a 'quasi-finalistic view'.[28]

PART FOUR

New Horizons

XII

FREE WILL IN A HIERARCHIC CONTEXT

I

'If Cleopatra's nose had been shorter,' remarked Pascal, 'the history of the world would have been different.' And if his contemporary, Descartes, had kept a poodle, the history of philosophy would have been different. The poodle would have taught Descartes that contrary to his doctrine, animals are not machines, and hence the human body is not a machine, forever separated from the mind, which he thought to be located in the pineal gland.

A diametrically opposite view is summed up in another unforgettable aphorism of Bergson's: 'The unconsciousness of a falling stone is something quite different from the unconsciousness of a growing cabbage.'

Bergson's attitude is close to panpsychism: the theory that some rudimentary kind of sentience is present throughout the animal kingdom and even in plants. Some speculatively inclined modern physicists would attribute a psychic element even to sub-atomic particles. Thus panpsychism postulates a continuum extending from the growing cabbage to human self-awareness, while Cartesian dualism regards consciousness as an exclusive possession of man, and places a kind of Iron Curtain between matter and mind.

Panpsychism and Cartesian dualism mark opposite ends of the philosophical spectrum. I shall not go into the various elaborations to which they have given rise – interactionism, parallelism, epiphenomenalism, identity-hypothesis, and so forth; instead I shall attempt to show that the concept of the multi-levelled holarchy is well suited to shed some new light on this very old problem. As we shall see, the hierarchic approach replaces the panpsychist's continuously ascending curve from cabbage to man by a whole series of discrete steps – a staircase instead of a slope; and it replaces the Cartesian single wall separating mind from body by a series of swing-gates as it were.

To start with, everyday experience tells us that consciousness is not an all-or-nothing affair but a *matter of degrees*. There are levels of consciousness which form ascending series from the unconsciousness under an anaesthetic, through the drowsiness induced by milder drugs, through the performance of complex routines like tying one's shoelaces automatically with an 'absent mind', through full awareness and self-awareness to the self's awareness of its awareness of itself – and so on, without hitting a ceiling.

In the downward direction we are also faced with a multiplicity of levels of consciousness or sentience which extend far below the human level. Ethologists who have a close *rapport* with animals generally refuse to draw a line indicating the lower limit of consciousness on the evolutionary ladder, while neurophysiologists talk of the 'spinal consciousness' in lower vertebrates and even of the 'protoplasmic consciousness' of protozoa. To mention a single example: Sir Alister Hardy has given us a vivid description of *Foraminifera* – single-celled miniature sea-animals related to amoeba, which build elaborate microscopic 'houses' out of the needle-like speculae of dead sponges – houses which Hardy calls 'marvels of engineering skill'.[1] Yet these primitive protozoans have neither eyes nor a nervous system and are but a gelatinous mass of flowing protoplasm. Thus the hierarchy appears to be open-ended both in the upward and downward direction.

To quote an eminent ethologist, W. H. Thorpe:

The evidence suggests that at the lower levels of the evolutionary scale consciousness, if it exists, must be of a very generalized kind, so to say unstructured; and that with the development of purposive behaviour and a powerful faculty of attention, consciousness associated with expectation will become more and more vivid and precise.[2]

However, it is essential to realize that these gradations in the 'structuring, vividness and precision' of consciousness are found not only along the evolutionary ladder, and in members of the same species at different stages of their ontogeny, but also within adult individuals when confronted by different situations. I am referring to the deceptively trivial fact that one and the same activity – driving a car – can be either performed *automatically*, without conscious awareness of one's own actions, or accompanied by varying *degrees of awareness*. Driving along a familiar road with little traffic on it, I can hand over to the 'automatic pilot' in my nervous system and think about something else. In other words, the task of controlling and coordinating my driving performance has been shifted from a higher to a lower level in my mental hierarchy. Vice versa, overtaking another car requires an *upward* shift of control to the level of semi-conscious routine; and overtaking in a tricky situation requires a further shift to full awareness of what I am doing.

There are several factors which determine how much, if any, conscious attention is paid by a person to the activity in which he is engaged. The most important of these factors in the present context is habit-formation. While learning a skill we must concentrate on every detail of what we are doing. We learn laboriously to recognize and name the printed letters of the alphabet, to ride a bicycle, to hit the right key on the piano or typewriter. But with increasing mastery and practice, the typist can let his fingers 'look after themselves'; we read, write, drive 'automatically', which is another way of saying that the rules which govern the exercise of the skill are now applied unconsciously. This condensation of learning into habit may be looked upon as a process *which transforms mental into mechanical activities* – mind-processes into machine-processes. It starts with infancy and never stops.

This tendency towards the progressive automatization of habits has a positive side: it conforms to the principle of parsimony. By manipulating the wheel of the car mechanically, I am able to carry on a conversation; and if the rules of grammar and syntax did not operate automatically I could not attend to meaning. But on the other hand the progressive mechanization of habits and routines threatens to turn us into automata. Man is not a machine, but most of the day we behave like machines – or sleepwalkers, without mentally attending to the activities we are engaged in. This applies not only to manipulative routines – wielding knife and fork at table, lighting a cigarette, or signing a letter – but also to mental activities: one can read a whole paragraph in a boring book 'absent-mindedly' without taking in a single word. Karl Lashley once quoted a colleague of his, a professor of psychology, who told him: 'When I have to give a lecture I turn my mouth loose and go to sleep.'

Thus consciousness may be described, somewhat perversely, as that special attribute of an activity which *decreases in direct proportion to habit formation*. The condensation of learning into habit is accompanied by a dimming of the lights of awareness. We expect therefore that the opposite process will take place when routine is disturbed by running into some unexpected obstacle or problem: that this will cause an instantaneous switch from 'mechanical' to 'minding' or 'mindful' behaviour. Let a kitten suddenly cross the road on which you have been driving absent-mindedly, and your previously absent mind will return in a flash to take over control, i.e., to make an instant decision whether to run over the kitten or risk the safety of your passengers by slamming on the brakes. What happens in such a crisis is a sudden transfer of control of an ongoing activity to a higher level of the multilevelled hierarchy, because the decision to be made is beyond the competence of the automatic pilot and must be referred to 'higher quarters'. In the present theory this sudden shift of the control of behaviour from a lower to a higher level of the hierarchy – analogous to the physicist's quantum jump – is the essence of conscious decision-making and of the subjective experience of free will.

The opposite process, as we have seen, is the mechanization of routines, the enslavement to habit. We thus arrive at a dynamic view of a continuous two-way traffic up and down the mind-body hierarchy. The automatization of habits and skills implies a steady *downward* motion as on a moving escalator, thus making room in the upper strata for more sophisticated activities – but also threatening to turn us into automata. Each downward step is a transition from the mental to the mechanical; each upward shift in the hierarchy produces more vivid and structured states of consciousness.

These alternations between robot-like and luminous behaviour are, as I said, a matter of everyday experience. On some rare occasions, however, creative people experience a quick oscillation – a *reculer pour mieux sauter* – from the over-articulated, over-specialized strata in the cognitive hierarchy down to more primitive and fluid levels, and up again to a re-structured upper level.

2

Classical dualism knows only a single mind–body barrier. The holarchic approach on which the present theory is based implies a *pluralistic instead of a dualistic view*: the transformation of physical events into mental events, and vice versa, is effected not by a single leap over a single barrier, but by a whole series of steps up or down through the swing-gates of the multi-levelled hierarchy.

As a concrete example, let us remember (Chapter I, 6) how we convert air-waves arriving at the ear-drum, which are physical events, into ideas, which are mental events. It isn't done 'in one go'. In order to decode the message which the air-pulsations carry the listener must perform a rapid series of 'quantum jumps' from one level of the language hierarchy to the next higher one: phonemes have no meaning and can only be interpreted on the level of morphemes; words must be referred to their context, sentences to a larger frame of reference. Active speech – the spelling out of a previously unverbalized idea or image – involves the reverse process: it converts mental events into the mechanical motions of the vocal cords. This again is achieved by a whole intermediate series of rapid but distinct steps, each of which triggers off linguistic routines of a more and more automatized type: the structuring of the intended message into a linear sequence, processing it according to the silent dictates of grammar and syntax; and lastly, innervating the entirely mechanical motion-patterns of the organs of speech. Noam Chomsky's psycholinguistic hierarchy was anticipated in *A Midsummer Night's Dream*:

> As imagination bodies forth
> The forms of things unknown, the poet's pen
> Turns them to shapes and gives to airy nothing
> A local habitation and a name.

Let me repeat: each downward step in the stepwise conversion of airy nothings into the physical motions of the vocal cords entails a transfer of control to more automatized automatisms; each step upward leads to more mentalistic processes of mentation. Thus the mind–body dichotomy is not localized along a single boundary or interface, as in classical dualism, but is present on every intermediary level of the hierarchy.

On this view, the categorical distinction between mind and body fades away, and instead of it 'mental' and 'mechanical' become complementary attributes of processes on every level. The dominance of one of these attributes over the other – whether the activity of knotting my tie is performed mindfully or mechanically – depends on the flow of traffic in the hierarchy, whether the shifts of control proceed in an upward or downward direction through the swing-gates. Thus even the lower, visceral reaches of the hierarchy, regulated by the autonomic nervous system, can apparently be brought under mental control through Yoga practices or biofeedback methods. And vice versa – to say it once more – when I am sleepy or bored, I can perform the supposedly mental activity of reading a paper – without 'taking in' a single word.

We are in the habit of talking of 'mind' as if it were a thing, which it is not – nor is matter, for that matter. Mentating, thinking, remembering, imagining are *processes* in a reciprocal or complementary relationship to mechanical processes. At this point of the argument modern physics provides us with a pertinent analogy: the so-called 'Principle of Complementarity', which is fundamental to its whole theoretical structure. It states, put into non-technical language, that the elementary constituents of matter – electrons, protons, neutrons, etc. – are ambiguous, Janus-faced entities which under certain conditions behave like solid corpuscles, but under other conditions behave like waves in a non-substantial medium. Werner Heisenberg, Nobel laureate and one of the pioneers in sub-atomic physics, commented:

The concept of Complementarity is meant to describe a situation in which we can look at one and the same event through two different frames of reference. These two frames mutually exclude each other, but they also complement each other, and only the juxtaposition of these contradictory frames provides an exhaustive view . . . What we call Complementarity accords very neatly with the Cartesian dualism of matter and mind.[3]

Although this refers to classical dualism and not to the plurality of levels proposed here, the analogy retains its attractiveness. The knowledge that an electron will behave as a particle or a wave, depending on the experimental set-up, makes it easier to accept that man too will, according to circumstances, function as an automaton or a conscious being.

Another Nobel laureate, Wolfgang Pauli, thought along similar lines:

The general problem of the relationship between mind and body, between the inward and the outward, cannot be said to have been solved . . . Modern science has perhaps brought us nearer to a more satisfactory understanding of this relationship by introducing the concept of complementarity into physics itself.[4]

One might add to these quotations almost any amount of similar pronouncements by the pioneers of contemporary physics. It is evident that they regard the parallel between the two types of complementarity – body/mind and corpuscle/wave – as more than a superficial analogy. It is, in fact, a very deep analogy, but in order to appreciate what it implies, we must try to get some inkling of what the physicist means by the 'waves' which constitute one of the two aspects of matter. Commonsense, that treacherous counsellor, tells us that to produce a wave, *there must be something that waves* – a vibrating piano-string, or undulating water, or air in motion. But the conception of 'matter-waves' *excludes by definition* any medium with material attributes as a carrier of the wave. Thus we are faced with the task of imagining the vibration of a string but without the string, or the grin of the Cheshire cat but without the cat. We may, however, derive some comfort from the analogy between the two complementarities. The contents of consciousness that pass through the mind, from the perception of colour to thoughts and images, are un-substantial 'airy nothings', yet they are somehow linked to the material brain, as the unsubstantial 'waves' of physics are somehow linked to the material aspects of the sub-atomic particles.

It seems that the dual aspect of man reflects the dual aspect of the ultimate constituents of the universe.

3

The 'spelling out' of an intention – whether it is the verbal articulation of an idea or just the stubbing out of a cigarette – is a process which triggers successive sub-routines into action – functional holons from arithmetical skills down to mechanical muscle-contractions: in other words, it is a process of *particularizations* of a general intent. Vice versa, the referring of decisions to higher levels is an *integrative* process which tends to produce a higher degree of coordination and wholeness of the experience. How does the problem of free will fit into this schema?

We have seen that all our bodily and mental skills are governed by *fixed rules* and more or less *flexible strategies*. The rules of chess define the permissible moves, strategy determines the choice of the actual move. The problem of free will then boils down to the question how such choices are made. The chess player's choice may be called 'free' in the sense that it is not determined by the rules. But though his choice is free in the above sense, it is certainly not random. On the contrary, it is guided by considerations of a much greater complexity – involving a higher level of the hierarchy – than the simple rules of the game. Compare the game of noughts and crosses with the game of chess. In both cases my strategic choice of the next move is 'free' in the sense of not being determined by the rules. But noughts and crosses offer only a few alternative choices guided by relatively simple strategies, whereas the chess player is guided by considerations on a much higher level of complexity with an incomparably larger variety of choices – that is, *more degrees of freedom.** Moreover, the strategic considerations which guide his choice again form an ascending hierarchy. On the lowest level are tactical precepts such as occupying the centre squares of the chessboard, avoiding loss of material, protecting the king – precepts which every duffer can master, but which the master is free to overrule by shifting his attention to higher levels of strategy where material may be sacrificed and the king exposed in an apparently crazy move which, however, is more promising from the viewpoint of the game as a whole. Thus in the course of the game decisions have to be constantly referred to higher echelons with more degrees of freedom, and each shift upward is accompanied by a heightening of awareness and the experience of making a free choice. Generally speaking, in these sophisticated domains the constraining code of rules (whether of chess or of the grammar of speech) operates more or less automatically, on unconscious or preconscious levels, whereas the strategic choices are aided by the beam of focal awareness.

To repeat: the degrees of freedom in the hierarchy increase with ascending order, and each upward shift of attention to higher levels, each handing over of a decision to higher echelons, is accompanied by the experience of free choice. But is it merely a subjective experience fraught with illusion? I do not think this is the case. After all, freedom cannot be defined in absolute, only in relative terms, as freedom *from* some specific constraint. The ordinary prisoner has more freedom than one in solitary confinement; democracy allows more freedom than tyranny; and so on. Similar gradations are found in the multilevelled hierarchies of

---

*The term 'degrees of freedom' is used in physics to denote the number of independent variables defining the state of a system.

thought and action, where with each step upwards to a higher level *the relative importance of the constraints decreases and the number of choices increases*. But this does not mean that there is a highest level free from all constraints. On the contrary, the present theory implies that the hierarchy is open-ended towards infinite regress, both in the upward and downward direction. We tend to believe that the ultimate responsibility rests with the apex of the hierarchy – but that apex is never at rest, it keeps receding. The self eludes the grasp of its own awareness. Facing downward and outward, a person is aware of the task in hand, an awareness that fades with each step down into the dimness of routine, the darkness of visceral processes, the various degrees of unawareness of the growing cabbage and the falling stone, and finally dissolves in the ambiguity of the Janus-faced electron. But in the upward direction the hierarchy is also open-ended and leads into the infinite regress of the self. Looking upwards, or inwards, man has a feeling of wholeness, of a solid core to his personality from which his decisions emanate, and which in Penfield's words, 'controls his thinking and directs the searchlight of his attention'. But this metaphor of the great neuro-surgeon is deceptive. When a priest chides a penitent for indulging in sinful thoughts, both priest and penitent tacitly assume that behind the agency which switches on the sinful thoughts, there is another agency which controls the switchboard, and so on *ad infinitum*. The ultimate culprit, the self which directs the searchlight of my attention, can never be caught in its focal beam. The experiencing subject can never fully become the object of his experience; at best he can achieve successive approximations. If learning and knowing consist in making oneself a private model of the universe, it follows that the model can never include a complete model of itself, because it must always lag one step behind the process which it is supposed to represent. With each upward-shift of awareness towards the apex of the hierarchy – the self as an integrated whole – it recedes like a mirage. 'Know thyself' is the most venerable and the most tantalizing command. Total awareness of the self, the identity of the knower and the known, though always in sight is never achieved. It could only be achieved by reaching the peak of the hierarchy which is always one step removed from the climber.

This is an old conundrum, but it seems to blossom into new life in the context of the open-ended holarchy. Determinism fades away not only on the sub-atomic quantum level, but also in the upward direction, where on successively higher levels the constraints diminish, and the degrees of freedom increase, *ad infinitum*. At the same time the nightmarish concept of predictability and predestination is swallowed up in the infinite regress. Man is neither a plaything of the gods, nor a marionette suspended on his chromosomes. To put it more soberly, similar conclusions are implied in Sir Karl Popper's proposition that no information-processing system can embody within itself an up-to-date representation of itself, *including that representation*.[5] Somewhat similar arguments have been advanced by Michael Polanyi[6] and Donald MacKay.[7]

Some philosophers dislike the concept of infinite regress because it reminds them of the little man inside the little man inside the little man. But we cannot get away from the infinite. What would mathematics, what would physics be without the infinitesimal calculus? Self-consciousness has been compared to a mirror in which the individual contemplates his own activities. It would perhaps be more appropriate to compare it to a Hall of Mirrors where one mirror reflects one's reflection in another mirror, and so on. Infinity stares us in the face, whether we look at the stars or search for our own identities. Reductionism has no use for it, but a true science of life must let infinity in and never lose sight of it.

4

The problem of Free Will versus Determinism has haunted philosophers and theologians from time immemorial. Ordinary mortals are rarely bothered by the paradox concerning the agency which directs one's thinking, and of the agency behind that agency, because, paradoxical or not, they take it for granted that 'I' am responsible for my actions. In *The Ghost in the Machine* I invented a short parable to illustrate the point. It took the form of a dialogue at high table at an Oxford college between an elderly don of strictly deterministic persuasion, and a young Australian guest of uninhibited temperament. The Australian exclaims: 'If you go on denying that I am free to make my own decisions, I'll punch you in the nose!'

The old man gets red in the face: 'I deplore your unpardonable behaviour.'

'I apologize. I lost my temper.

'You really ought to control yourself.'

'Thank you. The experiment was conclusive.'

It was indeed. 'Unpardonable', 'ought to', and 'control yourself' are all expressions which imply that the Australian's behaviour was *not* determined by his chromosomes and upbringing, that he was free to choose whether to behave politely or rudely. Whatever one's philosophical convictions, in everyday life it is impossible to carry on without the implicit belief in personal responsibility; and responsibility implies freedom of choice. The subjective experience of freedom is as much a given datum as the sensation of colour, or the feeling of pain.

Yet that experience is constantly being eroded by the formation of habits and mechanical routines, which tend to turn us into automata. When the Duke of Wellington was asked whether he agreed that habit was man's second nature he exclaimed: 'Second nature? It is ten times nature.' Habit is the denial of creativity and the negation of freedom; a self-imposed straitjacket of which the wearer is unaware.

Another enemy of freedom is passion, or more specifically, an excess of the self-asserting emotions. When these are aroused, the control of behaviour is taken over by those primitive levels in the hierarchy which are correlated to the 'old brain'. The loss of freedom resulting from this downward shift is reflected in the legal concept of 'diminished responsibility', and in the subjective feeling of acting under a compulsion – expressed by colloquialisms such as: 'I couldn't help it', 'I lost my head', 'I must have been out of my mind'.

It is at this point that the moral dilemma of judging others arises. Ruth Ellis was the last woman to be hanged in England –

for shooting her lover 'in cold blood', as it was said. How am I
to know, and how could the jury know, whether and to what
extent her responsibility was 'diminished' when she acted as she
did, and whether she could 'help it'? Compulsion and free will
are philosophical concepts at opposite ends of a scale, but there is
no pointer attached to the scale which I could read. In dilemmas
like this the safest procedure is to apply two different standards:
to ascribe a minimum of free will to the other, and a maximum
to oneself. There is an old French saying: *Tout comprendre c'est
tout pardonner* – to understand all is to forgive all. In the light of
the above, this should be altered to: *Tout comprendre, ne rien se
pardonner* : understand all – forgive yourself nothing.

It may be difficult to live up to, but at least it is a safe maxim.

XIII

PHYSICS AND METAPHYSICS

I

'Half of my friends accuse me of an excess of scientific pedantry; the other half of unscientific leanings towards preposterous subjects such as extra-sensory perception (ESP), which they include in the domain of the supernatural. However, it is comforting to know that the same accusations are levelled at an élite of scientists, who make excellent company in the dock.' Thus the opening paragraph of *The Roots of Coincidence*. Since then, the 'élite' of scientists has apparently grown into a majority. In 1973 the *New Scientist*, that much respected English weekly, sent out a questionnaire to its readers, inviting them to express their opinions on the subject of extra-sensory perception. Out of the 1,500 readers – nearly all of them scientists and engineers – who answered the questionnaire, 67 per cent regarded ESP either as an 'established fact' or 'a likely possibility'.[1]

Even earlier (1967), the New York Academy of Science held a symposium on parapsychology, and in 1969 the American Association for the Advancement of Science (the equivalent of the British Association) approved the application of the Parapsychology Association to become affiliated to that august body. Two previous applications had been rejected; the approval of the third was a sign of the changing intellectual climate; and for parapsychology the ultimate seal of respectability.

Accordingly, it seems to me unnecessary to recapitulate here the progress of parapsychology, from spiritistic seances in darkened Victorian drawing-rooms to a modern empirical science employing computerized statistics, Geiger counters and other sophisticated electronic equipment. In the pages that follow I shall no longer be concerned with the question whether telepathy and kindred phenomena *exist* – which, in view of the large body of accumulated evidence, I have come to take for granted* – but the implications of these phenomena for our world-view.

That world-view, in so far as the educated lamyan is concerned, places parapsychology and physics at opposite ends of the spectrum of knowledge and experience. Physics is regarded by the educated layman as the queen of the 'exact sciences', with direct access to the immutable 'laws of nature' which govern the material universe. In contrast to this, parapsychology deals with subjective, capricious and unpredictable phenomena which manifest themselves in apparently lawless ways, or in direct contradiction to the laws of nature. Physics is, as the academic jargon has it, a 'hard-nosed' science, completely down to earth, whereas parapsychologists float somewhere in nebulous Cloud-cuckoo-land.

This view of physics was indeed perfectly legitimate and immensely productive during the roughly two centuries when the term 'physics' was practically synonymous with Newtonian mechanics. To quote a contemporary physicist, Fritjof Capra:

Questions about the essential nature of things were answered in classical physics by the Newtonian mechanistic model of the universe which, much in the same way as the Democritean model in ancient Greece, reduced all phenomena to the motions and interactions of hard indestructible atoms. The properties of these atoms were abstracted from the macroscopic notion of billiard balls, and thus from sensory experience. Whether this notion could actually be applied to the world of atoms was not questioned.[2]

Or, in Newton's own words:

It seems probable to me that God in the beginning formed matter in solid, massy, hard, impenetrable, movable particles, of such sizes and figures, and with such other properties, and in such proportion to space, as most conduced to the end for which he formed them; and that these primitive particles being solids, are incomparably harder than any porous bodies compounded of them; even so very hard, as

*Some of this evidence is discussed in *The Roots of Coincidence*, *The Challenge of Chance* and several lectures included in *The Heel of Achilles*.

never to wear or break in pieces; no ordinary power being able to divide what God himself made one in the first creation.[3]

If you leave out the reference to God, the above quotation, dating from A.D. 1704, still reflects the implicit credo of our educated layman. Of course he knows that the formerly indivisible atoms can be split (with sinister results); but he believes – if he gives any thought to the matter – that *inside* the atom there are other, truly indivisible billiard balls called protons, neutrons, electrons, etc. However, if he were sufficiently interested, he would also discover that the giant atom-smashers have made mincemeat of protons, neutrons, etc.; that the ultimate (to date) elementary particles are called 'quarks',* and that some quarks have a physical attribute called 'charm'. The exotic terminology of sub-atomic physicists also includes 'the eightfold way', 'strangeness', and the 'bootstrap principle' – which goes to show that they are well aware of the surrealistic nature of the world they have created; behind the schoolboyish humour there is the awed recognition of mystery. For on this sub-microscopic level the criteria of reality are fundamentally different from those we apply on our macro-level; inside the atom our concepts of space, time, matter and causality are no longer valid, and physics turns into metaphysics with a strong flavour of mysticism. As a result of this development, the unthinkable phenomena of parapsychology appear somewhat less preposterous in the light of the unthinkable propositions of relativity and quantum physics.

One such proposition I have already mentioned: the Principle of Complementarity which turns the so-called 'elementary building-blocks' of classical physics into Janus-faced entities that behave under certain circumstances like hard little lumps of matter, but in other circumstances as waves or vibrations propagated in a vacuum. As Sir William Bragg put it, they seem to be waves on Mondays, Wednesdays and Fridays, and particles on Tuesdays, Thursdays and Saturdays. We have seen that some of the pioneers of quantum physics, as well as their con-

---

*A term borrowed from *Finnegans Wake*. Quark in German means curds or soft cheese of a pungent and generally evil-smelling sort.

temporary successors, regarded the Principle of Complementarity as a fitting paradigm for the mind–body dichotomy. This was cheering news to parapsychologists; we must remember, however, that Cartesian dualism recognizes only the two realms of mind and matter, whereas the present theory proposes a series of levels, equipped with 'swing-gates', opening now this way, now that. Both in our daily behaviour and on the sub-atomic level, the gates are kept swinging all the time.

2

The concept of matter-waves, launched in the 1920s by de Broglie and Schrödinger, completed the process of the *dematerialization of matter*. It had started much earlier, with Einstein's magic formula $E = mc^2$* which implies that the mass of a particle must not be conceived as some stable elementary material but as a concentrated pattern of energy, locked up in what appears to us as matter. The 'stuff' of which protons and electrons are made is rather like the stuff of which dreams are made, as a glance at the illustration on p. 246 suggests. It is an example of the type of events which takes place all the time in the physicists' bubble chambers, where high-energy 'elementary' particles collide and annihilate each other or create new particles which give rise to a new chain of events. The particles in question are of course infinitesimally small and many have a lifetime much shorter than a millionth of a second; yet they leave tracks in the bubble chamber comparable to the visible trails which invisible jet-planes leave in the sky. The length, thickness and curvature of the tracks enables the physicists to decide which of the two-hundred-odd 'elementary particles' has caused it, and also to identify 'particles' previously unknown.

But the fundamental lesson which the bubble chamber and other sophisticated instruments teach the physicist is that on the sub-atomic level our concepts of space, time, matter and conventional logic no longer apply. Thus two particles may collide and

*Where E stands for energy, m for mass, and c for the velocity of light.

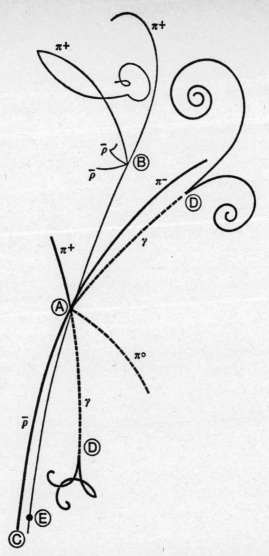

Diagram tracing a bubble-chamber photograph of subatomic events, from a Photo CERN – courtesy of European Organisation for Nuclear Research, Geneva. The caption (which leaves non-physicists none the wiser) reads: 'interaction in the heavy liquid bubble chamber, Gargamelle. At A an incident antiproton which enters the chamber at C (see plan) annihilates a resident proton giving rise to a +ve and −ve pion, a neutral pion, and two gamma rays each of which converts (at D) into an electron positron pair. A second event is recorded where a particle entering at E interacts at B and produces two antiprotons and two +ve pions one of which collides subsequently twice with resident particles.'

break into pieces, but these pieces may turn out to be not smaller than the original particles – because the kinetic energy liberated in the course of the collision has been transformed into 'mass'. Or a photon, the elementary unit of light, which has no mass, can give birth to an electron–positron pair which *does* have mass; and that pair might subsequently collide, and by the reverse process transform itself into a photon. The fantastic events in the bubble chamber have been compared to the dance of Shiva, with its rhythmic alternations of creation and destruction.*

All this is a long way from the beguilingly simple Rutherford–Bohr model of the beginning of our century, that represented atoms as miniature solar systems, in which negatively charged electrons circle like planets around a positively charged nucleus. Alas, the model ran into one paradox after another. The electrons were found to behave quite unlike planets – they kept jumping from one orbit into another without passing through the space between them – as if the earth were instantaneously transferred into the orbit of Mars in a single jump, ignoring space. The orbits themselves were not well-defined trajectories, but wide blurred tracks, appropriate to the wave-aspect of the electron which was 'smeared' all over the orbit, and it became as meaningless to ask at what exact point in space the electron was at a given moment, as it was meaningless to try to pin down a wave. As Bertrand Russell has put it:

The idea that there is a hard little lump there, which *is* the electron or proton, is an illegitimate intrusion of common sense notions derived from touch.[4]

The atomic *nuclei* in the model did not fare better than the orbiting 'planets'. The nuclei turned out to be compounds of particles, mainly protons and neutrons, held together by other particles and forces which defy any visual model or representation in terms of our sensory experience. According to one hypothesis, neutrons and protons race around inside the nucleus with veloci-

*Capra (1975).

ties of about 40,000 miles per second – a quarter of the speed of light. As Capra put it:

Nuclear matter is thus a form of matter entirely different from anything we experience 'up here' in our macroscopic environment. We can perhaps picture it best as tiny drops of an extremely dense liquid which is boiling and bubbling most fiercely.[5]

3

In earlier books[6] I have discussed some of the most notorious paradoxes of quantum physics: Thomson's experiments which made the same electron go through two minute holes in a screen at the same time (which, Sir Cyril Burt commented, 'is more than a ghost can do'); the paradox of 'Schrödinger's cat', which can be shown to be both alive and dead at the same time; Feynman's diagrams in which particles are made to move for a brief instant backward in time (which earned him the Nobel Prize in 1965); and the 'Einstein–Podolsky–Rosen paradox' (or EPR paradox) to which I shall briefly return. The situation has been summed up by Heisenberg himself, one of the chief architects of quantum theory:

The very attempt to conjure up a picture of elementary particles and think of them in visual terms is wholly to misinterpret them . . .[7]
Atoms are not *things*. The electrons which form an atom's shells are no longer things in the sense of classical physics, things which could be unambiguously described by concepts like location, velocity, energy, size. When we get down to the atomic level, the objective world in space and time no longer exists.[8]

4

Werner Heisenberg will probably be remembered as the great iconoclast who put an end to causal determinism in physics – and thereby in philosophy – by his celebrated 'Principle of Indeterminacy' which is as fundamental to modern physics as Newton's Laws of Motion were to classical mechanics. I have tried to convey its meaning by a rather simplistic analogy.[9] A certain static quality of many Renaissance paintings is due to the fact that the human figures in the foreground and the distant landscape in the background are both in sharp focus – which is optically impossible: when we focus on a close object the background gets blurred, and vice versa. The Principle of Indeterminacy implies that in studying the sub-atomic panorama the physicist is confronted with a similar predicament (though of course for quite different reasons). In classical physics a particle must at any time have a definite location and velocity; on the sub-atomic level, however, the situation turns out to be radically different. The more accurately the physicist is able to determine the location of an electron, for instance, the more uncertain its velocity becomes; and vice versa, the more exactly he is able to determine the particle's velocity, the more blurred, i.e., indeterminate, its location becomes. This indeterminacy is not caused by the imperfection of our techniques of observation, but by the inherently dual nature of the electron as both 'particle' and 'wavicle', which makes it both practically *and theoretically* impossible to pin down. But this implies nothing less than that down on the sub-atomic level the universe at any given moment is in a quasi-undecided state, and that its state in the next moment is to some extent indeterminate or 'free'. Thus if an ideal photographer with a perfect camera took a picture of the total universe at any given moment, the picture would be to some extent fuzzy, owing to the indeterminate state of its ultimate constituents.* Because of this fuzziness, physicists' statements about sub-atomic processes can only refer to probabilities, not to certainties; in the microworld the laws of probability supplant those of causality: 'nature is unpredictable' – to quote Heisenberg once more.

Thus for the last fifty years, since the advent of quantum theory, it has become a commonplace among physicists of the dominant school (the so-called Copenhagen School) that the strictly deterministic, mechanistic world-view can no longer be upheld; it has become a Victorian anachronism. The nineteenth-

---

*It can be shown that however short the exposure time, the Indeterminacy Principle will still blur the picture.

century model of the universe as a mechanical clockwork is a shambles and since the concept of matter itself has been de-materialized, *materialism can no longer claim to be a scientific philosophy.*

5

I have quoted some of the giants (most of them Nobel laureates)* who were jointly responsible for dismantling the antiquated clockwork, and attempted to replace it by a more sophisticated model, sufficiently flexible to accommodate logical paradoxes and wild theories previously considered unthinkable. During this half century countless new discoveries have been made – by radio-telescopes scanning the skies and in the bubble chambers recording the sub-atomic dance of Shiva – but no satisfactory model and no coherent philosophy has yet emerged comparable to that of classical, Newtonian physics. One might describe this post-Newtonian era as one of the periods of 'creative anarchy' which recur in the history of every science when the old concepts have become obsolete, and the breakthrough leading to a new synthesis is not yet in sight.† At the time of writing, theoretical physics itself seems to be immersed in a bubble chamber, with the weirdest hypotheses criss-crossing each other's tracks. I shall mention a few, which seem pertinent to our theme.

First, there have been some eminent physicists, among them Einstein, de Broglie, Schrödinger, Vigier, and David Bohm, who were unwilling to accept the indeterminacy and acausality of sub-atomic events – which in their opinion amounted to saying that these events were ruled by blind chance. (Einstein's famous phrase: 'God does not play dice with the world' reflects this attitude.) They were inclined to believe in the existence of a sub-stratum below the sub-atomic level, which ruled and deter-mined those seemingly indeterminate processes. This was called

*The frequent mention of Nobel awards is intended as a reassurance that the strange theories quoted in this chapter were propounded not by cranks but by physicists of international renown.

†cf above, Ch. VIII.

the theory of 'hidden variables' – which, however, has been abandoned even by its staunchest supporters because it seemed to lead simply nowhere.

But although unacceptable to the physicist, the 'hidden variables' provided a fertile field for metaphysical and parapsychological theorizings. Theologians proposed that Divine Providence might work from within the fuzzy gaps in the matrix of physical causality ('the god of the gaps'). Sir John Eccles, Nobel laureate in physiology, proposed that the quantum indeterminacy of 'critically poised' neurons in the brain made room for the exercise of free will:

In the active cerebral cortex within twenty milliseconds, the pattern of discharge of even hundreds of thousands of neurons would be modified as a result of an 'influence' that initially caused the discharge of merely one neuron . . .

Thus, the neurophysiological hypothesis is that the 'will' modifies the spatio-temporal activity of the neuronal network by exerting spatio-temporal 'fields of influence' that become affected through this unique detector function of the active cerebral cortex.[10]

The above applies to the action of individual minds on their 'own' brains. In the concluding sections of his book, however, Eccles includes ESP and PK (psychokinesis) in his theory. He accepts the experimental results of Rhine and his school as evidence for a generalized 'two-way traffic' between mind and matter, and of direct communication channels between mind and mind. He believes that ESP and PK are weak and irregular manifestations of the *same* principle which allows an individual's mental volition to influence his own material brain, and the material brain to give rise to conscious experiences.

The theory is not worked out in detail, but it is indicative of current trends of thought among enlightened neurophysiologists – from the late Sir Charles Sherrington to Penfield and Gray Walter, whom I have quoted in earlier works.

It is also interesting to note that Penfield, the neurologist, revived an unduly neglected hypothesis by Eddington, the astronomer, which postulated a 'correlated behaviour of the individual particles of matter, which he [Eddington] assumed to occur for matter in liaison with mind. The behaviour of such matter would stand in sharp contrast to the uncorrelated or random behaviour of particles that is postulated in physics.'[11]

Thus matter 'in liaison with mind' displays specific properties not otherwise found in the realm of physics – a proposition not far removed from panpsychism. Another astrononomer, V. A. Firsoff, suggested that 'mind was a universal entity or interaction of the same order as electricity or gravitation, and there must be a *modulus of transformation*, analogous to Einstein's famous equation $E = mc^2$.'[12]

In other words, as matter can be transformed into physical energy, so physical energy must be transformable into psychic energy, and vice versa.

In recent years, there has been a spate of such theories, intended to bridge the gap between quantum physics and parapsychology, which sound like science fiction – but the same remark applies, as we have seen, to the basic proposition of modern physics itself. Thus the brilliant Cambridge mathematician, Adrian Dobbs, has put forward an elaborate theory of telepathy and precognition, in which hypothetical 'psytrons', with properties similar to the neutrinos,* were regarded as the carriers of ESP phenomena, capable of impinging directly on neurons in the recipient's brain.[13] Among more recent writers, Dr E. Harris Walker, a ballistics expert, has developed an ingenious quantum–mechanical theory, in which the hypothetical 'hidden variables' are identified with consciousness as 'non-physical, but real entities', independent of space and time, and 'connected to the physical world by means of the quantum–mechanical wave function'.[14] His theory includes parapsychological phenomena, but it involves advanced mathematics and is altogether too technical to be discussed here.

Lifting our sights from the bubble chamber to the starry skies,

---

*Neutrinos are particles of cosmic origin, devoid of physical attributes (mass, weight, charge, magnetic field) traversing the earth (and our bodies) in swarms of billions at the speed of light.

our commonsense notions of space, time, and causality turn out to be as inadequate as when we try to apply them to the sub-atomic domain. In the relativistic universe space is curved and the flow of time is speeded up or slowed down according to the time-keeper's state of motion. Moreover, if parts of the universe are furnished with galaxies of anti-matter,* which many astro-nomers believe to be the case, there is a fair chance that in these galaxies the flow of time is reversed.

Switching back from macrocosmos to microcosmos, we remember that in Feynman's diagrams, particles are supposed to move for a short while backwards in time. Heisenberg himself endorsed this hypothesis:

The only consolation [when faced with the paradoxes of quantum theory] is the assumption that in very small regions of space–time of the order of magnitude of the elementary particles, the notions of space and time become unclear, i.e., in very small intervals even the concepts 'earlier' and 'later' can no longer be properly defined. Of course nothing is altered in space–time on the large scale, but we must bear in mind the possibility that experiment may well prove that small-scale space–time processes may run in reverse to the causal sequence.[15]

Thus our medium-sized world with its homely commonsense notions of space, time and causality appears to be sandwiched in between the macro- and micro-realms of reality, to which those parochial notions no longer apply. As Sir James Jeans wrote: 'The history of physical science in the twentieth century is one of progressive emancipation from the purely human angle of vision.'[16] On the macrocosmic scale of large distances and high speeds, relativity played havoc with that vision. On the micro-cosmic scale, relativity combined with quantum theory had the same effect. The physicist's concept of time is totally different today from what it was during Queen Victoria's reign. The most eminent among contemporary astronomers, Sir Fred Hoyle, has put it in his provocative way:

*Anti-matter consists of atoms in which the electric charges of their constituents are reversed.

You're stuck with a grotesque and absurd illusion . . . the idea of time as an ever-rolling stream . . . There's one thing quite certain in this business: the idea of time as a steady progression from past to future is wrong. I know very well we feel this way about it subjectively. But we're the victims of a confidence trick.[17]

But if the irreversibility of time is derived from a 'confidence trick' – that is, from a subjective illusion – we are no longer justified in excluding on *a priori* grounds the theoretical possibility of precognitive phenomena such as veridical dreams. The logical paradox that predicting a future event may prevent it or alter its course, is at least partly circumvented by the indeterminateness of the future in modern physics, and the probabilistic nature of all forecasts.

6

The revolution in physics which thus transformed our world-view took place in the 1920s. But in the second half of our century it took an even more surrealistic turn. At the time of writing, the universe appears to be pock-marked with so-called 'black holes'. The term was coined by John A. Wheeler, Professor of Physics at Princeton University, and a leading figure among contemporary physicists.* Black holes are hypothetical pits or sumps in distant space into which the mass of a burnt-out star which has suffered gravitational collapse is sucked at the speed of light, to be annihilated and vanish from our universe. The loci at which these apocalyptic events take place are referred to as 'singularities' in the continuum; here, according to the equations of general relativity, the curvature of space becomes infinite, time is frozen, and the laws of physics are invalidated. The universe is turning out to be a very odd place indeed, and we do not need ghosts to make our hair stand on end.

One might be tempted to ask the naive question where the matter which has fallen into the black hole 'goes' (for not all of

---

*Wheeler's book, *Geometrodynamics*, published in 1962, is considered a modern classic.

it can have been converted into energy). Wheeler has a tentative answer to that: it might emerge in the shape of a 'white hole' somewhere in another universe, located in superspace (his italics):

The stage on which the space of the universe moves is certainly not space itself. Nobody can be a stage for himself; he has to have a larger arena in which to move. The arena in which space does its changing is not even the space–time of Einstein, for space–time is the history of space changing with time. The arena must be a larger object: *super-space* . . . It is not endowed with three or four dimensions – it's endowed with an *infinite* number of dimensions. Any single point in superspace represents an entire, three-dimensional world; nearby points represent slightly different three-dimensional worlds.[18]

Superspace – or hyperspace – has been an old stand-by of science fiction, together with the notion of parallel universes and reversed or multidimensional time. Now, thanks to radio-telescopes and particle-accelerators, they are acquiring academic respectability. The stranger the hard, experimental data, the stranger the theories which attempt to account for them.

Wheeler's version of superspace has some remarkable features:

The space of quantum geometrodynamics can be compared to a carpet of foam spread over a slowly undulating landscape . . . The continual microscopic changes in the carpet of foam as new bubbles appear and old ones disappear symbolize the quantum fluctuations in the geometry . . .[19]

Another remarkable attribute of Wheeler's superspace is multiple connectivity. This means – put into simple and over-simplified language – that regions which in our homespun three-dimensional world are far apart, may be brought temporarily into direct contact through tunnels or 'holes' in superspace. They are called wormholes. The universe is supposed to be criss-crossed with these wormholes, which appear and disappear in immensely rapid fluctuations, resulting in ever-changing patterns – a cosmic kaleidoscope shaken by an invisible hand.

7

An essential feature of modern physics is its increasingly *holistic* trend, based on the insight that the whole is as necessary for the understanding of its parts as the parts are necessary for understanding the whole. An early expression of this trend, dating from the turn of the century, was 'Mach's Principle', endorsed by Einstein. It states that the inertial properties of terrestrial matter are determined by the total mass of the universe around us. There is no satisfactory causal explanation as to *how* this influence is exerted, yet Mach's Principle is an integral part of relativistic cosmology. The metaphysical implications are fundamental – for it follows from it not only that the universe as a whole influences local, terrestrial events, but also that local events have an influence, however small, on the universe as a whole. Philosophically-minded physicists are acutely aware of these implications – which remind one of the ancient Chinese proverb: 'If you cut a blade of grass, you shake the Universe.'

Bertrand Russell flippantly remarked that Mach's Principle, though formally correct, 'savours of astrology', while Henry Margenau, Professor of Physics at Yale, commented in an address to the American Society for Psychical Research:

Inertia is not intrinsic in the body; it is induced by the circumstance that the body is surrounded by the whole universe . . . We know of no physical effect conveying this action; very few people worry about a physical agency transmitting it. As far as I can see, Mach's Principle is as mysterious as your unexplained psychic phenomena, and its formulation seems to me almost as obscure . . .[20]

Switching once more from macro- to microcosmos, we are confronted with the famous 'Einstein–Podolsky–Rosen paradox'. It has been the subject of controversy ever since Einstein formulated it in 1933, and has recently been given a more precise expression by J. S. Bell, a theoretical physicist at CERN. 'Bell's Theorem' states that when two particles have interacted and then flown off in opposite directions, interference with one particle will instantly affect the other particle, regardless of the distance between them. The correctness of Bell's experimental results is not in dispute, but its interpretation poses a major problem because it seems to imply a sort of 'telepathy' between the particles in question. This is how David Bohm, Professor of Theoretical Physics at Birkbeck College, University of London, has summed up the situation (his italics):

It is generally acknowledged that the quantum theory has many strikingly novel features . . . However, there has been too little emphasis on what is, in our view, the most fundamentally different new feature of all, i.e. the intimate interconnection of different systems that are not in spatial contact. This has been especially clearly revealed through the . . . well-known experiments of Einstein, Podolsky and Rosen . . .

Recently interest in this question has been stimulated by the work of Bell, who obtained precise mathematical criteria, distinguishing the experimental consequences of this feature of 'quantum interconnectedness of distant systems'. . . . Thus, one is led to a new notion of *unbroken wholeness* which denies the classical idea of analysability of the world into separately and independently existent parts . . .[21]

I must mention one more apparently non-causal law of nature: the so-called Pauli Exclusion Principle. Wolfgang Pauli, whom I have quoted before, got the Nobel Prize in 1945 for having discovered it. It says (very roughly speaking) that any one of the 'planetary orbits' inside an atom can only be occupied by one electron at a time. If it were not so, chaos would result and the atom would collapse – but *why* is it so? The answer – or rather, absence of an answer – is vividly indicated in this passage quoted from Margenau (compressed):

Most of the organizing actions that occur in nature are brought about by the Pauli Principle, which is simply a principle of symmetry, a formal mathematical characteristic of the equations which in the end regulate phenomena in nature. Almost miraculously it calls into being the forces which bind atoms into molecules and molecules into crystals. The impenetrability of matter, its very stability, can be directly traced to the Pauli Exclusion Principle. Now, this principle has no dynamic aspect to it at all. It acts like a force though it is not a force. We cannot speak of it as doing anything by mechanical action. No, it is a very general and elusive thing; a mathematical symmetry imposed upon the basic equations of nature.[22]

These quotations (which could be multiplied indefinitely) do not represent solo voices, but rather a chorus of eminent physicists, aware of the revolutionary implications of quantum theory and of the new cosmology – which are bound to transform man's image of the universe even more radically than the Copernican revolution had done. But, as already said, the general public is slow in becoming aware of this change. The dogmas and taboos of nineteenth-century materialist science relating to space, time, matter and energy, contained within a rigid framework of causality and determinism, still dominate the habits of thought of the educated public which prides itself on its rational outlook, and feels compelled to deny the existence of ESP-type phenomena which seemingly contradict the 'Laws of Nature'. In fact our physicists have been engaged, over the last fifty years, in ruthlessly discarding previously sacrosanct 'Laws of Nature' and replacing them with obscure mental constructs which cannot be represented in three-dimensional space, and whose quasi-mystical implications are hidden in technical jargon and mathematical formalism. If Galileo were resurrected, he would certainly accuse Heisenberg, Pauli *et al.* of 'dabbling in occult fancies'.

Curiously enough, during the same period parapsychology took on a more 'hard-nosed' appearance by relying more and more on statistical methods, rigorous controls, mechanical gadgets and electronic computers. Thus the climate in the two camps seemed to be changing in opposite directions: Rhine's successors are sometimes accused of drab pedantry, while Einstein's successors have been accused of flirting with ghosts in the guise of particles which have no mass, no weight, nor any precise location in space. These convergent trends are certainly significant, but that does not mean that physics will provide explanations for the phenomena of parapsychology in the near or even in the distant future. What both have in common is an attitude defying commonsense and defying 'Laws of Nature' previously considered as inviolable. Both are provocative and iconoclastic. And, to say it once more, the baffling paradoxa of physics make the baffling phenomena of parapsychology appear a little less preposterous. If distant regions of the universe can be brought into contact through wormholes in superspace, is telepathy still unthinkable? The analogies can be treacherous – but it is encouraging to know that if the parapsychologist is out on a limb, the physicist is out on a tightrope.

8

There exists a type of phenomenon, even more mysterious than telepathy or precognition, which has puzzled man since the dawn of mythology: the seemingly accidental meeting of two unrelated causal chains in a coincidental event which appears both highly improbable and highly significant. Any theory which attempts to take such phenomena seriously must necessarily involve an even more radical break with our traditional categories of reasoning than the pronunciamentos of Einstein, Heisenberg or Feynman. It is certainly no coincidence that it was Wolfgang Pauli, discoverer of the Exclusion Principle, who collaborated with C. G. Jung on the latter's famous essay: 'Synchronicity: An Acausal Connecting Principle'. Jung coined the term 'synchronicity' for 'the simultaneous occurrence of two or more meaningfully but not causally connected events'[23]; and he claimed that the acausal factor behind such events is to be regarded as *equal in rank to causality as a principle of explanation*.[24]

'I have often come up against the phenomena in question,' Jung wrote, '. . . and could convince myself how much these inner experiences meant to my patients. In most cases they were things which people do not talk about for fear of exposing themselves to thoughtless ridicule. I was amazed to see how many people have had experiences of this kind and how carefully the secret was guarded.'[25]

Apparently the Swiss are more secretive by nature than the

British, for, ever since I wrote *The Roots of Coincidence* I have been inundated with coincidences in readers' letters. The most revealing among these were written by people who started by solemnly affirming that to attribute significance to coincidences is sheer nonsense, yet could not resist the urge to tell their own favourite believe-it-or-not story. Could it be that inside every hard-nosed sceptic there is a soft-nosed mystic crying to be let out?

Readers who share an interest in the collecting of coincidences will find a fair selection in *The Challenge of Chance*. While working through this vast amount of material, some distinct patterns began to emerge, although they often overlapped, while in other cases it seemed doubtful whether some event with astronomical odds against chance should be interpreted as a manifestation of 'classical' ESP or in terms of acausal 'synchronicity'. Thus in the *library* type of cases, you search for an elusive reference, open a fat volume at random, and there it is. In the *deus ex machina* type of episodes there is a seemingly providential interposition just in the nick of time to solve a problem, or avert a disaster, or fulfil a premonition. It is interesting to note that this intercession occurs indiscriminately on tragic or trivial occasions. A sub-category in this group is the seemingly miraculous recovery of *lost property*, usually of sentimental, not monetary value. In the *poltergeist* cases emotional tensions (usually in unstable adolescents) coincide with gross physical happenings – again regardless whether the effect is dramatic or grotesque. Among the most frequent 'convergent' or 'confluential' events (as one may call this type of coincidence) are unlikely *encounters*, although many of these might seem to be induced by ESP. Worst of all from a rational point of view are the clusterings of *names, numbers, addresses* and *dates*. Lastly, there is a wealth of well-authenticated cases of premonitions or *warnings* of impending disasters – but here it is particularly difficult to make a distinction between ESP and synchronicity, or 'confluential events'.

Even more frustrating is the attempt to draw a line between *significant* coincidences, which seem to be contrived by some unknown agency beyond physical causation, and *trivial* coincidences due to chance alone. For any such attempt must invoke the laws of probability, which are full of pitfalls – as we shall presently see.

9

Jung's essay on 'synchronicity', published in 1952,* was partly based on Paul Kammerer's book *Das Gesetz der Serie*,† published in 1919. Kammerer was the brilliant Viennese experimental biologist of Lamarckian persuasion who was accused of faking his results, and committed suicide in 1926, at the age of forty-five.†† He was throughout his life fascinated by coincidences and, from the age of twenty to forty, kept a log-book of them – as Jung also did.

Kammerer defined his concept of 'seriality' as the concurrence in space or recurrence in time of meaningfully but not causally connected events. His book contains exactly one hundred selected samples, classified with the meticulousness of a biologist devoted to taxonomy. He regarded single coincidences as merely the tips of the iceberg which happened to catch the eye among the ubiquitous manifestations of 'seriality'. He thus reversed the sceptic's argument that we tend to see significances everywhere because out of the multitude of random events we only remember those few which *are* significant. At the end of the first, classificatory part of his book, Kammerer concluded:

So far we have been concerned with the factual manifestations of recurrent series, without attempting an explanation. We have found that the recurrence of identical or similar data in contiguous areas of space or time is a simple empirical fact which has to be accepted and which cannot be explained by coincidence – or rather, which makes coincidence rule to such an extent that the concept of coincidence itself is negated.[26]

---

*Published in one volume together with Pauli's essay *'Der Einfluss Archetypischer Vorstellungen auf die Bildung Naturwissenschaftlicher Theorien bei Kepler'* (Jung-Pauli, *Naturerklärung und Psyche*, 1952).

†There is no English translation.

††See *The Case of the Midwife Toad.*

In the second, theoretical part of his book, Kammerer develops
his theory that coexistent with physical causality there is an
acausal principle active in the universe which tends towards
unity-in-variety. In some respects it is comparable to that other
mysterious force, universal gravity; but whereas gravity acts
indiscriminately on all matter, this hypothetical factor acts selectively to make like and like converge in space and time – it
correlates by affinity or some sort of selective resonance, like
tuning forks vibrating on the same wave-length. By what means
this acausal agency interferes with the causal order of things we
cannot know since it operates outside the known laws of physics.
In space it produces confluential events related by affinities of
form and function; in time, similarly related series:

We thus arrive at the image of a world-mosaic or cosmic kaleidoscope, which, in spite of constant shufflings and rearrangements, also
takes care of bringing like and like together . . .[27]

One need not be a professional gambler to feel attracted by
Kammerer's Law of Seriality. Most languages have a phrase or
proverb for it – 'Das Gesetz der Serie' is a cliché in German, the
equivalent of 'It never rains but it pours'. Some people seem to
become coincidence-prone as others become accident-prone. At
the end of his book Kammerer expresses his belief that seriality is

. . . ubiquitous and continuous in life, nature and cosmos. It is the
umbilical cord that connects thought, feeling, science and art with the
womb of the universe that gave birth to them.[28]

The main difference between Kammerer's seriality and Jung's
synchronicity is that the former emphasizes serial happenings in
time (though he also includes simultaneous coincidental events),
whereas the latter's emphasis is on simultaneous events (but also
includes precognitive dreams which may have occurred several
days before the event). Kammerer based his theory partly on the
analogy with gravity, partly on the periodic cycles in biology
and cosmology. Some of his excursions into physics contain

naive errors; other passages show tantalizing flashes of intuition – so much so that Einstein commented favourably on the book; he called it 'original and by no means absurd'.[29] Jung, on the other hand, used Pauli quasi as a tutor in theoretical physics, but in the end made little use of it; his explanations of the 'acausal factor' were utterly obscure, invoking the collective unconscious and its archetypes. This was sadly disappointing but it helped to turn synchronicity into a cult-word.

The part played by Pauli in these developments is of special interest. Pauli shared Kammerer's and Jung's belief in non-causal, non-physical factors operating in the universe – was not his own Exclusion Principle 'acting like a force though it is not a force'? He probably had a more profound insight than most of his colleagues into the limitations of science. Besides, like Jung, he was haunted all his life by poltergeist-like phenomena.[30] When he was fifty and a Nobel laureate, he wrote a penetrating study on science and mysticism, as exemplified in the works of Johannes Kepler.[31] It was first printed as a monograph by the Jung Institute in Zurich. Towards the end of the essay Pauli wrote (his italics):

Today we have the natural sciences, but no longer a philosophy of science. Since the discovery of the elementary quantum, physics was obliged to renounce its proud claim to be able to understand in principle the *whole* of the world. But this predicament may contain the seed of further developments which will correct the previous one-sided orientation and will move towards a unitary world-view in which science is only a part in the whole.[32]

This kind of philosophical doubt about 'the meaning behind it all' is not unusual among scientists when they reach the age of fifty: one might almost call it the rule. But Pauli went further than trying to devise physicalistic theories to explain ESP or synchronicity. He felt that this was hopeless, and that it was more honest to accept that these phenomena were the visible traces of invisible acausal factors – like the bubble-chamber tracks of invisible particles. Pauli's revolutionary proposal was to extend the concept of non-causal events from the micro-world (where its legitimacy was recognized) to the macro-world (where it was not). He may have hoped that by joining forces with Jung, they might be able to work out an acausal theory which made some sense of paranormal phenomena. The result, as already said, was disappointing. The upshot of Jung's essay on synchronicity was a curious diagram on which, Jung says, he and Pauli 'finally agreed'. This is the diagram:[33]

Indestructible energy

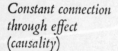
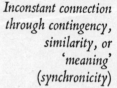

Constant connection through effect (causality)

Inconstant connection through contingency, similarity, or 'meaning' (synchronicity)

Space–Time continuum

Jung offers no explanation as to how the scheme is meant to work, and his comments on it are so obscure that I must leave it to the interested reader to look them up in the original. One cannot help being reminded of the biblical mountain whose labours gave birth to a mouse. But it was quite a symbolic mouse nevertheless. It was for the first time that the hypothesis of acausal factors at large in the universe was given the joint stamp of respectability by a psychologist and a physicist, both of international renown.

10

The belief in connections beyond physical causality did not, of course, originate with Kammerer or Jung. Its immediate ancestry can be traced back to Schopenhauer, who had considerable influence over both Freud and Jung. Schopenhauer taught that physical causality was *only one* of the principles ruling the world; the other was a metaphysical entity, a kind of universal consciousness, compared to which individual consciousness is 'as a dream compared to reality'. He wrote:

Coincidence is the simultaneous occurrence of causally unconnected events . . . If we visualize each causal chain progressing in time as a meridian on the globe, then we may represent simultaneous events by the parallel circles of latitude. . . . All the events in a man's life could accordingly stand in two fundamentally different connections.[34]

This idea of unity-in-diversity can be followed all the way back to the Pythagorean 'Harmony of the Spheres',* and the Hippocratics' 'sympathy of all things': 'there is one common flow, one common breathing, all things are in sympathy'. The doctrine that everything in the universe hangs together, partly by mechanical causes, but mainly by hidden affinities (which also account for apparent coincidences), provided not only the foundation for sympathetic magic, astrology and alchemy; it also runs as a *leit-motif* through the teachings of Taoism and Buddhism, the neo-Platonists, and the philosophers of the early Renaissance. It was neatly summed up by (among many others) Pico della Mirandola, A.D. 1550:

Firstly there is the unity in things whereby each thing is at one with itself, consists of itself, and coheres with itself. Secondly, there is the unity whereby one creature is united with the others and all parts of the world constitute one world.[35]

In the terms of the present theory, the first half of the above quotation reflects the working of the *self-assertive*, the second of the self-transcending or *integrative* tendency, on a universal level.

We may also compare Pico's statement with the consensus of contemporary physicists: 'It is impossible to separate any part of the universe from the rest.' The essence of both quotations, separated by four centuries, is a holistic view of the universe which transcends physical causality.

II

One of the best-kept secrets of the universe relates to the question how the sub-atomic micro-world of particles, which are at the same time wavicles, which defy strict determinism and mechanical

*For the influence of this conception on Elizabethan philosophy and poetry, see *The Sleepwalkers*, Part One, Ch. II.

causation – how this ambiguous 'undulating carpet of foam' gives
rise to the solid, orderly macro-world of everyday experience
ruled by strict causality.

The modern scientist's answer is that this seemingly miraculous
feat of creating order out of disorder must be seen in the light of
the theory of probability or the 'law of large numbers'. But this
law, like Pauli's Exclusion Principle, is not explainable by physical
forces; it hangs, so to speak, in the air. A few examples will
illustrate the point.

The first two are classic cases quoted from Warren Weaver's
book on the theory of probability.[36] The statistics of the New
York Department of Health show that in 1955 the average number of dogs biting people reported per day was 75·3; in 1956, 73·6;
in 1957, 73·5; in 1958, 74·5; in 1959, 72·4. A similar statistical
reliability was shown by cavalry horses administering fatal kicks
to soldiers in the German army of the last century; they were
apparently guided by the so-called Poisson equation of probability
theory. Murderers in England and Wales, however different in
character and motives, displayed the same respect for the laws of
statistics: since the end of the First World War, the average
number of murders over successive decades was: 1920–9, 3·84
per million of the population; 1930–9, 3·27 per million; 1940–9,
3·92 per million; 1950–9, 3·3 per million; 1960–9, approx 3·5
per million.

These bizarre examples illustrate the paradoxical nature of
probability, which has puzzled philosophers ever since Pascal
initiated that branch of mathematics – and which von Neumann,
the greatest mathematician of our century, called 'black magic'.
The paradox consists of the fact that the theory of probability
is able to predict with uncanny precision the overall result of a
large number of individual events, each of which is in itself
unpredictable. In other words, we are faced with *a large number
of uncertainties producing a certainty*, a large number of random
events creating a lawful total outcome.

But paradoxical or not, the law of large numbers *works*;
the mystery is why and how it works. It has become an indispensable tool of physics and genetics, of economic planners, insurance

companies, gambling casinos, and opinion polls – so much so that we take the black magic for granted. Thus when faced with such bizarre examples of probability-lore as the dogs or cavalry horses, we may be mildly puzzled or amused, without realizing the universal nature of the paradox and its relevance to the problem of chance and design, freedom and necessity.

In nuclear physics we find striking analogies to the unpredictable dogs producing predictable statistics. A classic example is radioactive decay, where totally unpredictable radioactive atoms produce exactly predictable overall results. The point in time at which a radioactive atom will suddenly disintegrate is totally unpredictable both theoretically and experimentally. It is not influenced by chemical or physical factors like temperature or pressure. In other words, it does not depend on the atom's past history, nor on its present environment; in the words of Professor Bohm, 'it does not have any causes', it is *completely arbitrary* in the sense that it has no relationship whatsoever to anything else that exists in the world or that ever has existed' (italics in the original).[37] And yet it *does* have a hidden, apparently acausal relationship with the rest of the world, because the so-called 'half-life' period of any grain of a radioactive substance (i.e. the time required for half of the atoms in the grain to disintegrate) is rigorously fixed and predictable. The half-life of uranium is four and a half million years. The half-life of radium A is 3·825 days. The half-life of thorium C is 60·5 minutes. And so on, down to millionths of seconds.

However, there may be fluctuations in the rate of decay of the grain; at some stages on the road to the half-life date there might be an excess or a deficit of decayed atoms which threatens to upset the time-table. But these deviations from the statistical mean will soon be corrected, and the half-life date rigorously kept. By what agency is this controlling and correcting influence exerted, since the decay of individual atoms is unaffected by what goes on in the rest of the grain? How do the dogs of New York know when to stop biting and when to make up the daily quota? How are the murderers in England and Wales made to stop at four victims per million? By what mysterious power is the roulette ball induced, after a glut of 'reds', to restore the balance in the long run? By 'the laws of probability' (or 'the law of large numbers') we are told. But that law has no physical powers to enforce its dictates. It is impotent – and yet virtually omnipotent.

It may seem that I am labouring the point out of sheer perversity, but this paradox is indeed vital to the problem of causality. Since the causal chains which lead to the decay of individual atoms are ostensibly independent from each other, we must either assume that the fulfilment of the statistical prediction that my sample of thorium C will have a half-life of 60·5 minutes is itself due to blind chance – which is absurd; or we must take the plunge and opt for some alternative hypothesis on the speculative lines of an 'acausal connecting agency', which is complementary to physical causality in the sense in which particle and wavicle, 'mechanical' and 'mental' complement each other. Such an agency would operate in different guises on different levels: in the shape of 'hidden variables' filling in the gaps in causality on the sub-atomic level; coordinating the activities of the physically independent thorium C atoms to make them respect the half-life date; bringing like and like together in the 'confluential events' of seriality and synchronicity; and perhaps generating the 'psi-field' of the parapsychologist.

This may sound like a tall proposition, but is in fact no taller than the paradoxical phenomena on which it is based. We live submerged in a universe of 'undulating quantum foam' which ceaselessly creates weird phenomena by means transcending the classical concepts of physical causation. The purpose and design of this acausal agency is unknown, and perhaps unknowable to us; but intuitively we feel it somehow to be related to that striving towards higher forms of order and unity-in-variety which we observe in the evolution of the universe at large, of life on earth, human consciousness, and lastly science and art. One ultimate mystery is easier to accept than a litter-basket of unrelated puzzles.

In his classic essay *What is Life?* which I have quoted before, Erwin Schrödinger took a similar line. He called the connecting link between the totally unpredictable sub-atomic events and their exactly predictable collective result 'the "order from disorder" principle'. He frankly admitted that it is beyond physical causation:

The disintegration of a single radioactive atom is observable (it emits a projectile which causes a visible scintillation on a fluorescent screen). But if you are given a single atom, its probable lifetime is much less certain than that of a healthy sparrow. Indeed, nothing more can be said about it than this: as long as it lives (and that may be for thousands of years) the chance of its blowing up within the next second, whether large or small, remains the same. This patent lack of individual determination nevertheless results in the exact exponential law of decay of a large number of radioactive atoms of the same kind.[38]

Robert Harvie, co-author (with Sir Alister Hardy and myself) of *The Challenge of Chance*, commented on this passage by Schrödinger:

Orthodox quantum theory attempts to resolve this paradox by asserting the probabilistic nature of matter at the microscopic level. But a further paradox remains – that of probability itself. The laws of probability describe *how* a collection of single random events can add up to a large-scale certainty, but not *why*. Why do not the million nuclei explode at once? Why should we expect that a symmetrically balanced penny will not fall 'heads' on every toss from now to eternity? The question is evidently unanswerable . . .

The 'order from disorder' principle seems to be irreducible, inexplicably 'just there'. To ask why is akin to asking 'Why is the universe?' or 'Why has space three dimensions?' (if indeed it has).[39]

In the present theory, the 'order from disorder' principle is represented by the integrative tendency. We have seen that this principle can be traced all the way back to the Pythagoreans. After its temporary eclipse during the reign of reductionist orthodoxies in physics and biology, it is once more gaining ascendancy in more sophisticated versions. I have mentioned the related concepts of Schrödinger's negentropy, Szent Györgyi's syntropy, Bergson's *élan vital*, etc.; one might add to the list the German biologist Woltereck who coined the term 'anamorphosis' – which von Bertalanffy adopted – for Nature's tendency to create new forms of life, and also L. L. Whyte's 'morphic principle', or 'the fundamental principle of the development of pattern'. What all these theories have in common is that they regard the morphic, or formative, or syntropic tendency, Nature's striving to create order out of disorder, cosmos out of chaos, as ultimate and irreducible principles beyond mechanical causation.*

The present theory is even more hazardous by explicitly suggesting that the integrative tendency operates in *both causal and acausal* ways, the two standing in a complementary relationship analogous to the particle–wave complementarity in physics. It is accordingly supposed to embrace not only the acausal agencies operating on the sub-atomic level, but also the phenomena of parapsychology and 'confluential events'. We have seen that ESP and 'synchronicity' often overlap, so that a supposedly paranormal event can be interpreted either as a result of ESP or as a case of 'synchronicity'. But we are perhaps mistaken when we try to make a categorical distinction between the two. Classical physics has taught us that there are various manifestations of energy, including kinetic, potential, thermal, electrical, nuclear and radiant energy which can be converted into one another by suitable procedures, like interchangeable currencies. The present theory suggests that in a similar way telepathy, clairvoyance, precognition, psychokinesis and synchronicity are merely *different manifestations under different conditions of the same universal principle* – i.e., the integrative tendency operating through both causal and acausal agencies. How this is done is beyond our understanding; but at least we can fit the evidence for paranormal phenomena into the unified design.

12

Among the basic requirements for the validation of a scientific experiment are its repeatability and predictability. Paranormal

---

*Although most of them do not expressly invoke acausal factors, these are implied in regarding the formative tendency as 'irreducible'.

events, however, whether produced in the laboratory or spontaneously, are unpredictable, capricious and relatively rare. This is one of the reasons why sceptics feel justified in rejecting the results of some forty years of rigorously controlled laboratory experiments in ESP and PK, in spite of the massive statistical evidence which, in any other field of research, would be considered as sufficient proof for the reality of the phenomena.

But the criterion of repeatability applies only when the experimental conditions are essentially the same as in the original experiment; and with sensitive human subjects the conditions are never quite the same in terms of mood, receptivity, or emotional rapport between subject and experimenter. Besides, ESP phenomena nearly always involve unconscious processes beyond voluntary control. And if the phenomena are in fact triggered by acausal agencies, it would be naive to expect that they can be produced at will.

There is, however, another explanation for the apparent rarity and capriciousness of paranormal phenomena, which is of special interest in our context. It was, I believe, originated by Henri Bergson and has been taken up by various writers on parapsychology. Thus, for instance, H. H. Price, former Wykeham Professor of Logic in Oxford:

It looks as if telepathically received impressions have some difficulty in crossing the threshold and manifesting themselves in consciousness. There seems to be some barrier or repressive mechanism which tends to shut them out from consciousness, a barrier which is rather difficult to pass, and they make use of all sorts of devices for overcoming it ... Often they can only emerge in a distorted and symbolic form (as other unconscious mental contents do). It is a plausible guess that many of our everyday thoughts and emotions are telepathic or partly telepathic in origin, but are not recognized to be so because they are so much distorted and mixed with other mental contents in crossing the threshold of consciousness.[40]

The Cambridge mathematician, Adrian Dobbs, commenting on the extract I have quoted, went straight to the heart of the matter:

This is a very interesting passage. It evokes the picture of either the mind or the brain as containing an assemblage of selective filters, designed to cut out unwanted signals on neighbouring frequencies, some of which get through in a distorted form, just as in ordinary radio reception.[41]

Cyril Burt, former Professor of Psychology, University College, London, took up the same idea:

Our sense organs and our brain operate as an intricate kind of filter which limits and directs the mind's clairvoyant powers, so that under normal conditions attention is concentrated on just those objects or situations that are of biological importance for the survival of the organism and its species . . . As a rule, it would seem, the mind rejects ideas coming from another mind as the body rejects grafts coming from another body.[42]

At this stage, the reader may have experienced a feeling of *déjà vu*, because earlier on I discussed some other 'filter-theories' related to the mechanisms of perception and the process of evolution. In fact, the hypothesis that there is a filtering apparatus which protects us against 'unwanted' ESP signals is merely an extrapolation from what we know about normal, sensory perception. We remember William James's famous 'blooming, buzzing multitude of sensations' which are constantly bombarding our sensory receptors, and particularly the eyes and ears. Our minds would be engulfed by chaos if we were to attend to each of these millions of stimuli impinging on them. Thus the central nervous system, and the brain, have to function as a multilevelled hierarchy of scanning, filtering and classifying devices 'which eliminate a large proportion of the sensory input as irrelevant "noise", and assemble the relevant information into coherent patterns before it is presented to consciousness'. By analogy, a similar filtering apparatus might protect our rational minds against the 'blooming, buzzing multitude' of messages, images, intuitions and coincidental happenings in the 'psycho-magnetic field' surrounding us.

We can draw a further analogy between the filtering hierarchies which protect the mind from irrelevant stimuli of sensory or extrasensory origin, and the genetic micro-hierarchies which protect the hereditary blueprint in the chromosomes against biochemical intrusions and harmful mutations which otherwise would play havoc with the stability and continuity of the species (see above, pp. 200 ff). Moreover, I also felt emboldened to suggest the existence of a Lamarckian micro-hierarchy of selective filters, which prevents acquired characteristics from interfering with the hereditary endowment – except for those select few which respond to some vital need of the species, resulting from persistent pressures of the environment over many generations, until they seep through the filter and become part of the hereditary endowment of the human embryo, like the thick skin on its soles. This is undeniably an acquired characteristic which has become hereditary – yet in conformity with the prevailing dogma we are asked to believe that it happened by pure chance.

In fact, the Lamarckians, as we have seen, found themselves in the same type of predicament as the parapsychologists: they were unable to produce a repeatable laboratory experiment. Even apparently clear-cut cases of Lamarckian inheritance were open to different interpretations, to polemics pursued with quasi-theological passions, and as a last resort, to accusations of fraud. Moreover, the Lamarckians were unable to provide a physiological explanation for the inheritance of acquired characteristics – just as the parapsychologists are unable to produce a physical explanation of ESP phenomena.

This curious parallel seems to have gone unnoticed by both Lamarckians and parapsychologists; I have found no mention of it in the literature of either school. Yet it seems to me relevant, because both heresies show up the shortcomings of scientific orthodoxies, without being able to offer a comprehensive alternative beyond Johannsen's 'great central mystery' or Grassé's 'It seems possible that confronted by these problems, biology is reduced to helplessness and must hand over to metaphysics.'[43]

XIV

A GLANCE THROUGH THE KEYHOLE

I

Approaching the end of this journey, it might be useful to look back at the Prologue, in which I discussed the sudden rise of the human neocortex, and its growth at a speed without precedent in the history of evolution. We have seen that one of the consequences of this explosive process was the chronic conflict between the new brain which endowed man with his reasoning powers, and the archaic old brain, governed by instinct and emotion. The outcome was a mentally unbalanced species, with a built-in paranoid streak, mercilessly revealed by its past and present history.

But the brain explosion in the late Pleistocene also led to other consequences – less dramatic, but no less far-reaching – which remain to be discussed.

The crucial point is, that in creating the human brain, evolution has wildly overshot the mark.

An instrument has been developed in advance of the needs of its possessor . . . Natural selection could only have endowed the savage with a brain a little superior to that of the ape, whereas he possesses one very little inferior to that of the average member of our learned societies . . .[1]

This was written by no less an authority than Alfred Russell Wallace, who co-fathered (if the expression is permitted) with Darwin the theory of evolution by natural selection.* Darwin instantly realized the potentially disastrous implications of the

*The first public unveiling of the theory was a joint communication to the Linnean Society by Darwin and Wallace in 1858.

argument, and wrote to Wallace. 'I hope you have not murdered completely your own and my child.'[2] But he had no satisfactory answer to Wallace's criticism, and his disciples swept it under the carpet.

Why was that criticism so important? There were two reasons. The first is merely of historical interest, in that Wallace's objection demolishes one of the cornerstones of the Darwinian edifice. Evolution in Darwinian and neo-Darwinian theory must proceed in very small steps, each of which confers some minimal selective advantage on the mutated organism – otherwise the whole conception makes no sense, as Darwin himself kept reiterating. But the rapid evolution of the human cerebrum, which some anthropologists have compared to a 'tumorous overgrowth',[3] could by no stretch of the imagination be fitted into this theory. Hence Darwin's agonized response, and the subsequent conspiracy of silence.

The second, and by far the more important, aspect of Wallace's criticism, he himself does not seem to have fully realized. He emphasized that the 'instrument' – the human brain – had been 'developed in advance of the needs of its possessor'.[4] But the evolution of the human brain not only overshot the needs of prehistoric man, it is also the only example of evolution *providing a species with an organ which it does not know how to use*; a luxury organ, which will take its owner thousands of years to learn to put to proper use – if he ever does.

The archaeological evidence indicates that the earliest representative of *homo sapiens* – Cro-Magnon man who enters the scene a hundred thousand years ago or earlier – was already endowed with a brain which in size and shape is indistinguishable from ours. But, however paradoxical it sounds, he hardly made any use of that luxury organ. He remained an illiterate cave-dweller and, for millennium after millennium, went on manufacturing spears, bows and arrows of the same primitive type, while the organ which was to take man to the moon was already there, ready for use, inside his skull. Thus the evolution of the brain overshot the mark by a time factor of astronomical magnitude. This paradox is not easy to grasp; in *The Ghost in the Machine* I tried to illustrate it by a bit of science fiction which I called 'the parable of the unsolicited gift':

There was once a poor, illiterate shopkeeper in an Arab bazaar, called Ali, who, not being very good at doing sums, was always cheated by his customers – instead of cheating *them*, as it should be. So he prayed every night to Allah for the present of an abacus – that venerable contraption for adding and subtracting by pushing beads along wires. But some malicious djin forwarded his prayers to the wrong branch of the heavenly Mail Order Department, and so one morning, arriving at the bazaar, Ali found his stall transformed into a multi-storey, steel-framed building, housing the latest I.B.M. computer with instrument panels covering all the walls, with thousands of fluorescent oscillators, dials, magic eyes, *et cetera*; and an instruction book of several hundred pages – which, being illiterate, he could not read. However, after days of useless fiddling with this or that dial, he flew into a rage and started kicking a shiny, delicate panel. The shocks disturbed one of the machine's millions of electronic circuits, and after a while Ali discovered to his delight that if he kicked that panel, say, three times and afterwards five times, one of the dials showed the figure eight. He thanked Allah for having sent him such a pretty abacus, and continued to use the machine to add up two and three – happily unaware that it was capable of deriving Einstein's equations in a jiffy, or predicting the orbits of planets and stars thousands of years ahead.

Ali's children, then his grandchildren, inherited the machine and the secret of kicking the same panel; but it took hundreds of generations until they learned to use it even for the purpose of simple multiplication. We ourselves are Ali's descendants, and though we have discovered many other ways of putting the machine to work, we have still only learned to utilise a very small fraction of the potentials of its millions of circuits. For the unsolicited gift is of course the human brain. As for the instruction book, it is lost – if it ever existed. Plato maintains that it did once – but that is hearsay.[5]

When biologists talk of 'mental evolution' superseding biological evolution as a specific characteristic in man and absent in animals, they generally fail to see the crux of the problem. For the learning potential in animals is inevitably limited by the fact that they, unlike man, make full use – or nearly full use – of all organs of their native equipment, including their brains. The capabilities of the computers inside the reptilian or lower mammalian skull are exploited almost to the full and thus leave no scope for cumulative learning and 'mental evolution'. Only in the case of *homo sapiens* has evolution anticipated his needs by a time factor of such magnitude that he is only beginning to utilize some of the unexploited, unexplored potentials of the brain's estimated ten thousand million neurons and their virtually inexhaustible synaptic cross-connections. The history of science, philosophy and art is, from this point of view, the slow process of the mind learning by experience to actualize the brain's potentials. The new frontiers to be conquered are in the convolutions of the cortex.

The reasons why this process of *learning to use our brains* was so slow, spasmodic and beset with reverses, can be summed up in a simple formula: the old brain got in the way of, or acted as a brake on, the new. The only periods in European history in which there was a truly cumulative growth of scientific knowledge were the three great centuries of Greece before the Macedonian conquest, and the four centuries from the Renaissance to the present. The organ to generate that knowledge was there inside the skulls of men all the time during the dark interregnum of two thousand years; but it was not allowed to generate that knowledge. For most of the time of recorded human history, and the much longer stretches of pre-history, the marvellous potentialities of the unsolicited gift were only allowed to manifest themselves in the service of archaic, emotion-based beliefs, saturated with taboos; in the magically motivated paintings of the Dordogne caves; in the translation of archetypal imagery into the language of mythology; in the religious art of Asia and the Christian Middle Ages. The task of reason was to act as *ancilla fidei*, the hand-maid of faith – whether it was the faith of sorcerers and medicine men, theologians, scholastics, dialectical materialists, devotees of Chairman Mao or King Mbo-Mba. The fault was not in our stars, but in the horse and crocodile which we carry inside our skulls.

2

The historical consequences of man's split personality have been discussed at length in earlier chapters; my purpose in bringing the subject up once more is to point out a quite different consequence of this condition, which raises basic philosophical problems. To stay for another moment with our metaphor: Ali's descendants were so impressed by and delighted with the apparently inexhaustible capabilities of the computer (in those happy periods when it was allowed to operate unimpeded) that they fell victim to the understandable illusion that the computer was *potentially omniscient*. This illusion was a direct consequence of evolution's overshooting the mark. In other words, the brain's powers of learning and reasoning turned out to be so enormous compared to those of other animals, and also compared to the immediate needs of its possessors, that they became convinced its untapped potentials were inexhaustible, and its powers of reasoning unlimited. There was indeed no reason to believe that problems existed to which the computer had no answer, because it was not 'programmed' to answer them. One might call this attitude the 'rationalist illusion' – the belief that it is only a question of time before the ultimate mysteries of the universe are solved, thanks to the brain's unlimited reasoning powers.

This illusion was shared by most of Ali's successors, including the most eminent among them. Aristotle thought that nearly everything worth discovering about the ways of the universe had already been discovered and that there were no unsolved problems left.[6] Descartes was so carried away by the success of applying mathematical methods to science that he believed he would be able to complete the whole edifice of the new physics by himself. His more cautious contemporaries among the pioneers of the scientific revolution thought it might take as much as two generations to wrest its last secret from Nature. 'The particular phenomena of the arts and sciences are in reality but a handful,' wrote Sir Francis Bacon. 'The invention of all causes and sciences would be a labour of but a few years.'[7] Two centuries later, in

1899, the eminent German biologist and apostle of Darwin, Ernst Haeckel, published his book *Die Welträtsel*, 'The Riddles of the Universe' (which became the bible of my youth). The book enumerated seven great riddles, of which six were 'definitively solved' – including the structure of matter and the origin of life. The seventh – the subjective experience of the freedom of will – was but 'an illusion having no real existence' – so there were no more unsolved riddles left, which was nice to know. Sir Julian Huxley probably shared this opinion when he wrote: 'In the field of evolution, genetics has given its basic answer, and evolutionary biologists are free to pursue other problems.'[8]

The philosophy of reductionism was a direct offspring of the rationalist illusion. 'The invention [i.e., discovery] of all causes and sciences would be a labour of but a few years.' Replace 'years' by 'centuries' and you get the essence of the reductionist credo that the potentially omniscient brain of man will eventually explain all the riddles of the universe by reducing them to 'nothing but' the interplay of electrons, protons and quarks. Dazzled by the benefits derived from the unsolicited gift, it did not occur to the beneficiaries that although the human brain's powers were in some respects immense, they were nevertheless severely limited in other respects, concerned with ultimate meanings. In other words, while evolution 'overshot' its target, it also grievously *undershot* it with respect to the ultimate, existential questions, for which it was not 'programmed'. These ultimates include the paradoxa of infinity and eternity ('If the universe started with the Big Bang, what was before the Bang?'); the curvature of space according to relativity; the notion of parallel and inter-penetrating universes; the phenomena of parapsychology and of acausal processes; and all questions related to ultimate meanings (of the universe, of life, of good and evil, etc.). To quote (for the last time) an eminent physicist, Professor Henry Margenau of the University of Yale:

An artifact occasionally invoked to explain precognition is to make time multidimensional. This allows a genuine backward passage of time, which might permit positive intervals in one time direction to become negative ('effect before cause') in another. In principle, this represents a valid scheme, and I know of no criticism that will rule it out as a scientific procedure. If it is to be acceptable, however, a completely new metric of space-time needs to be developed . . .[9]

But we are not 'programmed' for such a new metric; we are not able to visualize spatial dimensions added to length, width and height; nor time flowing from tomorrow towards yesterday, and so on. We are unable to visualise such phenomena, not because they are impossible but because the human brain and nervous system are not programmed for them.

The limitations of our programming – of our native equipment – are even more obvious in our sensory receptor organs. The human eye can perceive only a very small fraction of the spectrum of electromagnetic radiations; our hearing is restricted to a range of sound frequencies narrower than the dog's; our sense of smell is desultory and our capacity of spatial orientation cannot compare with the migrating bird's. Until about the thirteenth century man did not realize that he was surrounded by magnetic forces; nor does he have any sensory awareness of them; nor of the showers of neutrinos which penetrate and traverse his body in millions; nor of other unknown fields and influences operating inside and around him. If the *sensory* apparatus of our species is programmed to perceive only an infinitesimally small part of the cosmic phantasmagoria, then why not admit that its *cognitive* apparatus may be subject to equally severe limitations in programming – i.e., that it is unable to provide answers to the ultimate questions of 'the meaning of it all'? Such an admission would neither belittle the mind of man, nor discourage him from putting it to full use – for creative minds will always try to do just that, 'as if' the answers were just around the corner.

To admit the inherent limitations of man's reasoning power automatically leads to a more tolerant and open-minded attitude toward phenomena which seem to defy reason – like quantum physics, parapsychology and acausal events. Such a change of attitude would also put an end to the crude reductionist maxim that what cannot be explained cannot exist. A species of humans without eyes, such as the citizens of H. G. Wells's *Country of the Blind*, would reject our claim of being able to perceive distant objects without contact by touch, as occult nonsense. There is a Chinese proverb which tells us that it is useless to speak about the sea to a frog that lives at the bottom of a well.

We have heard a whole chorus of Nobel laureates assert that matter is merely energy in disguise, that causality is dead, determinism is dead. If that is so, they should be given a public funeral in the olive groves of Academe, with a requiem of electronic music. It is indeed time to get out of the strait-jacket which nineteenth-century materialism, combined with reductionism and the rationalist illusion, imposed on our philosophical outlook. Had that outlook kept abreast with the revolutionary messages from the bubble chambers and radio-telescopes, instead of lagging a century behind them, we would have been liberated from that strait-jacket a long time ago.

Once this simple fact is recognized, we might become more receptive to bizarre phenomena inside and around us which a one-sided emphasis on mechanical determinism made us ignore; might feel the draught that is blowing through the chinks of the causal edifice; include paranormal phenomena in our revised concepts of normality; and realize that we have been living in the Country of the Blind – or at the bottom of a well.

The consequences of such a shift of awareness are unforeseeable. In the words of Professor H. H. Price 'psychical research is one of the most important branches of investigation which the human mind has undertaken', and 'it may transform the whole intellectual outlook upon which our present civilisation is based'.[10] These are strong words coming from an Oxford Professor of Logic, but I do not think they overstate the case.

It is possible that in this particular field of psychic endowment we are – together with our other handicaps – an under-privileged species. The grand design of evolutionary strategy does not exclude the existence of biological freaks, like the koala bear, nor of self-destructive races, like our paranoid selves. If this is the case, we have to live 'as if' it were not so, and try to make the best of it – as we are trying to make the best of our suspended death-sentences *qua* individuals.

The limitations of Ali's computer may condemn us to the role of Peeping Toms at the keyhole of eternity. But at least we can try to take the stuffing out of the keyhole, which blocks even our limited view.

3

In the Prologue to this book I stressed the fact that our present situation is without precedent in history. To say it once more: in all previous generations man had to come to terms with the prospect of his death as an individual; the present generation is the first to face the prospect of the death of our species. *Homo sapiens* arrived on the scene about a hundred thousand years ago, which is but the blinking of an eye on the evolutionary time-scale. If he were to vanish now, his rise and fall would have been a brief episode, unsung and unlamented by other inhabitants of our galaxy. We know by now that other planets in the vastness of space are humming with life; that brief episode would probably never have come to their notice.

Only a few decades ago it was generally thought that the emergence of life out of inanimate chemical compounds must have been an extremely improbable, and therefore extremely rare event, which may have occurred only once, on this privileged planet of ours, and nowhere else. It was further thought that the formation of solar systems, such as ours, was also a rare event, and that planets capable of supporting life must be even rarer. But these assumptions, flavoured by 'earth-chauvinism', have been refuted by the rapid advances of astrophysics. It is now generally accepted by astronomers that the formation of planetary systems, including inhabitable planets, is 'a common event';* and that

*Professor Carl Sagan (Centre for Radiophysics and Space Research, Cornell University), at the CETI Congress, 1971. CETI (Communication with Extraterrestrial Intelligence) was sponsored by the US National Academy of Sciences and the Soviet Academy of Sciences and attended by leading scientists from both countries. Its proceedings (published by the MIT Press, 1973) represent a landmark in the study of the problems of extraterrestrial life, and of the possible methods of establishing contact with alien life-forms.

organic compounds, potentially capable of giving rise to life, are present both in our immediate neighbourhood, on Mars, and in the interstellar dust-clouds of distant nebulae. Moreover, a certain class of meteorites was found to contain organic materials whose spectra are the same as those of pollen-like spores in pre-Cambrian sediments.[11] Sir Fred Hoyle and his Indian colleague, Professor Chandra Wickranashinghe, proposed (in 1977) a theory, which regards 'pre-stellar molecular clouds such as are present in the Orion nebula, as the most natural "cradles" of life. Processes occurring in such clouds lead to the commencement and dispersal of biological activity in the Galaxy . . . It would now seem most likely that the transformation of inorganic matter into primitive biological systems is occurring more or less continually in the space between the stars.'[12]

As for the pollen-like structures in meteorites, the authors hold it to be possible that they 'represent primitive, interstellar "proto-cells" in a state of suspended animation'.[13] At present 'some hundred tons of meteoritic material enter the earth's atmosphere every day; but in earlier geological epochs the accumulation rate may have been much higher'. Part of this material may have originated in the 'cradles of life' – the dust-clouds pre-dating the formation of stars.

Thus the doctrines of 'terran chauvinism' have become untenable, like so many other cherished beliefs of nineteenth-century science. We are not alone in the universe – not the only spectators in the theatre, surrounded by empty seats. On the contrary, the universe around us is teeming with life, from primitive 'proto-cells', floating in interstellar space, to millions of advanced civilizations far ahead of us – where 'far' might mean the distance we have travelled from our reptilian or amoebic ancestry. I find this perspective comforting and exhilarating. In the first place, it is nice to know that we are not alone, that we have company out there among the stars – so that if we vanish, it does not matter too much, and the cosmic drama will not be played out before an empty house. The thought that we are the only conscious beings in this immensity, and that if we vanish, consciousness would vanish from it, is unbearable. Vice versa, the knowledge that there are billions of beings in our galaxy, and in other galaxies, infinitely more enlightened than our poor sick selves, may lead to that humility and self-transcendence which is the source of all religious experience.

This brings me to a perhaps naive, but I think plausible consideration regarding the nature of extraterrestrial intelligences and civilizations. Terrestrial civilization (from the start of agriculture, written language, etc.) is, at a generous estimate, around 10,000 years old. To make guesses about the nature of extraterrestrial civilizations a few *million* years older than ours is of course totally unrealistic. On the other hand, it is entirely reasonable to assume that sooner or later – within, say, its first 10,000 years – each of these civilizations would have discovered thermonuclear reactions – i.e., met the anno zero of its own calendar. From this point onward natural selection – or rather, the 'selective weed-killer' as I have called it – takes over on a cosmic scale. The sick civilizations engendered by biological misfits will sooner or later act as their own executioners and vanish from their polluted planet. Those civilizations which survive this and other tests of sanity will grow, or have already grown, into a cosmic élite of demi-gods. More soberly speaking, it is a comforting thought that owing to the action of the cosmic weed-killer, only the 'goodies' among these civilizations will survive, whereas the 'baddies' will annihilate themselves. It is nice to know that the universe is a place reserved for goodies and that we are surrounded by them. The established religions take a less charitable view of the cosmic administration.*

4

I shall conclude this book with a kind of *credo*, the origin of which dates some forty years back, to the Spanish Civil War. In 1937 I spent several months in the Nationalists' prison in Seville, as a uspected spy, threatened with execution.[14] During that period, in

---

*The oft-raised question why these advanced civilizations do not communicate with us lies outside the scope of this book; the reader will find a few remarks and bibliographical references on the subject in Appendix IV.

solitary confinement, I had some experiences which seemed to me close to the mystics' 'oceanic feeling' and which I subsequently tried to describe in an autobiographical account.* I called those experiences 'the hours by the window'. The extract which follows, though rather loosely formulated, reflects what one may call 'an agnostic's *credo*':

The 'hours by the window' had filled me with a direct certainty that a higher order of reality existed, and that it alone invested existence with meaning. I came to call it later on 'the reality of the third order'. The narrow world of sensory perception constituted the first order; this perceptual world was enveloped by the conceptual world which contained phenomena not directly perceivable, such as atoms, electromagnetic fields or curved space. This second order of reality filled in the gaps and gave meaning to the absurd patchiness of the sensory world.

In the same manner, the third order of reality enveloped, interpenetrated, and gave meaning to the second. It contained 'occult' phenomena which could not be apprehended or explained either on the sensory or on the conceptual level, and yet occasionally invaded them like spiritual meteors piercing the primitive's vaulted sky. Just as the conceptual order showed up the illusions and distortions of the senses, so the 'third order' revealed that time, space and causality, that the isolation, separateness and spatio–temporal limitations of the self were merely optical illusions on the next higher level. If illusions of the first type were taken at face value, then the sun was drowning every night in the sea, and a mote in the eye was larger than the moon; and if the conceptual world was mistaken for ultimate reality, the world became an equally absurd tale, told by an idiot or by idiot-electrons which caused little children to be run over by motor cars, and little Andalusian peasants to be shot through heart, mouth and eyes, without rhyme or reason. Just as one could not feel the pull of a magnet with one's skin, so one could not hope to grasp in cognate terms the nature of ultimate reality. It was a text written in invisible ink; and though one could not read it, the knowledge that it existed was sufficient to alter the texture of one's existence, and make one's actions conform to the text.

I liked to spin out this metaphor. The captain of a ship sets out with

The Invisible Writing (written in 1953).

a sealed order in his pocket which he is only permitted to open on the high seas. He looks forward to that moment which will end all uncertainty; but when the moment arrives and he tears the envelope open, he finds only an invisible text which defies all attempts at chemical treatment. Now and then a word becomes visible, or a figure denoting a meridian; then it fades again. He will never know the exact wording of the order; nor whether he has complied with it or failed in his mission. But his awareness of the order in his pocket, even though it cannot be deciphered, makes him think and act differently from the captain of a pleasure-cruiser or of a pirate ship.

I also liked to think that the founders of religions, prophets, saints and seers had at moments been able to read a fragment of the invisible text; after which they had so much padded, dramatized and ornamented it, that they themselves could no longer tell what parts of it were authentic.

APPENDICES

APPENDIX 1

BEYOND ATOMISM AND HOLISM – THE CONCEPT OF THE HOLON*

This is going to be an exercise in General Systems Theory – which seems to be all the more appropriate as Ludwig von Bertalanffy, its founding father, sits next to me. It seems equally appropriate that I should take as my text a sentence from Ludwig's *Problems of Life*[1]; it reads: 'Hierarchical organization on the one hand, and the characteristics of open systems on the other, are fundamental principles of living nature.'

If we combine these two fundamental principles, and add a dash of cybernetics to them, we get a system-theoretical model of Self-regulating Open Hierarchic Order, or SOHO for short. I intend to discuss some of the properties of this SOHO model as an alternative to the S–R model of linear causation, derived from classical mechanics, which we seem to be unanimous in rejecting. I can only give here a sketchy outline of the idea, but I have tried to tabulate the axioms and propositions relating to it in a more systematic way in an appendix to my last book,[2] which I have also appended to this paper, as a sort of *Tractatus Logico Hierarchicus*. Some of these propositions may appear trivial, others rest on incomplete evidence, still others will need correcting or qualifying. But they may provide a basis for discussion.

HIERARCHIES AND OLD HATS

When one talks about hierarchic organization as a fundamental principle of life, one often encounters a strong emotional resistance. For one thing, hierarchy is an ugly word, loaded with ecclesiastic and

---

*This edited version of a paper read at the *Beyond Reductionism* Symposium at Alpbach, 1968,[3] is intended as a summary of Part One, 'Outline of a System' (Chapters I-V). Unavoidably some passages are repetitive, others rather technical. The general reader can safely skip Appendices I-III.

military associations, and conveys to some people a wrong impression of a rigid or authoritarian structure. (Perhaps the assonance with 'hieratic', which is a quite different matter, plays a part in this confusion.) Apart from this, the term is often wrongly used to refer simply to order of rank on a linear scale or ladder (e.g. Clark Hull's 'habit-family hierarchies'). But that is not at all what the term is meant to signify. Its correct symbol is not a rigid ladder but a living tree – a multi-levelled, stratified, out-branching pattern of organization, a system branching into sub-systems, which branch into sub-systems of a lower order, and so on; a structure encapsulating sub-structures and so on; a process activating sub-processes and so on. As Paul Weiss said yesterday: 'The phenomenon of hierarchic structure is a real one, presented to us by the biological object, and not the fiction of a speculative mind.' It is at the same time a conceptual tool, a way of thinking, an alternative to the linear chaining of events torn from their multidimensionally stratified contexts.

All complex structures and processes of a relatively stable character display hierarchic organization, and this applies regardless whether we are considering inanimate systems, living organisms, social organizations, or patterns of behaviour. The linguist who thinks primarily in terms of Chomsky's[4] hierarchic model experiences a *déjà vu* reaction – as McNeill expressed it – towards the physiologist's intracellular hierarchy; and this may equally apply to Bruner's presentation of the hierarchic structure of voluntary action. In this essential respect – and in others that I shall mention – these processes in widely different fields are indeed isomorphic. The hierarchic tree diagram may serve equally well to represent the branching out of the evolution of species – the tree of life and its projection in taxonomy; it serves to represent the step-wise differentiation of tissues in embryonic development; it may serve as a structural diagram of the parts-within-parts architecture of organisms or galaxies, or as a functional schema for the analysis of instinctive behaviour by the ethologist;[5] or of the phrase-generating machinery by the psycholinguist. It may represent the locomotor hierarchy of limbs, joints, individual muscles, and so down to fibres, fibrils and filaments;[6] or, in reverse direction, the filtering and processing of the sensory input in its ascent from periphery to centre. It could also be regarded as a model for the subject-index of the Library of Congress, and for the organization of knowledge in our memory-stores; as an organizational chart for government administrations, military and business organizations; and so on.

This almost universal applicability of the hierarchic model may arouse the suspicion that it is logically empty; and this may be a further factor in the resistance against it. It usually takes the form of what one may call the 'so what' reaction: 'all this is old hat, it is self-evident' – followed by the *non sequitur* 'and anyway, where is your evidence?' Well, hierarchy may be old hat, but I would suggest that if you handle it with some affection, it can produce quite a few lively rabbits.

EVOLUTION AND HIERARCHIC ORDER

One of my favourite examples to illustrate the merits of hierarchic order is an amusing parable invented by Herbert Simon – whose absence we all regret. I have quoted it on other occasions, but I shall briefly quote it again. The parable concerns two watchmakers, Hora and Tempus. Both make watches consisting of a thousand parts each. Hora assembles his watches bit by bit; so when he pauses or drops a watch before it is finished, it falls to pieces and he has to start from scratch. Tempus, on the other hand, puts together sub-assemblies of ten parts each; ten of these sub-assemblies he makes into a larger sub-assembly of a hundred units; and ten of these make the whole watch. If there is a disturbance, Tempus has to repeat at worst nine assembling operations, and at best none at all. If you have a ratio of one disturbance in a hundred operations, then Hora will take four thousand times longer to assemble a watch – instead of one day, he will take eleven years. And if, for mechanical bits, we substitute amino-acids, protein molecules, organelles, and so on, the ratio between the time-scales becomes astronomical.

This is one basic advantage of employing the hierarchic method. The second is, of course, the incomparably greater stability and resilience to shock of the Tempus type of watch, and its amenability to repair and improvement. Simon concludes:

Complex systems will evolve from simple systems much more rapidly if there are stable intermediate forms than if there are not. The resulting complex forms in the former case will be hierarchic. We have only to turn the argument round to explain the observed predominance of hierarchies among the complex systems Nature presents to us. Among possible complex forms, hierarchies are the ones that had the time to evolve.[7]

If there is life on other planets, we may safely assume that, whatever its form, it must be hierarchically organized.

Motor manufacturers discovered long ago that it does not pay to design a new model from scratch by starting on the level of elementary components; they make use of already existing sub-assemblies – engines, brakes, etc. – each of which has developed from long previous experience, and then proceed by relatively small modifications of some of these. Evolution follows the same strategy. Once it has taken out a patent it sticks to it tenaciously – Thorpe remarked yesterday on its fixed conservative ways. The patented structure, organ or device acquires a kind of autonomous existence as a sub-assembly. The same make of organelles functions in the cells of mice and men; the same make of contractile protein serves the streaming motion of amoeba and the finger muscles of the piano-player; the same homologous design is maintained in the vertebrate forelimb of man, dog, bird and whale. Geoffroy de St Hilaire's *loi du balancement*, and d'Arcy Thompson's[8] transformation of a baboon's skull into a human skull by harmonious deformations of a Cartesian coordinate lattice, further illustrate the hierarchic constraints imposed on evolutionary design.

AUTONOMOUS HOLONS

The evolutionary stability of these sub-assemblies – organelles, organs, organ-systems – is reflected by their remarkable degree of *autonomy* or self-government. Each of them – a piece of tissue or a whole heart – is capable of functioning *in vitro* as a quasi-independent whole, even though isolated from the organism or transplanted into another organism. Each is a *sub-whole* which, towards its subordinated parts, behaves as a self-contained whole, and towards its superior controls as a dependent part. This relativity of the terms 'part' and 'whole' when applied to any of its sub-assemblies is a further general characteristic of hierarchies.

It is again the very obviousness of this feature which tends to make us overlook its implications. A part, as we generally use the word, means something fragmentary and incomplete, which by itself would have no legitimate existence. On the other hand, there is a tendency among holists to use the word 'whole' or '*Gestalt*' as something complete in itself which needs no further explanation. But wholes and parts in this absolute sense do not exist anywhere, either in the domain of living organisms or of social organizations. What we find are intermediary structures on a series of levels in ascending order of complexity, each of which has two faces looking in opposite directions: the face turned towards the lower levels is that of an autonomous whole, the one turned upward that of a dependent part. I have elsewhere[9] proposed the word 'holon' for these Janus-faced sub-assemblies.

The concept of the holon is meant to supply the missing link between atomism and holism, and to supplant the dualistic way of thinking in terms of 'parts' and 'wholes', which is so deeply engrained in our mental habits, by a multi-level, stratified approach. A hierarchically-organized whole cannot be 'reduced' to its elementary parts; but it can be 'dissected' into its constituent branches of holons, represented by the nodes of the tree-diagram, while the lines connecting the holons stand for channels of communication, control or transportation, as the case may be.

FIXED RULES AND FLEXIBLE STRATEGIES

The term holon may be applied to any stable sub-whole in an organismic, cognitive, or social hierarchy which displays rule-governed behaviour and/or structural Gestalt *constancy.* Thus biological holons are self-regulating 'open systems'[10] governed by a set of fixed rules which account for the holon's coherence, stability and its specific pattern of structure and function. This set of rules we may call *the canon of the holon.** The canon determines the fixed, invariant aspect of the open system in its steady state (*Fliessgleichgewicht* – dynamic equilibrium); it defines its pattern and structure. In other types of hierarchies, the canon represents the codes of conduct of social holons (family, tribe, nation, etc.); it incorporates the 'rules of the game' of instinctive rituals or acquired skills (behavioural holons); the rules of enunciation, grammar and syntax in the language hierarchy; Piaget's 'schemes' in cognitive hierarchies, and so on. *The canon represents the constraints imposed on any rule-governed process or behaviour.* But these constraints do not exhaust the system's degrees of freedom; they leave room for more or less *flexible strategies,* guided by the contingencies in the holon's local environment.

It is essential at this point to make a sharp, categorical distinction between the fixed, invariant canon of the system and its flexible (plastic, variable) strategies. A few examples will illustrate the validity of this distinction. In *ontogeny,* the apex of the hierarchy is the zygote, and the holons at successive levels represent successive stages in the development of tissues. Each step in differentiation and specialization imposes

---

*cf. the 'organizing relations' or 'laws of organization' of earlier writers on hierarchic organization (e.g., Woodger (1929), Needham (1941)), and the 'system-conditions' in general system theory.

further constraints on the genetic potential of the tissue, but at each step it retains sufficient developmental flexibility to follow this or that evolutionary pathway, within the range of its competence, guided by the contingencies of the cell's environment – Waddington's[11] 'strategy of the genes'. Turning from embryonic development to the *instinctive activities* of the mature animal, we find that spiders spin webs, birds build nests according to invariant species-specific canons, but again using flexible strategies, guided by the lie of the land: the spider may suspend its web from three, four or more points of attachment, but the result will always be a regular polygon. In *acquired skills* like chess, the rules of the game define the permissible moves, but the strategic choice of the actual move depends on the environment – the distribution of the chessmen on the board. In *symbolic operations*, the holons are rule-governed cognitive structures variously called 'frames of reference', 'universes of discourse', 'algorithms', etc., each with its specific 'grammar' or canon; and the strategies increase in complexity on higher levels of each hierarchy. It seems that life in all its manifestations, from morphogenesis to symbolic thought, is governed by rules of the game which lend it order and stability but also allow for flexibility; and that these rules, whether innate or acquired, are represented in coded form on various levels of the hierarchy, from the genetic code to the structures in the nervous system responsible for symbolic thought.

TRIGGERS AND SCANNERS

Let me discuss briefly some specific characteristics of what one might loosely call *output hierarchies*, regardless whether the 'output' is a baby, or a sentence spoken in English. However much their products differ, all output hierarchies seem to have a classic mode of operation, based on the trigger-releaser principle, where an implicit coded signal which may be relatively simple, releases complex, pre-set mechanisms.

Let me again run through a few examples. In *phylogeny*, Waddington[12] and others have convincingly shown that a single favourable gene-mutation can act as a trigger to release a kind of chain-reaction which affects a whole organ in a harmonious way. In *ontogeny*, the prick of a fine platinum needle on the unfertilized egg of a frog or sheep triggers off parthenogenesis. The genes act as chemical triggers, catalysing reactions. The implicit four-letter alphabet of the DNA chain is spelled out into the explicit, twenty-letter alphabet of amino-acids; the inducers or evocators, including Spemann's 'general organizer', again turn out to be relatively simple chemicals which need not even be species-specific to activate the genetic potentials of the tissue. In *instinct behaviour*, we have releasers of a very simple kind – the red belly of the stickleback, the spot under the herring-gull's beak, which trigger off the appropriate behaviour.[13] In the performance of *acquired skills* you have the same process of step-wise filling in the details of implicit commands issued from the apex of the hierarchy, such as 'strike a match and light this cigarette' or 'sign your name', or 'use your phrase-generating machine' to transform an unverbalized image into innervations of the vocal chords.

The point to emphasize is that this spelling-out process, from intent to execution, cannot be described in terms of a linear chain of S–R units, only as a series of discrete steps from one open sesame, activated by a combination lock, to the next. The activated holon, whether it is a government department or a living kidney, has its own canon which determines the pattern of its activity. Thus the signal from higher quarters does not have to specify what the holon is expected to do; the signal merely has to trigger the holon into action by a coded message. Once thrown into action, the holon will spell out the implicit command in explicit form by activating its sub-units in the appropriate strategic order, guided by feedbacks and feed-forwards from its environment. Generally speaking, *the holon is a system of relations which is represented on the next higher level as a unit, that is, a relatum.*

If we turn now to the *input hierarchies* of perception, the operations proceed, of course, in the reverse direction, from the peripheral twigs of the tree towards its apex; and instead of trigger-releasers we have the opposite type of mechanisms: a series of filters, scanners or classifiers through which the input traffic must pass in its ascent from periphery to cortex. First you have lateral inhibition, habituation and presumably some efferent control of receptors. On the higher levels are the mechanisms responsible for the visual and acoustic constancy phenomena, the scanning and filtering devices which account for the recognition of patterns in space and time, and enable us to abstract universals and discard particulars. The colloquial complaint: 'I have a memory like a sieve' may be derived from an intuitive grasp of these filtering devices that operate first all along the input channels, then along the storage channels.

How do we pick out a single instrument in a symphony? The whole medley of sounds arriving at the ear-drum is scrambled into a linear pressure-wave with a single variable. To reconstruct the timbre of an instrument, to identify harmonies and melodies, to appreciate phrasing, style and mood, we have to abstract patterns in time as we abstract visual patterns in space. But how does the nervous system do it? I will play you the opening bars of the *Archduke Trio*; watch your reactions, because no text-book on psychology that I know of will give you the faintest clue [opening bars of Beethoven's *Archduke Trio* played]. If one looks at the record with a magnifying glass, one is tempted to ask the naive question why the nervous system does not produce engrams by this simple method of coding, instead of being so damned complicated. The answer is, of course, that a linear engram of this kind would be completely useless for the purpose of analysing, matching and recognizing input patterns. The chain is a hopeless model; we cannot do without the tree.

In motor hierarchies, an implicit intention or generalized command is particularized, spelled out, step by step, in its descent to the periphery. In perceptual hierarchies, we have the opposite process. The peripheral input is more and more de-particularized, stripped of irrelevancies during its ascent to the centre. *The output hierarchy concretizes, the input hierarchy abstracts.* The former operates by means of triggering devices, the latter by means of filtering or scanning devices. When I intend to write the letter R, a trigger activates a functional holon, an automatic pattern of muscle contractions, which produces the letter R in my own particular hand-writing. When I read, a scanning device in my visual cortex identifies the letter R regardless of the particular hand that wrote it. Triggers release complex outputs by means of a simple coded signal. Scanners function the opposite way: they convert complex inputs into simple coded signals.

'ABSTRACT' AND 'SPOTLIGHT'

Let me briefly turn to the phenomena of *memory* and ask whether the hierarchic approach is capable of shedding some additional light on them. You watch a television play. The exact words of each actor are forgotten by the time he speaks his next line, and only their meaning remains; the next morning you can only remember the sequence of scenes which constituted the story; after a month, all you remember is that it was about a gangster on the run or about two men and a woman on a desert island. The same happens generally with the content of novels one has read, and episodes one has lived. The original experience has been stripped of detail, reduced to a schematic outline. Now this skeletonization of the input before it is put into storage, and the gradual decay of the stored material, would mean a terrible impoverishment of memory, if this were the whole story – memory would be a collection of dusty abstracts, the dehydrated sediments in the wine-glass, with all flavour gone. But there are compensating mechanisms. I can recognize a melody, regardless of the instrument on which it is played, and I can recognize the timbre of an instrument, regardless of the melody played on it. There are several interlocking hierarchies at work, each with its own criteria of relevance. One abstracts melody and treats everything else as noise, the other abstracts timbre and treats melody as noise. Thus not all the information discarded as irrelevant by one filtering system is irretrievably lost, because it may have been stored by another filtering hierarchy with different canons of relevance. Recall would then be made possible by the cooperation of several interlocking hierarchies, which may pertain to different sense modalities – sight and smell, for instance; or, what is less obvious, there may also be several distinct hierarchies with different criteria or relevance operating within the same sense modality. Recall could then be compared to the process of multi-coloured printing by the superimposition of several colour-blocks. This, of course, is speculative, but some modest evidence for the hypothesis can be found in a series of experiments by J. J. Jenkins and myself;[14]* and more tests on these lines can be designed without much difficulty.

I am aware that the hypothesis is in apparent contradiction to Penfield's[15] experiments eliciting what looks like total recall of past experiences by electrical stimulation of points on the patient's temporal lobe. But the contradiction may be resolved if we include in the criteria of relevance also criteria of *emotional* relevance which decide whether an input is worth storing. A detail might be emotionally relevant (on a conscious or unconscious level), and retained with almost photographic or cinematographic clarity. One might call this the *spotlight* type of memory which is stamped in, as distinct from *abstractive* memory which schematizes. Spotlight memories may be related to eidetic images; and they might even, unlike abstractive memories, originate in the limbic system.[16]

ARBORIZARION AND RETICULATION

I have used the term 'interlocking' or 'interlacing' hierarchies. Of

*See Appendix II.

course hierarchies do not operate in a vacuum. This truism regarding the interdependence of processes in an organism is probably the main cause of confusion which obscured from view its hierarchic structure. It is as if the sight of the foliage of the entwined branches in a forest made us forget that the branches originate in separate trees. The trees are vertical structures. The meeting points of branches from neighbouring trees form horizontal networks at several levels. Without the trees there could be no entwining, and no network. Without the networks, each tree would be isolated, and there would be no integration of functions. Arborization and reticulation seem to be complementary principles in the architecture of organisms. In symbolic universes of discourse arborization is reflected in the 'vertical' denotation (definition) of concepts, reticulation in their 'horizontal' connotations in associative networks. This calls to mind Hyden's proposal that the same neuron, or population of neurons, may be a member of several functional 'clubs'.

HIERARCHIC ORDER AND FEEDBACK CONTROL

The most obvious example of interlocking hierarchies is the sensory-motor system. The sensory hierarchy processes information and transmits it in a steady upward flow, some of which reaches the conscious ego at the apex; the ego makes decisions which are spelt out by the downward stream of impulses in the motor hierarchy. But the apex is not the only point of contact between the two systems; they are connected by entwining networks on various lower levels. The network on the lowest level consists of reflexes like the patellary. They are short-cuts between the ascending and descending flow, like loops connecting opposite traffic streams on a motor highway. On the next higher level are the networks of sensory–motor skills and habits, such as touch-typing or driving a car, which do not require the attention of the highest centres – unless some disturbance throws them out of gear. But let a little dog amble across the icy road in front of the driver, and he will have to make a 'top level' decision whether to slam on the brake, risking the safety of his passengers, or run over the dog. It is at this level, when the pros and cons are precariously balanced that the subjective experience of free choice and moral responsibility arises.

But the ordinary routines of existence do not require such moral decisions, and not even much conscious attention. They operate by means of feedback loops, and loops-within-loops, which form the multilevelled, reticulate networks between the input and output hierarchies. So long as all goes well and no dog crosses the road, the strategy of riding a bicycle or driving a car can be left to the automatic pilot in the nervous system – the cybernetic helmsman. But one must beware of using the principle of feedback control as a magic formula. The concept of feedback without the concept of hierarchic order is like the grin without the cat. All skilled routines follow a pre-set pattern according to certain rules of the game. These are fixed, but permit continual adjustments to variable environmental conditions. *Feedback can only operate within the limits set by the rules* – by the canon of the skill. The part which feedback plays is to report back on every step in the progress of the operation, whether it is over-shooting or falling short of the mark, how to keep it on an even keel, when to intensify the pace and when to stop. But it cannot alter the intrinsic pattern of the skill. To quote Paul Weiss[17] at the Hixon Symposium:

> The structure of the input does not produce the structure of the output, but merely modifies intrinsic nervous activities, which have a structural organization of their own.

One of the vital differences between the S–R and SOHO concepts is that according to the former, the environment determines behaviour, whereas according to the latter, feedback from the environment merely guides or corrects or stabilizes pre-existing patterns of behaviour.

Moreover, the cross-traffic between the sensory and motor hierarchies works both ways. The input guides the output and keeps it on an even keel; but motor activity in its turn guides perception. The eye must scan; its motions, large and small – drift, flicker, tremor – are indispensable to vision; an image stabilized on the retina disintegrates into darkness.[18] Similarly with audition: if you try to recall a tune, what do you do? You hum it. Stimuli and responses have been swallowed up by feedback loops within loops, along which impulses run in circles like kittens chasing their tails.

A HIERARCHY OF ENVIRONMENTS

Let us carry this inquiry into the meaning of current terminology a step further, and ask just what that convenient word 'environment' is meant to signify. When I am driving my car, the environment in contact with my right foot is the accelerator pedal, its elastic resistance to pressure provides a tactile feedback which helps keeping the speed of the car steady. The same applies to the 'feel' of the wheel under my hands. But my eyes encompass a much larger environment than my feet and hands; they determine the overall strategy of driving. The hierarchically organized creature that I am is in fact functioning in a hierarchy of environments, guided by a hierarchy of feedbacks.

One advantage of this operational interpretation is that the hierarchy of environments can be extended indefinitely. When the chess-player stares at the board in front of him, trying to visualize various situations three moves ahead, he is guided by feedbacks from imagined environments. Most of our thinking, planning and creating operates in such imaginary environments. But – to quote Bartlett[19] – 'all our perceptions are inferential constructs', coloured by imagination, and so the difference is merely one of degrees. The hierarchy is open-ended at the top.

MECHANIZATION AND FREEDOM

A skilled activity, such as writing a letter, branches into sub-skills which, on successively lower levels of the hierarchy, become increasingly mechanized, stereotyped and predictable. The choice of subjects to be discussed in a letter is vast; the next step, phrasing, still offers a great number of alternatives, but is more restricted by the rules of grammar, the limits of one's vocabulary, etc.; the rules of spelling are fixed, with no leeway for flexible strategies, and lastly, the muscle contractions which depress the typewriter keys are entirely automatized. Thus a *sub-skill or behavioural holon on the (n) level of the hierarchy has more degrees of freedom* (a larger variety of alternative strategic choices permitted by the canon) *than a holon on the (n–1) level.*

However, all skills tend with increasing mastery and practice to become automatized routines. While acquiring a skill we must concentrate on every detail of what we are doing; then learning begins to condense into habit as steam condenses into drops; with increasing practice we read, write, type, drive 'automatically' or 'mechanically'. Thus we are all the time transforming 'mental' into 'mechanical' activities. In unexpected contingencies, however, the process can be reversed. Driving along a familiar road is an automatized routine; but when that little dog crosses the road, a strategic choice has to be made which is beyond the competence of automatized routine, for which the automatic pilot in my nervous system has not been programmed, and the decision must be referred to higher quarters. The *shift of control* of an on-going activity from one level to a higher level of the hierarchy

– from 'mechanical' to 'mindful' behaviour – seems to be the essence of conscious decision-making and of the subjective experience of free will.

The tendency towards the progressive mechanization of skills has its positive side: it conforms to the principle of parsimony. If I could not hit the keys of the typewriter 'automatically' I could not attend to meaning. On the negative side, mechanization, like *rigor mortis*, affects first the extremities – the lower subordinate branches of the hierarchy, but it also tends to spread upward. If a skill is practised in the same unvarying conditions, following the same unvarying course, it tends to degenerate into stereotyped routine and its degrees of freedom freeze up. Monotony accelerates enslavement to habit; and if mechanization spreads to the apex of the hierarchy, the result is the rigid pedant, Bergson's *homme automate*. As von Bertalanffy wrote, 'organisms *are not* machines, but they can to a certain extent *become* machines, congeal into machines'.[20]

Vice versa, a variable environment demands flexible behaviour and reverses the trend towards mechanization. However, the challenge of the environment may exceed a critical limit where it can no longer be met by customary routines, however flexible – because the traditional 'rules of the game' are no longer adequate to cope with the situation. Then a crisis arises. The outcome is either a breakdown of behaviour – or alternatively the emergence of new forms of behaviour, of original solutions. They have been observed throughout the animal kingdom, from insects onward, through rats to chimpanzees, and point to the existence of unsuspected potentials in the living organism, which are inhibited or dormant in the normal routines of existence, and only make their appearance in exceptional circumstances. They foreshadow the phenomena of human creativity which must remain incomprehensible to the S–R theorist, but appear in a new light when approached from the hierarchic point of view.

SELF-ASSERTION AND INTEGRATION

The holons which constitute an organismic or social hierarchy are Janus-faced entities: facing upward, toward the apex, they function as dependent parts of a larger whole; facing downward, as autonomous wholes in their own right. 'Autonomy' in this context means that organelles, cells, muscles, neurons, organs, all have their intrinsic rhythm and pattern, often manifested spontaneously without external stimulation, and that they tend to persist in and assert their characteristic pattern of activity. This *self-assertive tendency* is a fundamental and universal characteristic of holons, manifested on every level of every type of hierarchy: in the regulative properties of the morphogenetic field, defying transplantation and experimental mutilation; in the stubbornness of instinct rituals, acquired habits, tribal traditions and social customs; and even in a person's handwriting, which he can modify but not sufficiently to fool the expert. Without this self-assertive tendency of their parts, organisms and societies would lose their articulation and stability.

The opposite aspect of the holon is its *integrative tendency* to function as an integral part of an existing or evolving larger whole. Its manifestations are equally ubiquitous, from the 'docility' of the embryonic tissues, through the symbiosis of organelles in the cell, to the various forms of cohesive bonds, from flock to insect state and human tribe.

We thus arrive at a polarity between the self-assertive and the integrative tendency of holons on every level. This polarity is of fundamental importance to the SOHO concept. It is in fact implied in the model of the multilevelled hierarchy, because the stability of the hierarchy depends on the equilibration of the two opposite tendencies of its holons. Empirically the postulated polarity can be traced in all phenomena of life; in its theoretical aspect it is not derived from any metaphysical dualism, but may rather be regarded as an application of Newton's Third Law of Motion (action and reaction) to hierarchic systems. We may even extend the polarity into inanimate nature: wherever there is a relatively stable dynamic system, from atoms to galaxies, stability is maintained by the equilibration of opposite forces, one of which may be centrifugal or separative or inertial, and the other a centripetal or attractive or cohesive force, which keep the parts in their place in the larger whole, and hold it together.

Perhaps the most fertile field of application of the SOHO schema is the study of emotions and emotional disorders on the individual and social scale. Under conditions of stress, the affected part of an organism may become overstimulated and tend to escape the restraining control of the whole.[21] This can lead to pathological changes of an irreversible nature, such as malignant growths with untrammelled proliferation of tissues that have escaped from genetic restraint. On a less extreme level, practically any organ or function may get temporarily and partially out of control. In rage and panic the sympathico–adrenal apparatus takes over from the higher centres which normally coordinate behaviour;

when sex is aroused the gonads seem to take over from the brain. The *idée fixe*, the obsession of the crank, are cognitive holons running riot. There is a whole gamut of mental disorders in which some subordinate part of the mental hierarchy exerts its tyrannical rule over the whole, from the insidious domination of 'repressed' complexes to the major psychoses, in which large chunks of the personality seem to have 'split off' and lead a quasi-independent existence. Aberrations of the human mind are frequently due to the obsessional pursuit of some part-truth, treated as if it were the whole truth – of a holon masquerading as a whole.

If we turn from organismic to *social hierarchies*, we again find that under normal conditions the holons (clans, tribes, nations, social classes, professional groups) live in a kind of dynamic equilibrium with their natural and social environment. However, under conditions of stress, when tensions exceed a critical limit, some social holon may get over-excited and tend to assert itself to the detriment of the whole, just like an over-excited organ. It should be noted that the canon which defines the identity and lends coherence to social holons (its laws, language, traditions, rules of conduct, systems of belief) represents not merely negative constraints imposed on its actions, but also positive precepts, maxims and moral imperatives.

The single individual constitutes the apex of the organismic hierarchy, and at the same time the lowest unit of the social hierarchy. Looking inward, he sees himself as a self-contained, unique whole, looking outward as a dependent part. No man is an island, he is a holon. His *self-assertive* tendency is the dynamic manifestation of his unique wholeness as an individual; his *integrative* tendency expresses his dependence on the larger whole to which he belongs, his partness. Under normal conditions, the two opposite tendencies are more or less evenly balanced. Under conditions of stress, the equilibrium is upset, as manifested in emotional behaviour. The emotions derived from the self-assertive tendencies are of the well-known aggressive–defensive, hunger, rage and fear type, including the possessive component of sex. The emotions derived from the integrative tendency have been largely neglected by contemporary psychology; one may call them the self-transcending or participatory type of emotions. They arise out of the human holon's need to be an integral part of some larger whole – which may be a social group, a personal bond, a belief-system, Nature or the *anima mundi*. The psychological processes through which this category of emotions operates are variously referred to as projection, identification, empathy, hypnotic rapport, devotion, love. It is one of the ironies of the human condition that both its glory and its predicament seem to derive not from the self-assertive but from the integrative potentials of the species. The glories of art and science, and the holocausts of history caused by misguided devotion, are both nurtured by the self-transcending emotions.

To conclude, even this fragmentary outline ought to make it clear that in the SOHO model there is no place for such a thing as an aggressive or destructive instinct in organisms; nor does it admit the reification of the sexual instinct as the *only* integrative force in human or animal society. Freud's Eros and Thanatos are relative late-comers on the stage of evolution: a host of creatures that multiply by fission or budding are ignorant of both. In the present view, Eros is an offspring of the integrative, destructive Thanatos of the self-assertive tendency, and Janus the symbol of the polarity of these two irreducible properties of living matter – that *coincidentia oppositorum* which von Bertalanffy is so fond of quoting, and which is inherent in the open-ended hierarchies of life.

SUMMARY: SOME GENERAL PROPERTIES OF SELF-REGULATING OPEN HIERARCHIC ORDER

1. *The Holon*

1.1 The organism in its structural aspect is not an aggregation of elementary parts, and in its functional aspects not a chain of elementary units of behaviour.

1.2 The organism is to be regarded as a multilevelled hierarchy of semi-autonomous sub-wholes, branching into sub-wholes of a lower order, and so on. Sub-wholes on any level of the hierarchy are referred to as *holons*.

1.3 Parts and wholes in an absolute sense do not exist in the domains of life. The concept of the holon is intended to reconcile the atomistic and holistic approaches.

1.4 Biological holons are self-regulating open systems which display both the autonomous properties of wholes and the dependent properties of parts. This dichotomy is present on every level of every type of hierarchic organization, and is referred to as the 'Janus phenomenon'.

1.5 More generally, the term 'holon' may be applied to any stable biological or social sub-whole which displays rule-governed behaviour and/or structural *Gestalt*-constancy. Thus organelles and homologous organs are evolutionary holons; morphogenetic fields are ontogenetic holons; the ethologist's 'fixed action-patterns' and the sub-routines of acquired skills are behavioural holons; phonemes, morphemes, words, phrases are linguistic holons; individuals, families, tribes, nations are social holons.

2. Dissectibility

2.1 Hierarchies are 'dissectible' into their constituent branches, on which the holons form the nodes; the branching lines represent the channels of communication and control.

2.2 The number of levels which a hierarchy comprises is a measure of its 'depth', and the number of holons on any given level is called its 'span' (Simon).

3. Rules and Strategies

3.1 Functional holons are governed by fixed sets of rules and display more or less flexible strategies.

3.2 The rules – referred to as the system's '*canon*' – determine its invariant properties, its structural configuration and/or functional pattern.

3.3 While the canon defines the permissible steps in the holon's activity, the strategic selection of the actual step among permissible choices is guided by the contingencies of the environment.

3.4 The canon determines the rules of the game, strategy decides the course of the game.

3.5 The evolutionary process plays variations on a limited number of canonical themes. The constraints imposed by the evolutionary canon are illustrated by the phenomena of homology, homeoplasy, parallelism, convergence and the *loi du balancement*.

3.6 In ontogeny, the holons at successive levels represent successive stages in the development of tissues. At each step in the process of differentiation, the genetic canon imposes further constraints on the holon's developmental potentials, but it retains sufficient flexibility to follow one or another alternative developmental pathway, within the range of its competence, guided by the contingencies of the environment.

3.7 Structurally, the mature organism is a hierarchy of parts within parts.

3.8 Functionally, the behaviour of organisms is governed by 'rules of the game' which account for its coherence, stability and specific pattern.

3.9 Skills, whether inborn or acquired, are functional hierarchies, with sub-skills as holons, governed by sub-rules.

4. *Integration and Self-Assertion*

4.1 Every holon has the dual tendency to preserve and assert its individuality as a quasi-autonomous whole; and to function as an integrated part of an (existing or evolving) larger whole. This polarity between the self-assertive and integrative tendencies is inherent in the concept of hierarchic order; and a universal characteristic of life.

The self-assertive tendencies are the dynamic expression of the holon's wholeness, the integrative tendencies of its partness.

4.2 An analogous polarity is found in the interplay of cohesive and separative forces in stable inorganic systems, from atoms to galaxies.

4.3 The most general manifestation of the integrative tendencies is the reversal of the Second Law of Thermodynamics in open systems feeding on negative entropy (Schrödinger), and the evolutionary trend towards 'spontaneously developing states of greater heterogeneity and complexity' (Herrick).

4.4 Its specific manifestations on different levels range from the symbiosis of organelles and colonial animals, through the cohesive forces in herds and flocks, to the integrative bonds in insect states and primate societies. The complementary manifestations of the self-assertive tendencies are competition, individualism, and the separative forces of tribalism, nationalism, etc.

4.5 In ontogeny, the polarity is reflected in the docility and determination of growing tissues.

4.6 In adult behaviour, the self-assertive tendency of functional holons is reflected in the stubbornness of instinct rituals (fixed action-patterns), of acquired habits (handwriting, spoken accent), and in the stereotyped routines of thought; the integrative tendency is reflected in flexible adaptations, improvisations, and creative acts which initiate new forms of behaviour.

4.7 Under conditions of stress, the self-assertive tendency is manifested in the aggressive–defensive, adrenergic type of emotions, the integrative tendency in the self-transcending (participatory, identificatory) type of emotions.

4.8 In social behaviour, the canon of a social holon represents not only constraints imposed on its actions, but also embodies maxims of conduct, moral imperatives and systems of value.

5. *Triggers and Scanners*

5.1   Output hierarchies generally operate on the trigger-releaser principle, where a relatively simple, implicit or coded signal releases complex, preset mechanisms.

5.2   In phylogeny, a favourable gene-mutation may, through homeorhesis (Waddington) affect the development of a whole organ in a harmonious way.

5.3   In ontogeny, chemical triggers (enzymes, inducers, hormones) release the genetic potentials of differentiating tissues.

5.4   In instinctive behaviour, sign-releasers of a simple kind trigger off innate releasive mechanisms (Lorenz).

5.5   In the performance of learnt skills, including verbal skills, a generalized implicit command is spelled out in explicit terms on successive lower echelons which, once triggered into action, activate their subunits in the appropriate strategic order, guided by feedbacks.

5.6   A holon on the n level of an output-hierarchy is represented on the $(n+1)$ level as a unit, and triggered into action as a unit. A holon, in other words, is a system of relata which is represented on the next higher level as a relatum.

5.7   In social hierarchies (military, administrative), the same principles apply.

5.8   Input hierarchies operate on the reverse principle; instead of triggers, they are equipped with 'filter'-type devices (scanners, 'resonators', classifiers) which strip the input of noise, abstract and digest its relevant contents, according to that particular hierarchy's criteria of relevance. 'Filters' operate on every echelon through which the flow of information must pass on its ascent from periphery to centre, in social hierarchies and in the nervous system.

5.9   Triggers convert coded signals into complex output patterns. Filters convert complex input patterns into coded signals. The former may be compared to digital-to-analogue converters, the latter to analogue-to-digital converters.[22]

5.10   In perceptual hierarchies, filtering devices range from habituation and the efferent control of receptors, through the constancy phenomena, to pattern-recognition in space or time, and to the decoding of linguistic and other forms of meaning.

5.11   Output hierarchies spell, concretize, particularize. Input hierarchies digest, abstract, generalize.

6.   Arborization and Reticulation

6.1   Hierarchies can be regarded as 'vertically' arborizing structures whose branches interlock with those of other hierarchies at a multiplicity of levels and form 'horizontal' networks: arborization and reticulation are complementary principles in the architecture of organisms and societies.

6.2   Conscious experience is enriched by the cooperation of several perceptual hierarchies in different sense-modalities, and within the same sense-modality.

6.3   Abstractive memories are stored in skeletonized form, stripped of irrelevant detail, according to the criteria of relevance of each perceptual hierarchy.

6.4   Vivid details of quasi-eidetic clarity are stored owing to their emotive relevance.

6.5   The impoverishment of experience in memory is counteracted to some extent by the cooperation in recall of different perceptual hierarchies with different criteria of relevance.

6.6   In sensory–motor coordination, local reflexes are short-cuts on the lowest level, like loops connecting traffic streams moving in opposite directions on a highway.

6.7   Skilled sensory–motor routines operate on higher levels through networks of proprioceptive and exteroceptive feedback loops within loops, which function as servo-mechanisms and keep the rider on his bicycle in a state of self-regulating, kinetic homeostasis.

6.8   While in S–R theory the contingencies of environment determine behaviour, in the present theory they merely guide, correct and stabilize pre-existing patterns of behaviour (Weiss).

6.9   While sensory feedbacks guide motor activities, perception in its turn is dependent on these activities, such as the various scanning motions of the eye, or the humming of a tune in aid of its auditory recall. The perceptual and motor hierarchies are so intimately cooperating on every level that to draw a categorical distinction between 'stimuli' and 'responses' becomes meaningless; they have become 'aspects of feed-back loops' (Miller *et al*).

6.10   Organisms and societies operate in a hierarchy of environments, from the local environment of each holon to the 'total field', which may include imaginary environments derived from extrapolation in space and time.

7. Regulation Channels

7.1 The higher echelons in a hierarchy are not normally in direct communication with lowly ones, and vice versa; signals are transmitted through 'regulation channels', one step at a time.

7.2 The pseudo-explanations of verbal behaviour and other human skills as the manipulation of words, or the chaining of operants, leaves a void between the apex of the hierarchy and its terminal branches, between thinking and spelling.

7.3 The short-circuiting of intermediary levels by directing conscious attention at processes which otherwise function automatically, tends to cause disturbances ranging from awkwardness to psychosomatic disorders.

8. Mechanization and Freedom

8.1 Holons on successively higher levels of the hierarchy show increasingly complex, more flexible and less predictable patterns of activity, while on successive lower levels we find increasingly mechanized, stereotyped and predictable patterns.

8.2 All skills, whether innate or acquired, tend with increasing practice to become automatized routines. This process can be described as the continual transformation of 'mental' into 'mechanical' activities.

8.3 Other things being equal, a monotonous environment facilitates mechanization.

8.4 Conversely, new or unexpected contingencies require decisions to be referred to higher levels of the hierarchy, an upward shift of controls from 'mechanical' to 'mindful' activities.

8.5 Each upward shift is reflected by a more vivid and precise consciousness of the ongoing activity; and, since the variety of alternative choices increases with the increasing complexity on higher levels, each upward shift is accompanied by the subjective experience of freedom of decision.

8.6 The hierarchic approach replaces dualistic theories by a serialistic hypothesis in which 'mental' and 'mechanical' appear as complementary attributes of a unitary process, the dominance of one or the other depending on changes in the level of control.

8.7 Consciousness appears as an emergent quality in phylogeny and ontogeny, which, from primitive beginnings, evolves towards more complex and precise states. It is the highest manifestation of the integrative tendency to extract order out of disorder, and information out of noise.

8.8 The self can never be completely represented in its own awareness, nor can its actions be completely predicted by any conceivable information-processing device. Both attempts lead to infinite regress.

9. Equilibrium and Disorder

9.1 An organism or society is said to be in dynamic equilibrium if the self-assertive and integrative tendencies of its holons counter-balance each other.

9.2 The term 'equilibrium' in a hierarchic system does not refer to relations between parts on the same level, but to the relation between part and whole (the whole being represented by the agency which controls the part from the next higher level).

9.3 Organisms live by transactions with their environment. Under normal conditions, the stresses set up in the holons involved in the transaction are of a transitory nature, and equilibrium will be restored on its completion.

9.4 If the challenge to the organism exceeds a critical limit, the balance may be upset, the over-excited holon may tend to get out of control, and to assert itself to the detriment of the whole, or monopolize its functions – whether the holon be an organ, a cognitive structure (*idée fixe*), an individual, or a social group. The same may happen if the coordinating powers of the whole are so weakened that it is no longer able to control its parts (Child).

9.5 The opposite type of disorder occurs when the power of the whole over its parts erodes their autonomy and individuality. This may lead to a regression of the integrative tendencies from mature forms of social integration to primitive forms of identification and to the quasi-hypnotic phenomena of group psychology.

9.6 The process of identification may arouse vicarious emotions of the aggressive type.

9.7 The rules of conduct of a social holon are not reducible to the rules of conduct of its members.

9.8 The egotism of the social holon feeds on the altruism of its members.

10.   *Regeneration*

10.1   Critical challenges to an organism or society can produce degenerative or regenerative effects.

10.2   The regenerative potential of organisms and societies manifests itself in fluctuations from the highest level of integration down to earlier, more primitive levels, and up again to a new, modified pattern. Processes of this type seem to play a major part in biological and mental evolution, and are symbolized in the universal death-and-rebirth motif in mythology.

APPENDIX II

AN EXPERIMENT IN PERCEPTION*

Arthur Koestler and James J. Jenkins

The writers are indebted to Donald Foss for collecting and coding the data. Thanks are also due to Professor Douglas Lawrence and Professor Ernest Hilgard of Stanford University and to Professor Arnold Mechanic and Joanne D'Andrea of California State College at Hayward for their generous facilitation of the study.

ABSTRACT

Experience suggests that a common error in processing visual sequences is inversion or transposition of two or more adjacent items. This phenomenon suggests that information concerning the identity of items and their positions may be partially separable. A perception experiment was performed with tachistoscopic exposure of 5-, 6-, and 7-digit sequences. Abundant evidence was found for transposition errors. Further, such errors were distributed in a serial position curve much like that found for errors of single items.

PROBLEM

While information-processing in visual perception has received increasing attention in recent years,[1] one common phenomenon of faulty processing which may have some theoretical significance seems to have been ignored. We refer to the inversion (or transposition) of adjacent items in a sequence of numbers shown in a tachistoscope. Though such errors are common enough in bookkeeping and have earned a special proofreader's mark, they are absent from discussions of visual perception or memory span in standard works such as Osgood[2] and Woodworth and Schlosberg.[3]

Apprehending a series of numerals and subsequently repeating them in their correct sequence must either involve the *ordered* storage of the individual items or the storage of information relating to

*See Chapter I, 13, and p. 297. Reprinted with permission from *Psychon. Sci.*, 1965, vol. 3, pp. 75–6.

that order. Both information identifying an item and information defining its place in the sequence must be available for the S for successful performance of the task.

The potential separability of the two kinds of information involved is not easy to demonstrate. If a subject makes a single error of identity, reporting either an incorrect number or a blank, it may indicate that he has lost only identity information. This argument, however, is inconclusive, because if the subject had acquired no information at all regarding the offending item, but complete information regarding other items, the outcome would be the same. The inversion of two digits or the permutation of three or more digits, on the other hand, furnishes a compelling argument because it is *prima facie* evidence that the identity information is accurate while the positional information is incomplete or distorted.

The purposes of the present study were to demonstrate that the phenomenon of transposition could be observed under laboratory conditions and to describe the locus of its probable occurrences in a given sequence.

METHOD

The stimulus materials were 80 4×6 notecards upon which digit sequences were typed in elite type. The 80 sequences were divided into four sets of 20 cards each. The first set showed sequences 5 digits in length; the second and third sets showed 6-digit sequences; the fourth set showed 7-digit sequences. The sequences contained the digits 1-9 with never more than a single digit repeated on a given card. The repeated digit, if any, never occurred without at least one intervening digit. The sets were presented in the order given above. A random arrangement was made of each set. This arrangement was used in the forward order for half the Ss and in reverse order for the remainder. The materials were presented in a mirror-type tachistoscope.

The Ss were 14 undergraduates in introductory psychology courses. The S held a plunger switch which activated the tachistoscope. The E gave a ready signal when the stimulus card was in place. The S activated the tachistoscope when he was ready. He was instructed to say the digit sequence aloud immediately after its appearance, and was encouraged to guess if he was not sure of one or several items. The S always knew how many digits were shown. Responses were recorded on a tape recorder. Only one exposure per sequence was given and the

S was not given any information about the correctness of his response.

Two practice sequences with ascending limits were given to accustom the S to the apparatus and to provide the E with some information on threshold. The test sets were then presented. One-minute rest periods were given after each set.

Exposure duration was individually adjusted for each S. Pilot work suggested that transpositions occurred most readily at the point where the S was beginning to miss single digits in the sequence. Therefore, the E attempted to have the exposure interval long enough that the proper number of digits would be reported but short enough that they were not always reported with complete accuracy. After every five cards the E decided whether to keep the exposure the same or to change it. Since there were practice effects in the task and since the task became appreciably more difficult, E continued to modify the presentation time during the course of the experiment. Generally 10-msec steps were employed in such changes but with an occasional S whose performance was markedly inferior the step span was increased.

RESULTS AND DISCUSSION

Responses were transcribed from the tape and scored. The following categories were employed:

C —correct
E —gross error
I —one digit incorrect, or 'blank' reported for a single missing digit
T —transposition of adjacent pairs of digits with rest of sequence correct
T^1 —transposition of three or more digits with remainder correct
IT —transposition of two or more digits *and* one digit incorrect
O —other errors, usually experimental or equipment errors

Results are given in terms of these scoring categories in Table I. Examination of the table shows that transposition provides an important source of errors. It is, however, difficult to find a statistical model which would provide a precise evaluation of the statistical significance of such errors. As Woodworth and Schlosberg[4] point out in their discussion of scoring memory span, any scoring system which attempts to provide separate credit for accuracy and order is arbitrary. Thus, any statistical model must make assumptions about the S's strategies on the

Table I. Distribution of Responses by Categories for Each Stimulus Set (280 items)

Scoring code	5 digits	6 digits	6 digits	7 digits
C	130	60	65	12
E	21	67	47	122
I	50	43	50	21
T	23	23	32	12
T¹	2	14	5	9
IT	44	64	73	96
O	10	9	8	8

one hand (e.g., Did the *S* note that digits can repeat within a sequence and, if so, did this alter his guessing behaviour in the appropriate manner?) and the interrelationships of error types (which we do not yet know) on the other. Fortunately, the question is not crucial for present purposes. The only question that need be asked here is whether there is more transposition than would be expected by chance (however chance is to be defined).

We think the answer to that is clear. Of the 140 errors on the 5-digit sequences, 69 involve transpositions; of the 211 and 207 errors on the 6-digit sequences, 101 and 110 respectively contain transpositions; of the 260 errors on the 7-digit set, 117 contain a transposition. It is evident that until the task becomes exceedingly difficult (and the response unscorable), approximately half the errors involve transpositions. No reasonable 'guessing' or chance model we have contrived can account for this finding. It seems simplest to conclude that in a large portion of the errors the *S* has the correct information as to the identity of some of the digits but has lost the information as to their precise location.

As a first step in describing the phenomenon the distribution of errors over positions was obtained for the simplest errors of both types. Table II shows the location of the error for each instance when one digit was incorrect (I error). Table III gives the location of the pair of items transposed when only single transposition was observed (T error). It can be seen that both sets of distributions for all sequence lengths show the same serial position effect, suggesting that both kinds of error are susceptible to the same form of interference. If one has all the individual items, he is least likely to have precise position information in the latter half of the sequence. Conversely, if one lacks the identity of an item, it is most likely to be one from a position in the latter half of the list. The most probable transposition for any particular length of sequence appears to involve the inversion in order of the item in the most difficult position in the sequence and the item immediately preceding it.

The psychological nature of each kind of error is not at all clear but it seems likely that future work will help narrow the alternatives. It would be particularly interesting to know, for example, whether transposition is equally common when the experiment is conducted with Sperling's procedure or with a rapid sequential procedure such as that used in short-term memory research.

While we cannot at present make any decision as to the underlying nature of the transposition phenomenon, we feel that this experiment concurs with common experience in pointing to a pervasive distortion in the visual perception and reporting system which theories of information processing must take into account.

Table II. Position of Errors in Cases of a Single Incorrect Digit

Sequence	Position						
	1	2	3	4	5	6	7
5-digit	1	1	4	34	10	–	–
6-digit	0	2	1	4	31	6	–
6-digit	0	1	3	11	25	10	–
7-digit	0	0	2	0	7	8	4

Table III. Position of Transposed Digits in Errors Involving a Single Transposition

Sequence	Positions transposed					
	1–2	2–3	3–4	4–5	5–6	6–7
5-digit	0	2	18	3	–	–
6-digit	0	2	1	17	3	–
6-digit	0	5	1	21	5	–
7-digit	0	0	0	3	7	2

APPENDIX III

NOTES ON THE AUTONOMIC NERVOUS SYSTEM*

In general (but there are, as we have seen, important exceptions) the action of the two divisions is mutually antagonistic: they equilibrate each other. The sympathetic division prepares the animal for emergency reactions under the stress of hunger, pain, rage and fear. It accelerates the pulse, increases blood pressure, provides added blood-sugar as a source of energy. The parasympathetic division does in almost every respect the opposite: it lowers blood pressure, slows the heart, neutralizes excesses of blood-sugar, facilitates digestion and the disposal of body wastes, activates the tear glands – it is generally calming and cathartic.

Both divisions of the autonomic nervous system are controlled by the limbic brain (the hypothalamus and adjacent structures). Different authors have described their functions in different terms. Allport[1] related the pleasurable emotions to the parasympathetic, the unpleasant ones to the sympathetic. Olds[2] distinguishes between 'positive' and 'negative' emotive systems, activated respectively by the parasympathetic and sympathetic centres in the hypothalamus. From a quite different theoretical approach, Hebb also arrived at the conclusion that a distinction should be made between two categories of emotion, 'those in which the tendency is to maintain or increase the original stimulating conditions (pleasurable or integrative emotions)' and 'those in which the tendency is to abolish or decrease the stimulus (rage, fear, disgust)'.[3] Pribram has made a similar distinction between 'preparatory' (warding-off) and 'participatory' emotions.[4] Hebb and Gellhorn distinguish between an ergotropic (energy-consuming) system operating through the sympathetic division to ward off threatening stimuli, and a trophotropic (energy-conserving) system which operates through the parasympathetic in response to peaceful or attractive stimuli.[5]

*See p. 140.

Gellhorn has summarized the emotional effects of two different types of drugs: on the one hand the 'pep pills', such as benzedrine, and on the other the tranquillizers, such as chlorpromazine. The former activates the sympathetic, the latter the parasympathetic, division. When administrated in small doses, the tranquillizers cause 'slight shifts in the hypothalamic balance to the parasympathetic side, resulting in calm and contentment, apparently similar to the state before falling asleep, whereas more marked alterations lead to a depressive mood'.[6] The benzedrine-type drugs, on the other hand, activate the sympathetic division, cause increased aggressiveness in animals, and in man in small doses alertness and euphoria, in larger doses over-excitation and manic behaviour. Lastly, *Cobb* has summed up the implicit contrast in a pointed form: 'Rage is called the most adrenergic, and love the most cholinergic characteristically parasympathetic reaction'.[7]

What this short survey indicates is, in the first place, a general trend among authorities in this field to distinguish between *two basic categories of emotion* – though the definitions of the categories differ. In the second place, there is a general feeling that the two categories are correlated to the two divisions of the autonomic nervous system.

APPENDIX IV

UFOs: A FESTIVAL OF ABSURDITY*

There is an understandable, but questionable connection in the public's mind between CETI (communication with extraterrestrial intelligence) and UFOs (unidentified flying objects, vulgarly called flying saucers). At the CETI conference in 1971,† UFOs were only mentioned in passing, and none of the participants suggested that they were of extra-terrestrial origin. The main reasons for this scepticism were summed up by the astrophysicist Carl Sagan:

> Such [advanced extraterrestrial] civilisations will be inconceivably in advance of our own. We have only to consider the changes in mankind in the last 10^4 years and the potential difficulties which our Pleistocene ancestors would have in accommodating to our present society to realize what an unfathomable gap 10^8 to 10^{10} years represents, even with a tiny rate of intellectual advance. Such societies will have discovered laws of nature and invented technologies whose applications will appear to us indistinguishable from magic. There is a serious question about whether such societies are concerned with communicating with us, any more than we are concerned with communicating with our protozoan or bacterial forebears. We may study microorganisms, but we do not usually communicate with them. I therefore raise the possibility that a horizon in communications interest exists in the evolution of technological societies, and that a civilization very much more advanced than we will be engaged in a busy communications traffic with its peers; but not with us, and *not via technologies accessible to us*. We may be like the inhabitants of the valleys of New Guinea who may communicate by runner or drum, but who are ignorant of the vast inter-national radio and cable traffic passing over, around and through them [my italics].[1]

The words that I italicized refer – as the context indicates – to the hypothesis that UFOs may be space-vehicles, or automated probes released from larger mother-ships (like the landers released from the

*See above, Chapter XIV.
†See above, p. 282a.

Viking orbiters). In spite of the aerial acrobatics which they are reported to perform, the appearance and behaviour of UFOs is too close to 'technologies accessible to us' to qualify as fit for magicians. As to the argument that we are too primitive to be worthy of study, one could of course object that our ethologists and anthropologists do not share this arrogant attitude towards lowlier forms of life and culture. But there is again a counter-argument: if our galaxy is as brimful with life as the astrophysicists tell us, then there must be some system of priorities for the magicians' exploratory survey-programmes, and even among lowly civilizations we may not be of special interest. If, on the other hand, we are as interesting as our terran chauvinism whispers into our ears, then why do UFOs so studiously avoid contact with us, by radio, or lasers or holographs – not to mention some advanced techniques of ESP? Evasion of contact is indeed the chief characteristic and common element in the antics of flying saucers. And as for the few cases in which contact with 'humanoid' UFO passengers is alleged, they represent, as one eminent ufologist wrote, 'a veritable festival of absurdity'.[2]

Why, then, bring up this disreputable subject at all? Firstly, because it seems to me that it would be cowardly, after discussing extraterrestrial civilizations, to pass over UFOs in silence – although, as I said, the two subjects may be unconnected. In the second place, UFOs – unidentified (or unexplained) flying objects as distinct from IFOs (identified flying objects) do seem to exist, whatever their origin. This belief is apparently shared by nearly a half of American astronomers. The following extract is from an article in the *New Scientist*:

Unidentified flying objects (UFOs) 'certainly', 'probably' or at least 'possibly' deserve scientific study, say 80 per cent of respondents to a questionnaire sent to members of the prestigious American Astronomical Society (AAS). Of the 2,611 members, 1,356 replied and of these only 20 per cent thought the study unnecessary.

This means that some 40 per cent of the AAS members would support a UFO investigation. Sixty-two respondents to the questionnaire even claimed to have seen a UFO, says a report from Stanford University, California, where the survey was conducted . . .

In five of the reported sightings the objects were seen through telescopes and in three cases through binoculars. In seven cases there were photographs; the organizer of the survey, Professor Peter Sturrock, a Stanford astrophysicist, believes he can find non-UFO explanations for two of them.

Sturrock is a strong supporter of a renewed investigation of UFOs. He criticizes the *Condon Report* of 1969, which dismissed the UFO phenomenon and closed 'Project Blue Book', the US Air Force's listing of UFO sightings by its personnel. 'It is essential that scientists begin an exchange of relevant information,' says Sturrock, 'if they are to contribute to the resolution of the UFO problem.'[3]

What is particularly impressive are those sixty-two astronomers – that is, five per cent of the respondents – who claimed to have *actually seen* a UFO. This is much more remarkable than the last Gallup poll on the subject, in 1973, which indicated that 15 million Americans had claimed to have seen UFOs, and that 51 per cent of the population believed that the UFO phenomenon exists.[4] Where the general population is concerned, such figures can always be explained, or explained away, as the result of mass-hysteria and optical illusions. But professional astronomers one assumes to be immune to such errors.

The term 'ufology' was coined by Air-Marshal Sir Victor Goddard in 1946, when he represented the Royal Air Force on the combined Chiefs of Staff advisory committee in Washington. He then thought UFOs were a hoax, and was instrumental in persuading President Truman to call off the search for UFOs by the US Air Force, which Truman had inaugurated earlier to probe the rumours of intruders in the American air space. But later on Goddard changed his mind. In his book, *Flight Towards Reality*, he writes:

In nearly thirty years there must have been two hundred thousand claims of UFO sightings recorded in one hundred countries at the least. That is the kind of basis of UFO statistics now available in North and South America. Reports upon ten thousand thorough-going checks have furnished evidence which leads to two conclusions: The first is that only six per cent of so-called UFO sightings remain unsolved and unexplained; the second is that, of the unsolved residue – twelve thousand unidentified by now – some surely were quite rightly held to be what they were claimed to be – objects of reality but unknown in origin and technicality. . . So, they *were* UFO – nothing else – and that is not to be denied even by sceptics of the deepest dye.[5]

There exist now UFO research groups in various countries of Europe and America, mostly run by astronomers and other scientists as a hobby. The USA Center for UFO Studies has a computer file of some 80,000 catalogued and classified reports. This centre was created and is directed by Dr J. Allen Hynek, Chairman of the Department of Astronomy, North-Western University, formerly Associate Director

of the Smithsonian Astrophysical Observatory and Astronomical
Consultant of the US Air Force on 'Project Blue Book' of reported
UFO sightings.

Why then in view of all this, is ufology still in disrepute? Part of the
answer is provided by an amusing historical analogy. The extract
which follows is from *Principles of Meteoritics* by E. L. Krinov:

During the period of vigorous scientific development which took place
during the eighteenth century, scientists came to the conclusion that the falling
of meteorites upon the Earth is impossible; all reports of such cases were
declared to be absurd fiction. Thus, for example . . . the Swiss mineralogist J. A.
Deluc stated that 'if he saw a fall of a meteorite himself, he would not believe
his own eyes'. But especially astonishing is the fact that even the well-known
chemist Lavoisier signed a memorandum in 1772 with scientists of the Paris
Academy of Sciences, which concluded . . . that 'the falling of stones from the
sky is physically impossible'. Finally, when the meteorite Barbotan fell in
France in 1790 and the fall was witnessed by the mayor and the city council,
the French scientist Berthollet wrote: 'How sad it is that the entire municipality
enters folk tales upon an official record, presenting them as something actually
seen, while they cannot be explained by physics nor by anything reasonable.'[6]

If you think of it, for eighteenth-century minds meteors were no
easier to swallow than UFOs for us. Hence the same choking and
spluttering reaction. This was particularly in evidence in the course of
the so-called 'Condon Report' scandal, which grew into a kind of
academic Watergate. One of the best *résumés* of this complicated
affair – which led to the shelving of the US Air Force 'Project Blue
Book' and to the official taboo on UFOs – was written by Charles H.
Gibbs-Smith, the eminent aviation historian. Here is an abbreviated
version of his account (italics in the original):[7]

For the purposes of this article, I am not concerned whether UFOs are
vehicles from outer space, hamburgers tossed from balloons, or spots in front
of the eyes of neurotic tabby cats. I am concerned with the status and standing
of a scientific report, the 'Condon Report of the Scientific Study of Unidentified Flying Objects', completed in 1968, and released to the Press in January
1969.

On August 9, 1966, a confidential memorandum was written by a Mr
Robert J. Low to officials of the University of Colorado, concerning the proposed contract between this University and the US Air Force, for the former
to conduct research into UFOs, and be paid for this project out of public funds

to the tune of some half a million dollars. The project was to be under the direction of Dr Edward U. Condon, with Mr Low (a member of the University staff) as the project co-ordinator and 'key operations man'. The memorandum in question was written *before* the contract was signed between the University and the Air Force.

The Low memorandum was entitled 'Some Thoughts on the UFO Project', and included the following passages (my italics):

'. . . Our study would be conducted almost exclusively by non-believers who, though they couldn't possibly *prove* a negative result, could and probably would add an impressive body of evidence that there is no reality to the observations. *The trick would be, I think, to describe the project so that, to the public, it would appear a totally objective study, but, to the scientific community, would present the image of a group of non-believers trying their best to be objective,* but having an almost zero expectation of finding a saucer. One way to do this would be to stress investigation, not of the physical phenomena, but rather of the people who do the observing – psychology and sociology of persons and groups who report seeing UFOs. *If the emphasis were put here, rather than on examination of the old question of the physical reality of the saucer, I think the scientific community would quickly get the message.* . . I'm inclined to feel at this early stage that, if we set up the thing right and take pains to get the proper people involved and have success *in presenting the image we want to present to the scientific community, we* could *carry the job off to our benefit* . . .'

This memorandum was accidentally discovered by a researcher late in 1967, and was revealed to the public in *Look* magazine in May of 1968 . . .

The Low memorandum can only be viewed as a deliberate act calculated to deceive; to deceive first the scientific community, and, through them, the public at large. I know of no modern parallel to such a cynical act of duplicity on the part of a university official . . . By the writing of such a document, the integrity of the entire project was shattered in advance. Mr Low's words disclose that everything in the report – unbeknown to the reader, be he scientist or layman – could ultimately play its part in presenting the angled case whereby the 'scientific community would quickly get the message'. This, in plain language, means that a deliberate perversion of the truth was planned *before* the contract with the Air Force was signed; which, in turn, points to an *agreement* with someone, or some body, as to what that 'message' should be. Thus the spirit of perversion must inevitably have pervaded the whole fabric of the report; conditioned what was included, and what was excluded; what was played up, and what was played down; what was said in a particular manner, and what was not said; what was implied, and what was not implied . . .

The Low memorandum also conveys an implied contempt for the subject of the UFOs which the University was being handsomely paid to investigate. . .

What underlines the dishonesty which surrounds the whole project is the fact that *at no time has the Low memorandum been repudiated, or even deplored, by any of the parties to the deal.* Neither the University of Colorado nor the Air Force has had a word of explanation to offer for behaviour which cuts at the very roots of scientific integrity.

The explanation of the conspiracy – there seems to be no other word to describe it – is not difficult to guess. Some of the scientists on the committee had a genuine horror of getting involved with 'little green men from Venus' and refused to make a distinction between serious UFO research and the tales of crackpots and hoaxers. There are plenty of precedents for such an attitude in the history of science; long before the denial of meteors, some of Galileo's fellow-astronomers denied the existence of Jupiter's moons which he had discovered, and refused even to look through his telescope because they felt sure that those moons were an optical illusion.*

As for the Air Force and other official agencies, they well remembered the mass-hysteria and panic released by Orson Welles's 1938 broadcast about a Martian invasion, and were anxious to prevent a repetition. Moreover, Government agencies do not like to admit that there are things going on in the nation's sky which they are unable to explain. The upshot of it all was that in December 1969, the US Secretary for Air officially announced that further research 'cannot be justified on the ground of national security or in the interest of science', and closed 'Project Blue Book' down.

In contrast to the American attitude, French Government agencies frankly admitted that they took a lively interest in UFOs, encouraged the population to report sightings to the nearest gendarmerie, and ordered the gendarmes to report their investigations through official channels. More than that: in a remarkable radio interview in 1975, the French Minister of Defence, Robert Galley, explained in some detail the methods used to collect evidence on UFOs, insisted repeatedly on the necessity 'to keep an open mind', and affirmed that in his opinion the phenomena in question were 'to date unexplained or badly explained'. He also came out in favour of a suggestion by Claude Poher, Head of Research of the National Agency for Space Research, to construct automated observation posts to establish correlations between variations of the earth's magnetic field and passing UFOs. And yet the French are supposed to be a nation of sceptics.

What are we to conclude? Open-minded scientists, when confronted

*See *The Sleepwalkers*, Ch. VIII, 6.

with *prima facie* evidence for phenomena which they cannot explain, go on collecting data in the hope that an explanation will eventually be found. This hope may be spurious, a product of the rationalist illusion, but there is no alternative strategy in science – except the ostrich's, who follows the maxim: 'What I cannot explain cannot exist.' Granted that even the best-documented UFO cases resemble a 'festival of absurdity', we must also realize that when we approach the borders of science, whether in ESP or quantum physics or ufology, we must expect to encounter phenomena which seem to us paradoxical or absurd. To quote once more Aimé Michel:[8]

It must never be forgotten that in any manifestation of a superhuman nature the apparently absurd is what one must expect. 'Why do you take so much trouble about your food and your house?' one of my cats asked me one day. 'What an absurd lot of upheaval, when everything can be found in the dust-bins, and there is good shelter under the cars.'

REFERENCES

Prologue: The New Calendar (pages 1 to 20)

1. *Time*, New York, 29 January 1965.
2. Vaihinger (1911).
3. von Bertalanffy (1956).
4. MacLean (1962).
5. MacLean (1973).
6. MacLean (1958).
7. Gaskell (1908), pp. 65–7.
8. Wood Jones and Porteus (1929), pp. 27–8.
9. Lorenz (1966).
10. Russell (1950), p. 141.

PART ONE: OUTLINE OF A SYSTEM

Chapter I: The Holarchy (pages 23 to 56)

1. Frankl (1969), pp. 397–8.
2. Morris (1967).
3. Quoted by Frankl (1969).
4. Smuts (1926).
5. Pattee (1970).
6. Weiss (1969), p. 193.
7. Needham, J. (1936).
8. Needham, J. (1945).
9. Koestler (1964, 1967).
10. Koestler (1967).
11. Jevons (1972), p. 64.
12. Ruyer (1974).
13. Gerard (1957).
14. Gerard (1969), p. 228.
15. Thorpe (1974), p. 35.
16. Bonner (1965). p. 136.

17. Waddington (1957).
18. de St Hilaire (1818).
19. Simon (1962).
20. Miller (1964).
21. Koestler (1969a).
22. Jaensch (1930).
23. Kluever (1933).
24. Penfield and Roberts (1959).
25. Frankl (1969).

Chapter II: Beyond Eros and Thanatos (pages 57 to 69)

1. Freud (1920), p. 63.
2. ibid., pp. 3–5.
3. Jones (1953), Vol. I, p. 142.
4. Horney (1939).
5. Pearl in *Enc. Brit.*, 14th ed.
6. ibid.
7. Thomas (1974), p. 28.
8. ibid.
9. ibid., pp. 28–30.

Chapter IV: Ad Majorem Gloriam . . . (pages 77 to 97).

1. Hayek (1966).
2. Milgram (1975), p. 18.
3. ibid.
4. Milgram (1974), p. 166.
5. ibid., p. 71.
6. ibid., p. 167.
7. ibid.
8. ibid., p. 131.
9. ibid., p. 132.
10. ibid.
11. ibid., p. 8.
12. ibid., p. 9.
13. ibid., p. 148.
14. Milgram (1975), p. 20.
15. Milgram (1974), p. 188.
16. Calder (1976), pp. 124–7.

17. Calder (1976).
18. Calder (1976a), p. 127.
19. Prescott (1964), p. 62.
20. *The Times*, London, 27 July 1966.

Chapter V: *An Alternative to Despair (pages 98 to 106)*

  1. Hyden (1961).
  2. Koestler (1967).

PART TWO: THE CREATIVE MIND

Chapter VI: *Humour and Wit (pages 109 to 130)*

  1. Koestler (1948, 1959, 1964 and 1967).
  2. Koestler (1974).
  3. de Boulogne (1862).
  4. Foss (1961).
  5. Freud (1940), Vol. VI.
  6. Huxley, A. (1961).

Chapter VIII: *The Discoveries of Art (pages 137 to 161)*

  1. Jones (1957), Vol. 3, p. 364.
  2. Pribram *et al.* (1960), p. 9.
  3. Gellhorn (1957).
  4. See Koestler (1964), Book I, Ch. v–xi.
  5. Hadamard (1949).
  6. Popper (1975).
  7. ibid.
  8. Koestler (1964, 1968, etc.).
  9. Szent-Györgyi (1957).
  10. Gombrich (1962), pp. 9, 120.

PART THREE: CREATIVE EVOLUTION

Chapter IX: *Crumbling Citadels (pages 165 to 192)*

  1. Skinner (1953), pp. 30–1.
  2. Jaynes (1976), p. xx.

3. Watson (1928), pp. 198 f.
4. Skinner (1953), p. 252.
5. ibid., pp. 108–9.
6. Skinner (1957), p. 163.
7. ibid., p. 438.
8. ibid., p. 439.
9. ibid., p. 150.
10. ibid., p. 206.
11. Koestler (1967), p. 12n.
12. Chomsky (1959).
13. cf., e.g., Macbeth (1971).
14. Huxley, J. (1957) quoted by Eisley (1961), p. 336.
15. Waddington (1957), pp. 64–5.
16. von Bertalanffy (1969), p. 67.
17. ibid.
18. Hardy (1965), p. 207.
19. von Bertalanffy (1969), p. 65.
20. Huxley, J. (1954), p. 14.
21. Waddington (1952).
22. Monod (1971), p. 121.
23. ibid., p. 122.
24. ibid.
25. ibid., p. 146.
26. Darwin, quoted by Macbeth (1971), p. 101.
27. Koestler (1967), pp. 128–9.
28. Grassé (1973).
29. Tinbergen (1951), p. 189.
30. ibid., p. 9.
31. Macbeth (1971), pp. 71–2.
32. von Bertalanffy (1969), p. 66.
33. Jenkin (1867).
34. Hardy (1965), p. 80.
35. Darwin, F., quoted by Hardy (1965), p. 81.
36. Bateson (1902).
37. Grassé (1973), p. 21.
38. ibid., p. 351.
39. ibid.
40. ibid.
41. Bateson, G., private communication, 2 July 1970.
42. Bateson, W (1913), p. 248.

43. Johannsen (1923), p. 140.
44. Butler (1951 ed.), p. 167, quoted by Himmelfarb (1959), p. 362.
45. Monod (1971), p. 118.
46. Beadle (1963).
47. Grassé (1973), p. 369.
48. Simpson, Pittendrigh and Tiffany (1957), p. 330.
49. Grassé (1973).
50. Gorini (1966).
51. Koestler (1967), p. 133 – based on de Beer (1940), p. 148, and Hardy (1965), p. 212.
52. Cannon (1958), p. 118.
53. Monod (1971), p. 9.
54. ibid., pp. 21–2.
55. Grassé (1973), p. 277.

Chapter X: Lamarck Revisited (pages 193 to 204)

1. Kammerer in New York Evening Post, 23 February 1924.
2. Simpson (1950) quoted by Hardy (1965), p. 14.
3. Thomson (1908) quoted by Wood Jones (1943), p. 9.
4. Darlington in preface to reprint of On the Origin ofSpecies(1950).
5. Spencer (1893), Vol. I, p. 621.
6. Haldane (1940), p. 39.
7. Huxley, J. (1954), p. 14.
8. McConnell (1965).
9. The Times, London, 26 June 1970.
10. Grassé (1973), p. 366.
11. ibid., p. 367.
12. Koestler (1971), p. 130.
13. Koestler (1967), pp. 158–9.
14. Waddington (1957), p. 182.
15. ibid.
16. Koestler and Smythies (1969), pp. 382 f.
17. Wood Jones (1943), p. 22.
18. Quoted by Smith (1975), pp. 162–3.

Chapter XI: Strategies and Purpose in Evolution (page 205 to 226)

1. Simpson, Pittendrigh and Tiffany (1957), p. 472.
2. Simpson (1949), p. 180.

3. Spurway (1949).
4. Whyte (1965).
5. Waddington (1957), p. 79.
6. Hardy (1965), p. 211.
7. Koestler (1967), pp. 148–9.
8. Simpson (1950), quoted by Hardy (1965), p. 14.
9. Sinnott (1961), p. 45.
10. Muller (1943), quoted by Sinnott (1961), p. 45.
11. Coghill (1929).
12. Hardy (1965), p. 176.
13. ibid., pp. 172, 192–3.
14. Huxley, J. (1964), p. 13.
15. Hardy (1965), de Beer (1940), Takhtajan (1972) and Koltsov (1936).
16. Koestler (1967), pp. 163–4.
17. Young (1950), p. 74.
18. de Beer (1940), p. 118.
19. Quoted by Takhtajan (1972).
20. ibid.
21. Koestler (1967), p. 166.
22. Hamburger (1973).
23. Herrick (1961).
24. Schrödinger (1944), p. 72.
25. Szent–Györgyi (1974)
26. ibid.
27. Grassé (1973), p. 401.
28. Waddington (1961).

PART FOUR: NEW HORIZONS

Chapter XII: Free Will in a Hierarchic Context (pages 229 to 241)

1. Hardy (1965), p. 229.
2. Thorpe (1966a).
3. Heisenberg (1969), p. 113.
4. Pauli (1952), p. 164.
5. Popper (1950).
6. Polanyi (1966).
7. MacKay (1966).

Chapter XIII: Physics and Metaphysics (pages 242 to 273)

1. *New Scientist*, 25 January 1973, p. 209.
2. Capra (1975), p. 52.
3. Newton, quoted by Capra (1975), p. 57.
4. Russell (1927), p. 163.
5. Capra (1975), p. 77.
6. Koestler (1972, 1973 and 1976).
7. Heisenberg quoted by Burt (1967), p. 80.
8. Heisenberg (1969), pp. 63–4.
9. Koestler (1972), p. 51.
10. Eccles (1953), pp. 276–7.
11. ibid., p. 279.
12. Firsoff (1967), pp. 102–3.
13. Dobbs (1967).
14. Walker (1973).
15. Heisenberg (1958), pp. 48–9.
16. Jeans (1937).
17. Hoyle (1966).
18. Wheeler quoted by Chase (1972).
19. Wheeler (1967), p. 246.
20. Margenau (1967), p. 218.
21. Bohm and Hiley (1974).
22. Margenau (1967), p. 218.
23. Jung (1960), p. 318.
24. ibid., p. 435.
25. ibid., p. 420.
26. Kammerer (1919), p. 93.
27. ibid., p. 165.
28. ibid., p. 456.
29. Quoted by Przibram (1926).
30. Koestler (1973), pp. 191–3.
31. Pauli (1952).
32. ibid., p. 164.
33. Jung (1960), p. 514.
34. Schopenhauer (1859).
35. della Mirandola (1557), p. 40.
36. Weaver (1963).
37. Bohm (1951).
38. Schrödinger (1944), p. 83.

39. Harvie (1973), p. 133.
40. Price quoted by Dobbs (1967), p. 239.
41. Dobbs (1967), p. 239.
42. Burt (1968), pp. 50, 58–9.
43. Grassé (1973), p. 401.

Chapter XIV: A Glance through the Keyhole (pages 274 to 286)

1. Wallace quoted by Macbeth (1971), p. 103.
2. Quoted by Macbeth (1971), p. 103.
3. Herrick (1961), pp. 398–9.
4. Wallace quoted by Macbeth (1971), p. 103.
5. Koestler (1967), pp. 297 f.
6. Koestler (1959), p. 55 and (1964), p. 342.
7. Butterfield (1924), p. 104.
8. Huxley, J. (1954), p. 12.
9. Margenau (1967), pp. 223–4.
10. Price (1949), pp. 105–13.
11. *New Scientist*, 21 April 1977.
12. ibid.
13. ibid.
14. Koestler (1937 and 1954).

APPENDICES

*Appendix I: Beyond Atomism and Holism – The Concept of the Holon
(pages 289 to 311)*

1. von Bertalanffy (1952).
2. Koestler (1967).
3. Koestler and Smythies, eds. (1969).
4. Chomsky (1965).
5. Tinbergen (1951); Thorpe (1956).
6. Herrick (1981); Weiss, ed. (1950), etc.
7. Simon (1962).
8. Thompson (1942).
9. Koestler (1967).
10. von Bertalanffy (1952).
11. Waddington (1957).
12. ibid.

13. Tinbergen (1951).
14. Koestler and Jenkins (1965).
15. Penfield and Roberts (1969).
16. MacLean (1958).
17. Weiss in Jeffress, ed. (1951).
18. Hebb (1958).
19. Bartlett (1958).
20. von Bertalanffy (1952).
21. Child (1925).
22. Miller *et al.* (1960).

Appendix II: An Experiment in Perception (pages 312 to 316)

1. e.g. Sperling (1960); Averbach (1963); Broadbent (1963).
2. Osgood (1953).
3. Woodworth and Schlosberg (1954).
4. ibid., p. 697.

Appendix III: Notes on the Autonomic Nervous System (pages 317 to 318)

1. Allport (1924).
2. Olds (1960).
3. Hebb (1949).
4. Pribram (1966).
5. Gellhorn (1963).
6. ibid.
7. Cobb (1950).
8. Pribram (1966), p. 9.
9. Gellhorn (1957).

Appendix IV: UFOs: A Festival of Absurdity (pages 319 to 325)

1. Sagan (1973), pp. 366–7.
2. Michel (1974).
3. *New Scientist*, 31 March 1977.
4. *International Herald Tribune*, 22 April 1977.
5. Goddard (1975), pp. 106–7.
6. Krinov (1960), p. 9.
7. Gibbs-Smith (1970).
8. Michel (1974), p. 255.

BIBLIOGRAPHY

ALLPORT, F. H., *Social Psychology* (New York, 1924).

ATKINSON, see Hilgard and Atkinson, eds. (1967).

AVERBACH, E., in *J. Verb. Learn. Verb. Behav.*, Vol. 2, pp. 60–4 (1963).

BARTLETT, F. C., *Thinking* (London, 1958).

BATESON, W., *Mendel's Principles of Heredity: A Defence* (Cambridge, 1902).

—, *Problems of Genetics* (London, 1913).

BEADLE, G. W., *Genetics and Modern Biology* (Philadelphia, 1963).

DE BEER, G., *Embryos and Ancestors* (Oxford, 1940).

BERGSON, H. L., *Le Rire* (15th ed. Paris, 1916).

VON BERTALANFFY, L., *Problems of Life* (New York, 1952).

—, in *Scientific Monthly* (January 1956).

—, in *Beyond Reductionism* – see Koestler and Smythies, eds. (1969).

—, *Festschrift* – see Gray and Rizzo, eds. (1973).

BOAG, T. J., and CAMPBELL, D., eds., *A Triune Concept of the Brain and Behaviour* (Toronto, 1973).

BOHM, D., *Quantum Theory* (London, 1951).

— and HILEY, B., 'On the Intuitive Understanding of Non-Locality as Implied by Quantum Theory' (Preprint, Birkbeck College, Univ. of London, 1974).

BOLK, J., *Das Problem der Menschwerdung* (Jena, 1926).

BONNER, J., *The Molecular Biology of Development* (Oxford, 1965).

BOWEN, C., *The Humanoids* (London, Futura ed., 1974).

DE BOULOGNE, D., *Le Mécanisme de la Physionomie Humaine* (Paris, 1862).

BROADBENT, D. E., in *J. Verb. Learn. Verb. Behav.*, Vol. 2, pp. 34–9 (1963).

BURT, SIR C., in *Science and ESP* (see Smythies, ed., 1967).

—, *Psychology and Psychical Research. The Seventeenth Frederick W. H. Myers Memorial Lecture* (London, 1968).

BUTLER, S., *Evolution Old and New* (1879).

—, *Notebooks*, ed. G. Keynes and B. Hill (New York, 1951).

BUTTERFIELD, SIR H., *The Origins of Modern Science* (London, 1924).

CALDER, N., *The Human Conspiracy* (London, 1976).
—, in *The Times*, London, 25 February 1976a.
CAMPBELL, D., see Boag and Campbell, eds. (1973).
CANNON, H. GRAHAM, *The Evolution of Living Things* (Manchester, 1958).
CAPRA, F., *The Tao of Physics* (London, 1975).
CHASE, L. B., in *University, A Princeton Quarterly* (Summer, 1972).
CHILD, C. M., *Physiological Foundations of Behaviour* (New York, 1925).
CHOMSKY, N., in *Language*, Vol. 35, No. 1, pp. 26–58 (1959).
—, *Aspects of the Theory of Syntax* (Cambridge, Mass., 1965).
COBB, S., *Emotions and Clinical Medicine* (New York, 1950).
COGHILL, G. E., *Anatomy and the Problem of Behaviour* (Cambridge, 1929).
DARLINGTON, C. D., in preface to *On the Origin of Species* (reprint of 1st ed., London, 1950).
DARWIN, C., *The Variation of Animals and Plants under Domestication*, 2 vols. (London, 1868).
—, *On the Origin of Species* (reprint of 1st ed., London, 1950).
DOBBS, A., in *Science and ESP* – see Smythies, ed. (1967).
EASTMAN, M., *The Enjoyment of Laughter* (New York, 1936).
ECCLES, SIR J., *The Neurophysiological Basis of Mind* (Oxford, 1953).
—, ed., *Brain and Conscious Experience* (New York, 1966a).
EISLEY, L., *The Immense Journey* (New York, 1958).
—, *Darwin's Century* (New York, 1961).
FARBER, S. M., and WILSON, R. H. L., eds., *Control of the Mind* (New York, 1961).
FIELD, J., ed., *Handbook of Physiology: Neurophysiology*, vol. III (Washington D.C., 1961).
FIRSOFF, V. A., *Life, Mind and Galaxies* (Edinburgh and London, 1967).
FORD, E. B., see Huxley, Hardy and Ford, eds. (1954).
FOSS, B., in *New Scientist*, 6 July 1961.
FRANKL, V. E., in *Beyond Reductionism* – see Koestler and Smythies, eds. (1969).
FREUD, S., *Jenseits des Lustprinzips* (1920).
—, *Gesammelte Werke*, Vols. I–XVIII (London, 1940–52).
GALANTER, E., see Miller, Galanter and Pribram (1960).
GARSTANG, W., in *J. Linnean Soc. London, Zoology*, 35, 81, 1922.
—, in *Quarterly J. Microscopical Sci.*, 72, 51, 1928.
GASKELL, W. H., *The Origin of Vertebrates* (1908).

GELLHORN, E., *Autonomic Imbalance* (New York, 1957).

— and LOOFBOURROW, G. N., *Emotions and Emotional Disorders* (New York, 1963).

GERARD, R. W., in *Science*, Vol. 125, pp. 429–33 (1957).

—, in *Hierarchical Structures* – see Whyte, Wilson and Wilson, eds. (1969).

GIBBS-SMITH, C. H., in *Flying Saucer Review* (July/August 1970).

GODDARD, SIR V., *Flight Towards Reality* (London, 1975).

GOLDING, W., *The Inheritors* (London, 1955).

GOMBRICH, SIR E., *Art and Illusion* (London, 1962).

GORINI, L., in *Scientific American* (April 1966).

GRASSÉ, P., *L'Évolution du Vivant* (Paris, 1973).

GRAY, W., and RIZZO, N. D., eds., *Unity through Diversity –A Festschrift for Ludwig von Bertalanffy* (New York, London, Paris, 1973).

HADAMARD, J., *The Psychology of Invention in the Mathematical Field* (Princeton, 1949).

HAECKEL, E., *Die Welträtsel* (1899).

HALDANE, J. B. S., *Possible Worlds* (1940).

HAMBURGER, V., in *Encyclopaedia Britannica*, Vol. 19, 78c (1973).

HARDY, SIR A. See Huxley, Hardy and Ford, eds. (1954).

—, *The Living Stream* (London, 1965).

—, *The Divine Flame* (London, 1966).

—, HARVIE, R., and KOESTLER, A., *The Challenge of Chance* (London, 1973).

—, *The Biology of God* (London, 1975).

HARRÉ, R., ed., *Problems of Scientific Revolution* (Oxford, 1975).

HARRIS, H., ed., *Astride the Two Cultures* (London, 1975).

HARVIE, R., see Hardy, Harvie and Koestler (1973).

VON HAYEK, F. A., in *Studies in Philosophy, Politics and Economics* (London, 1966).

HEBB, D. O., *Organization of Behaviour* (New York, 1949).

—, *A Textbook of Psychology* (Philadelphia and London, 1958).

HEISENBERG, W., *The Physicist's Conception of Nature* (London, 1958).

—, *Der Teil und das Ganze* (Munich, 1969). English tr. *Physics and Beyond* (London, 1971).

HERRICK, C. J., *The Evolution of Human Nature* (New York, 1961)

HILEY, B., see Bohm and Hiley (1974).

HILGARD, E. R., and ATKINSON, *Introduction to Psychology* (4th ed., 1967).

HIMMELFARB, G., *Darwin and the Darwinian Revolution* (London, 1959).

HORNEY, K., *New Ways in Psychoanalysis* (London, 1939).

HOYLE, SIR F., *October the First is Too Late* (London, 1966).

HUXLEY, A., in *Control of the Mind* – see Farber and Wilson, eds. (1961).

HUXLEY, SIR J., HARDY, SIR A., and FORD, E. B., eds., *Evolution as a Process* (New York, 1954).

—, *Evolution in Action* (New York, 1957).

—, *Man in the Modern World* (New York, 1964).

HYDEN, H., in *Control of the Mind* – see Farber and Wilson, eds. (1961).

HYNEK, J. A., *The UFO Experience* (London, 1972).

JAENSCH, E. R., *Eidetic Imagery* (London, 1930).

JAMES, W., *The Varieties of Religious Experience* (London, 1902).

JAYNES, J., *The Origin of Consciousness in the Breakdown of the Bicameral Mind* (Boston, 1976).

JEANS, SIR J., *The Mysterious Universe* (Cambridge, 1937).

JEFFRESS, L. A., ed., *Cerebral Mechanisms in Behaviour* – *The Hixon Symposium* (New York, 1951).

JENKIN, Fleeming, in *North British Review*, June 1867.

JENKINS, J. J., see Koestler and Jenkins (1965).

JEVONS, F. R., in *The Rules of the Game* – see Shanin, ed. (1972).

JOHANNSEN, W., in *Hereditas*, Vol. IV, p. 140 (1923).

JOKEL, V., 'Epidemic: Torture' (Amnesty International, London, n.d., *c.* 1975).

JONES, E., *Sigmund Freud*, Vols. I and III (London, 1953–7).

JUNG, C. G., and PAULI, W., *Naturerklärung und Psyche. Studien aus dem C. G. Jung-Institut, Zürich, IV* (1952).

—, *The Structure and Dynamics of the Psyche, Collected Works*, Vol. VIII, tr. R. F. C. Hull (London, 1960).

KAMMERER, P. *Das Gesetz der Serie* (Stuttgart, 1919).

KLUEVER, O., in *A Handbook of Child Psychology* – see Murchison, ed. (1933).

KOESTLER, A., *Twilight Bar* (London, 1945).

—, *Insight and Outlook* (London, 1948).

—, *Dialogue with Death* (London, 1954).

—, *The Invisible Writing* (London, 1954).

—, *The Sleepwalkers* (London, 1959).

—, in *Control of the Mind* – see Farber and Wilson, eds. (1961).

—, *The Act of Creation* (London, 1964).

— and JENKINS, J., in *Psychon. Sci.*, Vol. 3 (1965) [appears as Appendix II in this volume].

—, *The Ghost in the Machine* (London, 1967).

—, *Drinkers of Infinity* (London, 1968).

— and SMYTHIES, J. R., eds., *Beyond Reductionism – The Alpbach Symposium* (London, 1969).

—, in *The Pathology of Memory* – see Talland and Waugh (1969a).

—, *The Case of the Midwife Toad* (London, 1971).

—, *The Roots of Coincidence* (London, 1972).

—, in *The Challenge of Chance* – see Hardy, Harvie and Koestler (1973).

—, 'Humour and Wit' in *Encyclopaedia Britannica* (15th ed., 1974).

—, *The Heel of Achilles* (London, 1974).

—, in *Life After Death* – see Toynbee, Koestler *et al.* (1976).

KÖHLER, W., *The Mentality of Apes* (London, 1925).

KOLTSOV, N., *The Organisation of the Cell* (in Russian) (Moscow, 1936).

KRETSCHMER, E. A., *A Textbook of Medical Psychology* (London, 1934).

KRINOV, E. L., *Principles of Meteoritics*, tr. I. Vidziunas (Oxford, London, New York, Paris, 1960).

KUHN, T., *The Structure of Scientific Revolutions* (Chicago, 1962).

LAMARCK, J. P., *Philosophie Zoologique*, 2 vols., ed. C. Martins (2nd ed., Paris, 1873).

LASHLEY, K. S., *The Neuro-Psychology of Lashley*: Selected Papers (New York, 1960).

LOOFBOURROW, G. N., see Gellhorn and Loofbourrow (1963).

LORENZ, K., *On Aggression* (London, 1966).

MACBETH, N., *Darwin Retried* (London and Boston, 1971).

MCCONNELL, J. V., *The Worm Re-Turns* (Englewood Cliffs, N. J., 1965).

MACKAY, D. M., in *Brain and Conscious Experience* – see Eccles (1966).

MACLEAN, P. D., in *Psychosom. Med.*, Vol. II, pp. 338–53 (1949).

—, in *Am. J. of Medicine*, Vol. XXV, No. 4, pp. 611–26, (October 1958).

—, in *Handbook of Physiology: Neurophysiology*, Vol. III – see Field, ed. (1961).

—, in *J. of Nervous and Mental Disease*, Vol. 135, No. 4 (October 1962).

—, in *A Triune Concept of the Brain and Behaviour* – see Boag and Campbell, eds. (1973).

MARGENAU, H., in *Science and ESP* – see Smythies, ed. (1967).

MAYR, E., *Animal Species and Evolution* (Harvard, 1963).

MENDEL, G., in *Proc. of the Natural History Society of Brüm* (1865).

MICHEL, A., in *The Humanoids* – see Bowen, ed. (1974).

MILGRAM, S., *Obedience to Authority* (New York, 1974).

—, in *Dialogue*, Vol. 8, No. 3/4 (Washington, 1975).

MILLER, G. A., GALANTER, E., and PRIBRAM, K. H., *Plans and the Structure of Behaviour* (New York, 1960).

DELLA MIRANDOLA, PICO, *Opera Omnia* (Basle, 1557).

MONOD, J., *Chance and Necessity* (New York, 1971).

MORRIS, D., *The Naked Ape* (London, 1967).

MULLER, H. J., *Science and Criticism* (New Haven, Conn., 1943).

MURCHISON, C., ed., *A Handbook of Child Psychology* (Worcester, Mass., 1933).

NEEDHAM, J., *Order and Life* (New Haven, Conn., 1936).

—, *Time, the Refreshing River* (London, 1941).

OLDS, J., in *Psychiatric Research Reports of the American Psychiatric Association* (January, 1960).

OSGOOD, C. E., *Method and Theory in Experimental Psychology* (London and New York, 1953).

PATTEE, H. H., in *Towards a Theoretical Biology* – see Waddington, ed. (1970).

PAULI, W., see Jung and Pauli (1952).

PEARL, in *Encyclopaedia Britannica*, 14th ed., Vol. VIII, pp. 110 f.

PENFIELD, W., and ROBERTS, L., *Speech and Brain Mechanisms* (Princeton, 1959).

PITTENDRIGH, G. S., see Simpson, Pittendrigh and Tiffany (1957).

POLANYI, M., *The Tacit Dimension* (New York, 1966).

POPPER, SIR K., in *Br. J. Phil. Sci.*, Part I and II (1950).

—, in *Problems of Scientific Revolution* – see Harré, ed. (1975).

PORTEUS, S. D., see Wood Jones and Porteus (1929).

PRESCOTT, O., *The Conquest of Mexico* (New York, 1964).

PRIBRAM, K. H., see Miller, Galanter and Pribram (1960).

PRICE, H. H., in *Hibbert J.*, Vol. XLVII (1949).

PRZIBRAM, H., in *Monistische Monatshefte* (November 1926).

RIZZO, N. D., see Gray and Rizzo, eds. (1973).

ROBERTS, L., see Penfield and Roberts (1959).

RUSSELL, B., *An outline of Philosophy* (London, 1927).

— *Unpopular Essays* (1950).

RUYER, R., *La Gnose de Princeton* (Paris, 1974).

SAGAN, C., ed., *Communication with Extraterrestrial Intelligences (CETI)* (Cambridge, Mass. and London, 1973).

DE ST HILAIRE, G., *Philosophie Anatomique* (Paris, 1818).

SCHLOSBERG, H., see Woodworth and Schlosberg (1954).

SCHOPENHAUER, A., *Sämtliche Werke*, Vol. VIII (Stuttgart, 1859).

SCHRÖDINGER, E., *What is Life?* (Cambridge, 1944).

SHANIN, T., ed., *The Rules of the Game* (London, 1972).
SIMON, H. J., in *Proc. Am. Philos. Soc.*, Vol. 106, No. 6 (December 1962).
SIMPSON, G. G., *The Meaning of Evolution* (New Haven, Conn., 1949, and Oxford, 1950).
—, PITTENDRIGH, C. S., and TIFFANY, L. H., *Life: An Introduction to Biology* (New York, 1957).
—, *This View of Life* (New York, 1964).
SINNOTT, E. W., *Cell and Psyche – The Biology of Purpose* (New York, 1961).
SKINNER, B. F., *The Behaviour of Organisms* (New York, 1938).
—, *Science and Human Behaviour* (New York, 1953).
—, *Verbal Behaviour* (New York, 1957).
—, *Beyond Freedom and Dignity* (New York, 1973).
SMITH, E. LESTER, ed., *Intelligence Came First* (Wheaton, Ill., 1975).
SMUTS, J. C., *Holism and Evolution* (London, 1926).
SMYTHIES, J. R., ed., *Science and ESP* (London, 1967).
—, see Koestler and Smythies, eds. (1969).
SPENCER, H., *Principles of Biology* (1893).
—, in *Essays on Education and Kindred Subjects* (London, 1911).
SPERLING, G., in *Psychol. Monogr.*, 74 (11, Whole No. 498), 1960.
SPURWAY, H., in *Supplemento. La Ricerca Scientifica (Pallanza Symposium) 18* (Rome, 1949).
SZENT-GYÖRGYI, A., *Bioenergetics* (New York, 1957).
—, in *Synthesis* (Spring 1974).
TALLAND, G. A., and WAUGH, N. C., eds., *The Pathology of Memory.* (New York and London, 1969a).
TAKHTAJAN, A., in *Phytomorphology*, Vol. 22, No. 2 (June 1972).
THOMAS, L., *The Lives of a Cell* (New York, 1974).
THOMPSON, D. W., *On Growth and Form* (Cambridge, 1942).
THOMSON, SIR J. A., *Heredity* (London, 1908).
THORPE, W. H., *Learning and Instinct in Animals* (London, 1956).
—, in *Nature*, 14 May 1966.
—, in *Brain and Conscious Experience* – see Eccles, ed. (1966a).
—, in *Beyond Reductionism* – see Koestler and Smythies, eds. (1969).
—, *Animal Nature and Human Nature* (Cambridge, 1974).
TIFFANY, L. H., see Simpson, Pittendrigh and Tiffany (1957).
TINBERGEN, N., *The Study of Instinct* (Oxford, 1951).
TOYNBEE, A., KOESTLER, A. et al., *Life After Death* (London, 1976).

VAIHINGER, H., *Die Philosophie des Als Ob*, 1911 (English tr. C. K. Ogden, London, 1924).

WADDINGTON, C. H., in *The Listener*, 13 February 1952.

—, *The Strategy of the Genes* (London, 1957).

—, *The Nature of Life* (London, 1961).

—, in *Beyond Reductionism* – see Koestler and Smythies, eds. (1969).

—, ed., *Towards a Theoretical Biology* (Edinburgh, 1970).

WALKER, E. HARRIS, in *J. for the Study of Consciousness* (1973).

WALTER, W. GREY, *Observations on Man, his Frame, his Duty and his Expectations* (Cambridge, 1969).

WATSON, J. B., *Behaviourism* (London, 1928).

WAUGH, N. C., see Talland and Waugh, eds. (1969a).

WEAVER, W., *Lady Luck and the Theory of Probability* (New York, 1963).

WEISS, P. A., ed., *Genetic Neurology* (Chicago, 1950).

—, in *Cerebral Mechanisms in Behaviour* – see Jeffress, ed. (1951).

—, in *Beyond Reductionism* – see Koestler and Smythies, eds. (1969).

WHEELER, J. A., *Geometrodynamics* (1962).

—, in *Batelle Recontres* (1967).

WHYTE, L. L., *The Unitary Principle in Physics and Biology* (London, 1949).

WHYTE, L. L., *Internal Factors in Evolution* (New York, 1965).

—, WILSON, A. G., and WILSON, D., eds., *Hierarchical Structures* (New York, 1969).

WILSON, A. G., see Whyte, Wilson and Wilson, eds. (1969).

WILSON, D., see Whyte, Wilson and Wilson, eds. (1969).

WILSON, R. H. L., see Farber and Wilson, eds. (1961).

WOLSKY, A., see Wolsky and Wolsky (1976).

WOLSKY, M. DE I., and WOLSKY, A., *The Mechanism of Evolution* (Basle, Munich, Paris, London, New York, 1976).

WOOD JONES, F., and PORTEUS, S. D., *The Matrix of the Mind* (London, 1929).

—, *Habit and Heritage* (London, 1943).

WOODGER, J. H., *Biological Principles* (London, 1929).

WOODWORTH, R. S., and SCHLOSBERG, H., *Experimental Psychology* (rev. ed., New York, 1954).

YOUNG, J. Z., *The Life of Vertebrates* (Oxford, 1950).

INDEX

Birkbeck College, London, 257
Birth control, 101
Bisociation, 113, 118, 123, 129–30, 141–7, 149, 151, 156
Black holes, 254–5
Bohm, David, 250, 257, 267
Bohr, N., 247
Bolk, J., 218
Bonner, James, 40
Botticelli, Sandro, 154
Bragg, Sir William, 244
Brain: functions of the, 12–13, 276–7; structures of the, 9–11, 20; types of, 12
Brave New World, 103
Bristol University, 91–2
Broad, C. D., 32
Bruner, Blanche, 23 n
Bruner, J. S., 23 n, 290
Buddhism, 7, 8, 265
Burt, Sir Cyril, 248, 272
Buss, A. H., 88
Butler, Samuel, 185, 193, 202

Calder, Nigel, 91–2
California, University of, 101
Caligula, Roman emperor, 77
Cambridge, University of, 184, 271
Canons, *see* Codes
Capra, Fritjof, 243, 247 n, 248
Caricature, 114, 122–3, 126, 128–9, 133
Carrell, Alexis, 30
Carroll, Lewis, 121
Cartesian dualism, 229–30, 233–5, 245
Cartoons, 114, 118, 123, 128
Caruso, 51
Case of the Midwife Toad, The, 180 n, 193 n, 198 n, 200, 261 n
Causality, physical, 259–65, 268–9
Cell: body, 40–1; nucleus, 40, 182
Cells, 27–30, 39–42, 44, 58, 68, 225
Centripetal versus centrifugal, 62

CETI (communication with extraterrestrial intelligence), 319–25
Cézanne, Paul, 141, 154
Chain-response theory, 39 n
Challenge of Chance, The, 243 n, 260, 269
Chance and Necessity, 67, 191
Chaplin, Charles, 115, 117
Child, C. M., 310
Chomsky, Noam, 31, 170, 234, 290
Chopin, Frédéric, 127
Chromosomes, 39–42, 44, 181–2, 185, 186 n, 187, 197–9, 202–3, 215, 273
Cicero, 115, 124
Civilization and its Discontents, 63
Clausius, 222
Cleopatra, queen of Egypt, 229
Clerk Maxwell, James, 135
Cobb, S., 318
Code governing holon's structure, 38–9
Codes of conduct, 38–45, 59, 61, 63, 81–2, 89, 112, 145, 148; incompatible, 144
Coghill, G. E., 214
Cognitive code, 45–6
Cognitive hierarchy, 47, 59, 226, 233
Cognitive holons, 112, 121, 131–2
Coincidence, 144, 259–65
Colorado, University of, 323–4
Comedy, 125, 129, 144–5
Comic devices, 123–4
Comic opera, 127
Comic verse, 121
Communicating ideas, 35
Communication theory, 34, 53, 53 n
Communication with extraterrestrial intelligence (CETI), 319–25
Complementarity, Principle of, 61, 234–5, 244–5
Condon, E. U., 323
Conflict, 145

ABOUT THE AUTHOR

ARTHUR KOESTLER was born in 1905 in Budapest. Though he studied science and psychology in Vienna, at the age of twenty he became a foreign correspondent and worked for various European newspapers in the Middle East, Paris, Berlin, Russia and Spain. During the Spanish Civil War, which he covered from the Republican side, he was captured and imprisoned for several months by the Nationalists, but was exchanged after international protest. In 1939–40 he was interned in a French detention camp. After his release, due to British government intervention, he joined the French Foreign Legion, subsequently escaped to England, and joined the British Army.

Like many other intellectuals in the thirties, Koestler saw in the Soviet experiment the only hope and alternative to fascism. He became a member of the Communist Party in 1931, but left it in disillusionment during the Moscow purges in 1938. His earlier books were mainly concerned with these experiences, either in autobiographical form or in essays or political novels. Among the latter, *Darkness At Noon* has been translated into thirty-three languages.

After World War II, Mr. Koestler became a British citizen, and all his books since 1940 have been written in English. He now lives in London, but he frequently lectures at American universities, and was a Fellow at the Center for Advanced Study in the Behavioral Sciences at Stanford in 1964–65.

In 1968 Mr. Koestler received the Sonning Prize at the University of Copenhagen for his contributions to European culture. He is also a Commander of the Order of the British Empire, as well as one of the ten Companions of Literature, elected by the Royal Society of Literature. His works are now being republished in a collected edition of twenty volumes.